SEARCH ENGINE VISIBILITY

SECOND EDITION

SHARI THUROW

New Riders

1249 Eighth Street, Berkeley, CA 94710

An Imprint of Peachpit, A Division of Pearson Education

Search Engine Visibility, Second Edition

Shari Thurow

New Riders
1249 Eighth Street
Berkeley, CA 94710
510/524-2178
510/524-2221 (fax)

Find us on the Web at: www.newriders.com
To report errors, please send a note to errata@peachpit.com

New Riders is an imprint of Peachpit, a division of Pearson Education

Project Editor: Michael J. Nolan
Development Editor: Doug Adrianson
Production Editor: Myrna Vladic
Technical Editors: Erik Daffron and James Gunn
Copy Editor and Proofreader: Hope Frazier
Compositor: David Van Ness
Indexer: Joy Dean Lee
Cover & interior designer: Aren Howell

ISBN 13: 978-0-321-50324-4
ISBN 10: 0-321-50324-4

9 8 7 6 5 4 3 2 1

Printed and bound in the United States of America

About the Author

Shari Thurow is a sought-after speaker and trainer on the topics of search engine friendly Web site design, search usability, Web copywriting, and link development. A popular speaker at Search Engine Strategies, Web site design, and online marketing conferences worldwide, Shari's sessions are very popular and four-star rated.

Shari is the also founder and SEO director for Omni Marketing Interactive, a full-service search engine marketing, Web usability and design firm. She has successfully designed and promoted Web sites since 1995, and she is outsourced to many firms throughout the United States. She has a 100 percent success rate for getting client sites ranked at the top of search engine and directory queries.

Shari has designed and successfully marketed Web sites for businesses in fields such as medicine, science, biotechnology, accounting and finance, computers and software, manufacturing, real estate, law, ecommerce and online stores, art and design, marketing, insurance, employment, education, and travel. Her clients include Microsoft, America Online, Yahoo, National Cancer Institute, HSBC, Deloitte and Touche, WebMD and MedicineNet.com, ABC News, Court TV, Wharton School of the University of Pennsylvania, and Dow Corning.

Shari has been featured in many publications, including *USA Today*, *Wired* magazine, *PC World*, *Entrepreneur*, *Internet Retailer*, *Fortune Small Business*, *Crain's Chicago Business, Inc.* magazine, *MacWorld*, and ComputerUser.com. She has also received numerous design awards and content awards, including top site honors from Lycos, Business 2.0, and *Computer User* magazine.

Dedication

N'oubliez jamais ceux qui apportent un sourire à votre âme.

In loving memory
Harold Paul Thurow · Marion Louise Thurow
Jerry Carlock · Richard Crowell · Nani Crowell
Jerry Bussewitz · Mooseman

Acknowledgements

This book took years of testing and experience to get a final product. It also took the knowledge and support of some very important people.

Again, I would like to show my highest gratitude to my two "cyber-mentors," Danny Sullivan and John Audette. Back in 1995 when I created my first Web site and was assigned the task to market it as well, I stumbled onto your sites. I am still in awe of your knowledge, intelligence, and the way that you communicated your knowledge to your readers. I listened to everything you said and followed your advice. I learned by example. My success as a Web designer and online marketer, my clients' successes, and this book can all be traced back to the day I discovered your Web sites. I thank you both for sharing your knowledge with myself and others, for publishing my posts and my articles, and for allowing me to speak at your conferences.

I extend another special thank you to Chris Sherman and Gary Price, two of the most knowledgeable people in the field of information retrieval in the world. I never tire of reading anything you write or listening to anything you have to say about the topic.

Thank you to all of the staff at Peachpit Press—Doug Adrianson, Michael Nolan, and all of the production and marketing staff. Your incredible patience, attention to detail, and enthusiasm were crucial in shaping this book. And thank you to my technical editors—Erik Dafforn and James Gunn—for your attention to detail and for not letting me get away with anything that is not factually accurate. You are great technical editors, colleagues, and friends.

A special thank you to all of my search engine marketing, design, and usability colleagues: Adam Audette, Doug Ausbury, Matt Bailey, Christine Churchill, Bruce Clay, Grant Crowell, Liana Evans, Matthew Finlay, Andrew Goodman, Mike Grehan, Graham Hansell, Patrick Harris, Kristjan Mar Hauksson, Peter Hershberg, Jonathan Hochman, Gord Hotchkiss, Anthony Iaffaldano, Detlev Johnson, Kim Krause, Jennifer Laycock, Rebecca Lieb, Gregory Markel, John Marshall, Elisabeth Osmeloski, Alan Perkins, Mike Rende, Jeffrey Rohrs, Kevin Ryan, Catherine Seda, Jim Stob, Joshua Stylman, Mikkel deMib Svendsen, Naveen Thattil, Dana Todd, Amanda Watlington, Jill Whalen, and Stacy Williams. Your years of experience and wisdom have been beneficial to myself and to our online communities.

Thank you to all of the folks at Incisive Media and Search Marketing Expo—Karen DeWeese, Chris Elwell, Barry Schwartz, Stewart Quealy, and Marilyn Crafts—for providing me with a venue to present this topic. You have been wonderful, supportive colleagues and friends.

My success in this industry clearly lies with the existence of the commercial Web search engines and their vast knowledge of information retrieval and search usability. I extend my heartfelt thanks to my search engine colleagues: Tim Converse, Dan Crow, Matt Cutts, Vanessa Fox, Jon Glick, Peter Kelly, Amit Kumar, Tim Mayer, Paul Gardi, Priyank Shanker Garg, Karen Howe, Peter Kelly, Rajat Mukherjee, Tomi Poutanen, John Riccardi, Craig Silverstein, Amit Singhal, Bryan White, and Michael Yang.

A very special thanks goes out to my four "muses": Mel Carson, Dixon Jones, Jonathan Forster, and Francois Roux. Inspiration for writing and different ways of explaining ideas comes from many sources. Even laughter can be inspiring. Just being in your presence inspired considerable portions of this book.

And finally, thank you to all of my clients and non-clients who agreed to be showcased in this book. And thank you to my colleagues who had the kindness and generosity to listen to my ideas.

Table of Contents

Foreword

"If you build it, they will come" is the famous quote from the book and movie *Field of Dreams*. As all too many webmasters and designers have discovered, however, just building a Web site is no guarantee of receiving visitors.

There are many ways that people may come to a Web site, but one of the leading methods is through search engines. Survey after survey attests to the popularity of these tools among Web surfers. How you build your Web site can have a major impact on whether those users will find you through search engines.

Build it right, and you can easily tap into "natural" traffic and gain quality visitors for free, saving your money to spend on ads to target areas in which you don't naturally do well. Build it wrong, and you'll find yourself in the morass of constantly trying to win the search engine game with strikes against you from the outset. You then should expect to spend significant time and money to raise your profile.

Building a site right needn't be hard. "Search engine friendly" design, which I've been preaching about since 1997, isn't about using myriad tricks to fool search engines into favoring your Web site. Rather, making a site search engine friendly often means implementing small and easy changes that usually have a big impact in gaining search engine visibility.

Far too often, designers spend time ensuring that their Web sites are compatible with the two major Web browsers while ignoring what I call the "third browser" search engines. Building a site that's accessible and friendly to search engines that crawl the Web is just as important as thinking about humans who use Internet Explorer and Firefox. Why? Because many of those humans will "tune in" to your Web site by means of crawler-based search engines. If those crawlers have problems reaching you, they can't direct the human visitors you want to your Web site.

Fortunately, building a site for the third browser of crawler-based search engines doesn't mean ostracizing your human visitors. In fact, thinking about crawlers can often make your site's usability for humans better than it was before.

Shari Thurow has been a leader in helping guide people toward better search engine design through her writing and speaking. She has consistently been one of the best-rated speakers at search marketing conferences I have produced. Now Shari has put her knowledge into book format, and it is a great companion for anyone involved in constructing Web sites.

Search engine friendly design isn't just about pleasing crawlers. How sites are listed in human-powered search engines can also be positively—or negatively—impacted by site design. Shari addresses these issues, as well as offering tips on improving the submission process to human-backed search engines.

Build it right with the help of this book, and you should indeed find that they come!

Danny Sullivan
Editor-in-Chief, SearchEngineLand.com

Introduction

This book is a guide to help Web designers, Web developers, programmers, usability professionals, ad agencies, online marketers, copywriters, and anyone who creates Web sites build a better site, one that can be found via the major commercial Web search engines.

The foundation of a successful search engine optimization campaign begins with a genuinely effective Web site, one that delivers content site visitors are searching for. This book is about building a strong foundation. Without a strong foundation, a search engine optimization campaign will ultimately fail, costing Web site owners wasted time and expenses.

Therefore, this book will not teach you a "secret recipe" for each search engine. It will not teach you a "magic formula" to get your site at the top of search engine results. Rather, it will teach you the foundation of a successful search engine optimization campaign, one that works with all of the major commercial search engines and delivers long-term search engine visibility, not quick fixes.

This book is not based on my personal design preferences. Everyone has opinions on what constitutes good and bad design. I might look at a site and think it is ugly, but the site might be successfully generating millions of dollars in sales. On the flip side, an award-winning, beautifully designed site might receive plenty of traffic, create buzz in Web logs (blogs) and other online publications—and generate no sales. But that is not what this book is based on. This book is based on my years of experience, formal education and training, resulting expertise, and my 100% success rate at increasing search engine visibility, site traffic, and sales on my own sites and client sites since 1995 without incurring any search engine spam penalties whatsoever.

The content of this second edition is based on client data that I have gathered since 1995. One of the many jobs I have held over the years is online marketing manager at various Web design firms. Even though I did not design every site created by these design firms, I did have to optimize and market many them.

I had access to site statistics for thousands of Web sites. I was able to see which types of Web site designs search engine spiders indexed easily and which designs they had problems with. I was able to see the types of sites Web directory editors accepted and rejected. I was able to see the types of sites and individual Web pages that people liked to link to, and the types of sites that must resort to purchasing thousands of dollars in links because the site's content and usability were substandard. With that knowledge, I was able to build Web sites that search engines easily crawled, Web directory editors approved, and site visitors linked to.

Although search engine visibility is important, it is not the ultimate goal. For a Web site to be successful, its end users, or target audience, have to like the site and actually use it. Site visitors must take a desired action (Add to Cart, Subscribe to Newsletter, Enroll in

Class, etc.) in order for a site to meet business goals. To my pleasant surprise, I found that sites that are naturally search engine friendly are also user friendly. Therefore, this book is not based on my personal preferences; it is based on years of data on actual user behavior. This book will help you build a Web site that is both search engine friendly and user friendly.

New in This Edition

"Why the second edition?" some colleagues and other readers have asked me. The most common assumption is that search engines change their algorithms on a daily basis. Some of my esteemed colleagues publish their search engine optimization books online for this very reason. Their belief is that no standard print book about search engine optimization (SEO) can possibly keep up with the vast amount of search engine changes.

Nonetheless, I have never clung to the delusion that I know every single mathematical equation that constitutes a search engine algorithm for every type or part of a search engine (news, local, audio, graphic image, video, ads, main search results, etc.). In fact, there is no software engineer at Google who knows every single equation that constitutes all of Google's search engine algorithms. The same holds true for the other currently popular crawler-based search engines: Yahoo, Microsoft's Live, and Ask.

No search engine representative will reveal his or her top-secret means of organizing Web content. No patent application will reveal key ingredients to the "secret sauce." Therefore, no search engine optimization professional, including myself, knows the splendid, convoluted mathematical equations that constitute a search engine algorithm.

What I do understand, however, is users' search behavior, not only querying behavior. I focus on principles. I take the time to gather data from a wide variety of resources, carefully analyze this data for patterns of search behavior, and then draw conclusions. The result? Search usability™ principles that are applicable years after a book is published, even when new search engines emerge and others cease to exist.

I believe a Web site should be redesigned every two to four years because browsers, code, and programming languages evolve. With two to four years of data from usability testing, focus groups, Web analytics software, and pay-per-click search engine advertising, Web site owners can continually build sites that satisfy user expectations, accomplish business goals, and meet the terms and conditions set forth by the major commercial Web search engines.

The principles from the first edition have not changed: the Five Basic Rules of Web Design and the building blocks of successful search engine optimization (text component, link component, popularity component).

What has changed is the emerging popularity of different file types, both text-based and nontext files. I have optimized non-HTML files for many years. But non-HTML files were not very popular when I wrote the first edition of *Search Engine Visibility*. Since I wrote the first edition, I have accumulated more data on searcher and user behavior, and I am now sharing my recommendations and conclusions with you.

How This Book Is Organized

The best way to read this book is in chronological order, from beginning to end, whether you are new to search engine marketing or are an expert.

Why?

Too many search engine marketers, advertising agencies, and Web design firms are focused on quick fixes and short-term results, not principles. Even self-proclaimed search engine "experts" do not understand search optimization principles and, therefore, do not incorporate these principles into Web sites. This book focuses on the very core of a successful search engine optimization campaign. Once this foundation is in place, and once all search usability principles are followed, Web site owners can save thousands or millions of dollars in maintenance time and expenses.

In Part 1, I define the different types of search services and how the most popular commercial Web search engines display search results. Most search results present data from a variety of resources, and the search engine listings displayed depend on the words typed into a search box. Before building any Web site and embarking on any type of search engine marketing campaign, all Web site owners should analyze how search engines display search listings.

Part 1 also addresses the fundamental components of a successful Web site design and the foundation of an effective search engine optimization campaign. Site design and search engine visibility are inextricably interrelated. As I mentioned previously, many advanced search engine optimization professionals do not understand the principles of search usability. Parts 1 and 2 provide explanations and examples of search usability principles.

Part 2 addresses text-based Web documents. I go into great detail about the foundation of a successful search engine optimization campaign using a fictional Web site. Each component of the foundation is addressed. This section contains information on how to write search engine friendly copy for your whole Web site and individual HTML tags.

Part 2 presents solutions to navigation schemes that are problematic, showing actual search engine friendly Web pages. If your site uses frames, DHTML, Cascading Style Sheets, and other technologies, there are ways to make them more search engine friendly. This section also contains guidelines for building a solid link development campaign.

Part 3 addresses optimization guidelines and recommendations for nontext documents, including graphic images, audio, and video files. Though many readers might be tempted to skip to Part 3 of this book, at the time of this writing search engines are not as advanced as they can be when it comes to nontext information retrieval. The information presented in Part 2 provides the context for nontext file optimization.

Part 4 outlines the submission process to search engines and Web directories. It contains detailed checklists to use before the submission process. And the section provides tips, guidelines, and actual email letters to use in the event a submission is rejected. The guidelines for search engine and Web directory submission are also applicable for other types of external, third party link development.

Parts 1 through 4 teach you what to do. Part 5 will tell you what *not* to do. Part 5 addresses best practices, i.e. what to do and what not do to. It will also debunk common search engine marketing myths. The contents of this section can help you select a reputable, professional search engine marketing firm, determining if it follows best practices.

Companion Web Site

To supplement this book, I have created a companion Web site at www.searchenginesbook.com. As you are well aware, search engines change all the time, and some of the content in this book can become outdated as soon as a search engine and directory change partnerships, new search engines emerge, etc. The companion Web site will contain the most recent tips and guidelines for optimization, along with a glossary of search engine optimization terms and an extensive list of online and print resources.

Also, HTML code, style sheets, and JavaScript can be difficult to retype. So I have created the companion site for you to use in your site designs. For example, if I find that a rollover script is more search engine friendly than other scripts, I will post that information (and the code for the script) on the companion site for your use.

Furthermore, search engines are becoming better at indexing different types of Web pages and documents. As the search engines continually develop, so will search engine friendly Web design tips. Any new or updated information will be presented on the companion site.

Part 1:

Before You Build

Search engine optimization (SEO) is a powerful online marketing strategy. When implemented appropriately, millions of online searchers can find your site among millions of top search results.

Many Web site owners consider SEO an afterthought, after a site has already been built. If you are preparing to create a new site or redesign an existing one, understanding how the search engines work, how your target audience searches, and how best to design your site from the outset can save your company thousands or millions of dollars in time and money.

Why Search Engine Visibility Is Important

Search engines are the main way Internet users discover Web sites. According to Nielsen//NetRatings, 256 million people—81% of the global Internet population—visited a search engine in December 2006. As of this writing, the average searcher viewed 93 search engine results pages (SERPs) per month and spent an average of 27 minutes per month searching for information. In other words, people search. The number of people searching, and the time people spend searching, continues to increase.

The commercial Web search engines average over 6.4 billion searches per day. In other words, people search for information online. Properly preparing your Web site for search engine visibility increases the probability that Web searchers will visit your site.

Additionally, think about your own personal experience. Where do you go to search for information about a company or a product on the Web? Where do you go to find a site whose Web address you do not know or cannot remember? In these cases, you will probably use a commercial Web search engine to find that information.

Web searchers are not random visitors. When searchers enter a series of words into a search engine query, they are actively seeking a specific product or service. So the traffic your site receives from the search engines is already targeted. In other words, Web searchers are self-qualified prospects for your business.

Of course, search engines are not the only way people discover Web sites. People may find a Web address in offline sources such as print, television, or radio. They might click a link to a Web site in an email document or an online advertisement. Word of mouth (referral marketing) is a popular method of attracting visitors to sites. People also locate sites by clicking links from one site to another, commonly known as surfing or browsing the Web.

Since millions of people use search engines to discover Web sites, maximizing your site's search engine visibility can be a powerful and cost-effective part of an online marketing plan. A properly performed search engine marketing campaign can provide a tremendous, long-term return on investment (ROI).

Understanding Search Results

Most SERPs present information from a variety of sources, including but not limited to:

- Crawler-based or spider-based search engines

- Search engine advertisements

- Human-based search engines, also known as Web directories

- Specialty or topical search engines, also known as vertical search engines

What does this mean to you, the Web site owner? Most SERPs present hybrid results. Hybrid search results generally get most listings from one source; thus, hybrid search engines are classified according to the main source used. For example, if a hybrid search service gets its primary results from a Web directory and its secondary results from a search engine, the search service is generally classified as a directory.

The first step of any search engine marketing campaign should be to review how each major search engine displays links to Web sites. Begin with a small, but targeted, keyword list. Type a number of keyword phrases into all of the major search engines to see what types of search resources dominate the search results. Analyze how your pages might display in search results. Analyze how your keyword competitors' pages look in search results. All future search engine marketing campaigns should be based on how search engines display listings, your target audience's search behavior, and your business goals.

Anatomy of a Search Engine Results Page

As I mentioned previously, most search engine results pages present information from a variety of sources. The following is a list and description of the various places from which search engines receive and retrieve data for their search results:

Crawler-Based Search Engines

A Web directory consists of sites that have been added by human editors. Search engine databases are compiled using special software robots, called spiders, to retrieve information from Web pages.

Figures 1-1 and 1-2 show where crawler-based listings appear in Yahoo and Google:

Figure 1-1

The majority of Yahoo search listings come from spidered listings. Notice how much screen real estate on the first page of search results is allocated to spidered listings.

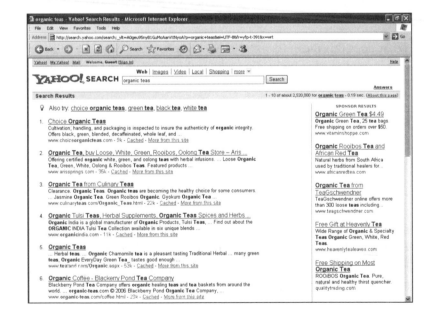

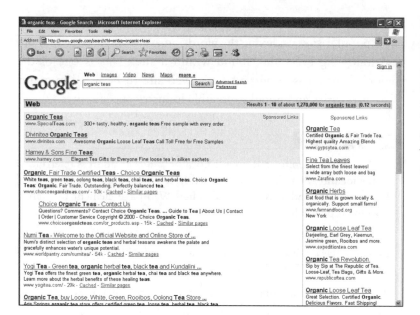

Figure 1-2
Likewise, the majority of Google listings currently come from spidered listings. Spidered listings are frequently referred to as "organic" or "natural" search engine listings because these listings come from the natural spidering process.

Crawler- or spider-based search engines perform three basic tasks:

1. Search engine *spiders* find and fetch Web pages, a process called crawling or spidering, and build lists of words and phrases found on each Web page.

2. Search engines keep an index (or database) of the words and phrases they find on each Web page they are able to crawl. The part of the search engine that places the Web pages into the database is called an *indexer*.

3. Search engines then allow end users to search for keywords and keyword phrases found in their indices. Search engines try to match the words typed in a search query with the Web page that is most likely to have the information end users are searching for. This part of the search engine is called the *query processor*.

How do search engines begin finding Web pages? The usual starting points are lists of heavily used servers from major Internet service providers (ISPs), such as America Online, and frequently visited Web sites such as the Yahoo directory, the Open Directory and other major directories. Search engine spiders will begin crawling these popular sites, indexing the words on every single page of a site and following every link found within a site. This is one of the major reasons it is important for a Web site to be listed in major Web directories and popular, credible industry-specific sites.

What Is a URL?

URL stands for Uniform Resource Locator and is an address referring to the location of a file on the Internet. In terms of search engine marketing, it is the address of an individual Web page element or Web document on the Internet.

Many people believe a URL is the same as a domain name or home page, but this is not so. Every Web document and Web graphic image on a Web site has a URL. The syntax of a URL consists of three elements:

The protocol, or the communication language, the URL uses.

The domain name, or the exclusive name that identifies a Web site.

The path name of the file to be retrieved, usually related to the path name of a file on the server. The file can contain any type of data, but only certain files are interpreted directly by most browsers, usually an HTML document or a graphic image.

For example, the URL for a home page is commonly written as:

http://www.companyname.com/index.html

- The http:// is the protocol (hypertext transfer protocol).
- The www.companyname.com is the domain name.
- The index.html is the path name or file name. In this example, it is an HTML document named index.

The URL for an About Us page for a company called TranquiliTeas is commonly written as:

http://www.tranquiliteasorganic.com/about.html

- The http:// is the protocol.
- The www.tranquiliteasorganic.com is the domain name.
- The about.html is the path name.

As a general rule of thumb, whenever you see an Add URL or Submit URL to the search engines, remember that every Web page should have a unique URL with unique content.

Figure 1-3 outlines the search engine crawling process for a single Web page:

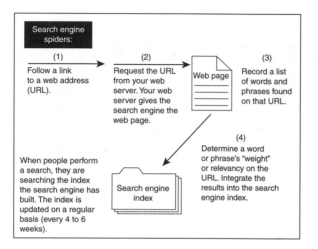

Figure 1-3
How search engines crawl
Web pages.

Since search engine spiders are continuously crawling the Web, their indices are constantly receiving new and updated data. Search engines regularly update their indices, generally every two to four weeks, though news search engines must update their available information on a daily or hourly basis.

A search engine index contains full-text indices of Web pages. Thus, when you perform a search query on a search engine, you are searching this full-text index of retrieved Web pages, not the Web itself.

To determine the most relevant URL for a search query, most search engines take the text information on a Web page and assign a "weight" to the individual words and phrases on that page. An engine might give more weight to the number of times a word appears on a page. An engine might assign more weight to words that appear in the title tags, meta tags, and subheadings. An engine might assign more weight to words that appear at the top of a document. This assigning of weight to a set of words on a Web page is part of a search engine's algorithm, which is a scientific/mathematical formula that determines how Web pages are ranked. Every search engine has a different formula for assigning weight to the words and phrases in its index.

Search engine algorithms are kept highly confidential and change almost every day. Thus, no search engine optimization expert can ever know an exact search engine algorithm at a specified point in time.

Submission Forms vs. Natural Spidering

Search engines also find Web pages via the submission forms, generally labeled as Add URL or Submit URL. The Submit URL form allows Web site owners to notify the search engines of a Web page's existence and its Web address (URL).

Unfortunately, unethical search engine marketers (called spammers) create automated submission tools that bombard submission forms with thousands of URLs. These URLs point to poorly written and constructed Web pages that are of no use to a Web site owner's target audience.

In fact, most of the major search engines state that 95% of submissions made via the Add URL form are considered spam.

Because of the overwhelming spam problems, submitting a Web page through an Add URL form does not guarantee that the search engines will accept your Web page.

Therefore, it is generally more beneficial for Web pages to be discovered by a search engine spider during its normal crawling process. In fact, if the only way search engines are able to discover new or updated content through submission forms or site map submission, it is often a clear indication that a site's information architecture is substandard.

What a search engine optimization expert can do is:

1. Ensure that your targeted words and phrases are placed in a strategic manner on your Web pages, no matter what the current algorithms are.

2. Ensure that the spiders are able to access your Web pages.

The key to understanding search engine optimization is comprehending Figure 1-3 because search engine spiders are always going to index text on Web pages, and they are always going to find Web pages by crawling links from Web page to Web page, from Web site to Web site. *Anything that interferes with the process outlined in Figure 1-3 will negatively impact a site's search engine positions.* If a search engine spider is not able to access your Web pages, then those pages will not rank well. If a search engine can access your Web pages but cannot find your targeted keyword phrases on those Web pages, then those pages will not rank well.

Pay-for-inclusion models

With a pay-for-inclusion model, a search engine will include pages from a Web site in its index in exchange for payment. This model is beneficial to search engine marketers and Web site owners because (a) they know their Web pages will not be dropped from a search engine index, and (b) any new information added to their Web pages will be reflected in the search engines very quickly.

This type of program guarantees that your submitted Web pages will not be dropped from the search engine index for a specified period of time, generally six months or a year. To keep your guaranteed inclusion in the index, you must renew your payment.

Submitting Web pages in a pay-for-inclusion program does *not* guarantee that the pages will appear in top positions. Thus, it is best that those pages be optimized.

Search engine marketers find pay-for-inclusion programs save them considerable time and expense because a Web page cannot rank if it is not included in the search engine index. Furthermore, pay-for-inclusion programs allow dynamic Web pages to be included in the search engine index without having to implement costly workarounds.

Search Engine Advertising

Search engine advertising includes sponsorships and pay-for-placement (PFP) advertising, though the two terms are often synonymous. Search engine advertising generally follows a pay-for-placement model. A pay-for-placement search engine guarantees top positions in that search engine in exchange for payment. With pay-for-placement search engines, participants "bid" against each other to obtain top positions on the search site and within its distribution network for specified keywords or keyword phrases. Typically, the higher the bid, the more prominently the search engine ad appears in search results.

Many search engines have outstanding distribution networks, and the top two or three ads are often displayed in other search engines, portals, verticals (specialty search engines), and Web directories. Paid placement advertisements are generally marked on partnered sites as "Featured Listings," "Sponsored Links," etc.

Figure 1-4 shows where search engine advertising appears on Google:

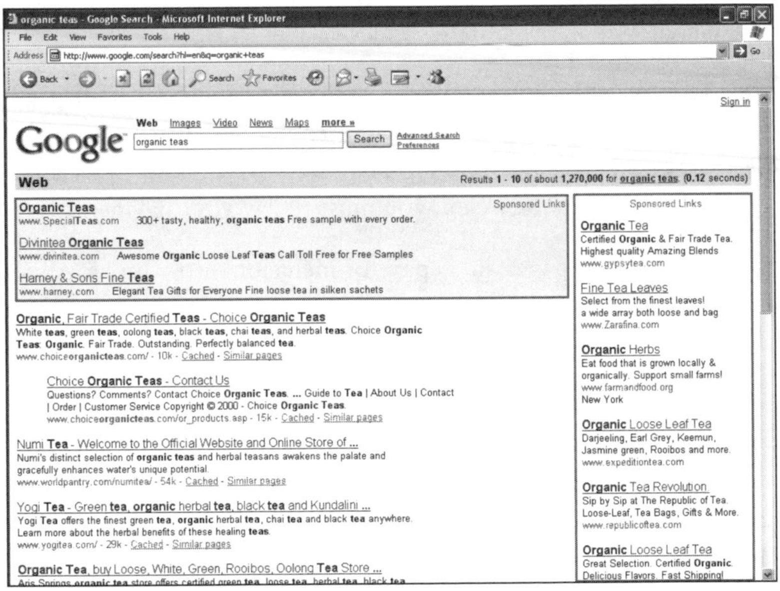

Figure 1-4

The phrase "Sponsored Links" or "Featured Listings" appears next to search engine ads.

Successful search engine advertising campaigns depend on five main factors:

- Keyword selection
- Bid price
- Ad copy
- Ad distribution
- Effective landing pages

Participating in search engine advertising programs can get expensive, which is one of the reasons any search engine optimization can result in a better, long-term return on investment for many Web site owners.

Web Directories

Web directories use human editors to create their listings and are often referred to as human-based search engines. When you submit a site to be included in a Web directory, a human editor reviews your site and determines whether to include your site in the directory. Human editors also discover sites on their own by searching or browsing the Web.

Every Web page (or site) listed in a directory is categorized in some way. The categories are typically hierarchical, branching off into different subcategories. Web searchers can find sites in directories by browsing categories, or they can perform a keyword search for information.

For example, a company that sells organic teas might be listed in the Yahoo directory category:

Directory > Business and Economy > Shopping and Services > Food and Drinks > Drinks > Tea > Organic

If we place the categories in a vertical hierarchy, it will look like this:

Directory
    Business and Economy
        Shopping and Services
            Food and Drinks
                Drinks
                    Tea
                        Organic

In this example, the top-level category in the directory is called Business and Economy. A subcategory of Business and Economy is

Shopping and Services. A subcategory of Shopping and Services is Food and Drinks, and so on. As we move down (drill down) the category structure, notice that the categories get more and more specific.

A company that sells herbal teas might be listed in a different Yahoo directory category:

Directory > Business and Economy > Shopping and Services > Food and Drinks > Drinks > Tea > Herbal

Let's place this categorization into a vertical hierarchy:

Directory

Business and Economy

Shopping and Services

Food and Drinks

Drinks

Tea

Herbal

A company that sells a variety of teas might be listed in a less specific Yahoo directory category:

Directory

Business and Economy

Shopping and Services

Food and Drinks

Drinks

Tea

Web directories are structured in this manner to make it easier for their end users to find sites.

Web pages are generally displayed in directories with a Title and a Description. The Title and Description originate either from the directory editors themselves (upon reviewing a site) or are adapted from site owner submissions. It is important to remember that directories do *not* necessarily use the HTML <title> tag or the description contained in your site's meta tags, like some crawler-based search engines do.

Since most Web directories tend to be small, directory results are often supplemented with additional results from a search engine partner. These supplemental results are commonly referred to as "fall-through" results. In fact, many people mistakenly believe that their sites are listed in a directory when they are actually appearing in the fall-through results from a search engine.

Web directories tend to list Web sites, not individual Web pages. A Web site is a collection of Web pages that generally focuses on a specific topic. In other words, a Web page is part of a Web site. A Web directory is most likely to list only your domain name (www.companyname.com) and not individual Web pages.

However, if a section of a Web site, or an individual page on a Web site, contains unique and valuable information about a particular topic, Web directory editors will include links to these resources under different categories. Glossaries and how-to tips are examples of content-rich sections of Web sites that can receive additional directory listings. A link to a section of a Web site will usually lead to a main category or channel page. A link to a single Web page with substantial and unique content will, of course, lead to that individual URL.

In contrast, crawler-based search engine result pages display links to individual Web pages.

Paid submission programs

A Web directory that uses a paid submission program will charge a submission fee to process a request to be included in its index. Payment of the submission fee guarantees that your site will be reviewed within a specified period of time (generally 48 hours to ten days).

If you wish to have individual, content-rich Web pages included in separate directory categories, in most cases you must pay an additional submission fee for another review. Some Web directories will accept content-rich pages without payment, but directory editors generally will not review those pages as quickly as the paid submissions.

The main advantage of paid submission is speed. You know your Web site is being reviewed quickly, and, if the editors find your site acceptable, your listing will be added to the Web directory database within days.

Furthermore, once your site is added to a legitimate, professional Web directory, the listing gives your site a significant popularity boost in the crawler-based search engines.

The Yahoo directory is an example of a Web directory that has a paid submission program.

Web directory category pages, particularly those that originate from high-quality, industry-specific directories, commonly appear at the top of crawler-based search results. Web directory listings are extremely important for link development campaigns, which are discussed in Part 4 of this book.

Specialty Search Engine Results

The commercial Web search engines constantly gather data about searcher behavior. As a result, search engine results pages have evolved to include information from specialty search engines including but not limited to:

- News search engines
- Local search engines
- Shopping search engines

For example, if a searcher types a keyword phrase that includes a local qualifier (such as "Chicago") into a search box, local search results often appear at the top of the screen beneath the ads. Figure 1-5 shows where information from the local search database at Google appears when a person searches for a pizza restaurant in Chicago:

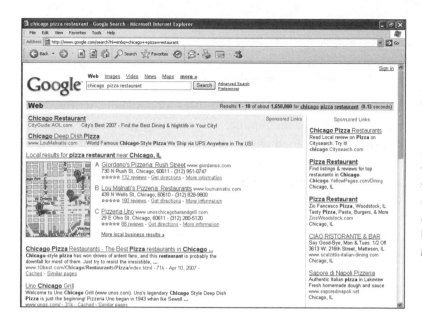

Figure 1-5
Local search listings typically appear beneath search engine advertising when a searcher types a local quali-fier keyword in the search box. Google and the other major crawler-based search engines have determined that searchers who enter this type of keyword phrase (chicago pizza restaurant) are more interested in local search results than general search results.

Analyzing search engine results pages should be the first step before implementing any search engine marketing campaign. Reviewing and analyzing search results will help Web site owners determine the types of search engine marketing that best suit their businesses and organizations.

Search Engine Optimization Strategies

One of the most widespread beliefs about search engine marketing is search engine *advertising* equals search engine *marketing*. Although this belief is common, it is hardly accurate. Search engine marketing encompasses multiple search engine strategies, including but not limited to:

- Search engine optimization

- Search engine advertising

- Search engine paid inclusion

continues

- Web directory paid inclusion

- Specialized/vertical search optimization

- Multimedia search optimization

Search engine optimization is the process of designing, writing, coding (in HTML), programming, and scripting your entire Web site so that there is a good chance that your Web pages will appear at the top of search engine queries for your selected keywords. Optimization is a means of helping your potential customers find your Web site.

To get the best overall, long-term search engine visibility, three components must be present on a Web page:

- Text component

- Link component

- Popularity component

All of the major search engines (Google, Yahoo, MSN's Live, Ask, etc.) use these components as a part of their search engine algorithm. Figure 1-6 illustrates the "ideal" Web page that is designed and written for the search engines:

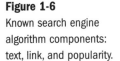

Figure 1-6

Known search engine algorithm components: text, link, and popularity.

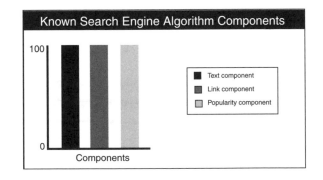

Very few Web pages can attain the "ideal" match for all search engine algorithms. In reality, most Web pages have different combinations of these components, as illustrated in Figure 1-7:

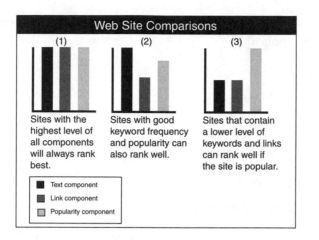

Figure 1-7
Web site comparisons.

Sites that (a) have all of the components on their Web pages and (b) have optimal levels of all the components perform well in the search engines overall.

Text Component—An Overview

Since the search engines build lists of words and phrases on URLs, it naturally follows that in order to do well on the search engines, you must place these words on your Web pages in the strategic HTML tags.

The most important part of the text component of a search engine algorithm is keyword selection. In order for your target audience to find your site on the search engines, your pages must contain keyword phrases that match the phrases your target audience is typing into search queries.

Once you have determined the best keyword phrases to use on your Web pages, you will need to place them within your HTML tags. Search engines do not place emphasis on the same HTML tags. For example, Yahoo places some emphasis on meta-tag content; Google rarely uses meta-tag content to determine relevancy. Thus, in order to do well on all of the search engines, it is best to place keywords in all of the HTML tags possible, without keyword stuffing. So no matter what the search engine algorithm is, you know that your keywords are contained in your documents.

Keywords should be placed in the following places, whenever possible and applicable:

- Title tags

- Visible body text

- Anchor text

- Meta tags

- Graphic images (alternative text)

- Domain and file names

The two most important tags to place keywords are in the title tag and in the visible body text, because all of the search engines index this text and place significant weight on this text.

Keywords in Your Domain Name and File Names

Many search engine marketers believe that placing keywords in your domain name and your file names has a major impact on search engine positioning, whereas others believe that the boost is miniscule.

One reason people believe the position boost is significant is that the words or phrases matching the words you typed in a query are highlighted when you view the search results. This occurrence is called search-term highlighting or term highlighting.

Search engines and Web directories may use term highlighting for usability purposes. The process is done dynamically using a highlighting application. This application simply takes your query words and highlights them in the search results for quick reference. Term highlighting merely indicates that query terms were passed through the application. In other words, in search results, just because a word is highlighted in your domain name does not necessarily mean that the domain name received a significant boost in search results.

Many other factors determine whether a site will or will not rank, and the three components (text, link, popularity) have more impact on search engine visibility than using a keyword in a domain and/or a file name.

Link Component—An Overview

The strategy of placing keyword-rich text in your Web pages is useless if the search engine spiders have no way of accessing that text. Therefore, the way your pages are linked to each other, and the way your Web site is linked to other Web sites, has a significant impact your site's search engine visibility.

Even though search engine spiders are powerful data-gathering programs, HTML coding or scripting can prevent a spider from crawling your pages. Examples of site navigation schemes that can be problematic are:

1. **Poor HTML coding on all navigation schemes:** Browsers can display Web pages with sloppy HTML coding; search engine spiders are not as forgiving as browsers are.

2. **Image maps:** Many search engines have a difficult time following the links in some types of image maps.

3. **JavaScript:** All of the major search engines will not follow many of the links embedded in many types of JavaScript, including but not limited to mouseovers/rollovers, arrays, and navigation menus.

4. **Dynamic or database-driven Web pages:** Pages that are generated via scripts, databases, and/or have a ?, &, $, =, +, or % in the URL often pose problems for search engine spiders. URLs with CGI-BIN in them can also be problematic.

5. **Flash:** Currently, few search engines can follow the links embedded in Flash documents.

When designing Web pages, be sure to include a navigation scheme so that the spiders have the means to record the words on your Web pages. Usually that means having two forms of navigation on a Web site: one that pleases your target audience visually and one that the search engines spiders can follow.

For example, let's say that a Web site's main navigation scheme is a series of drop-down menus coded with JavaScript. Figure 1-8 illustrates why sites without JavaScript in the navigation scheme consistently rank higher than sites with JavaScript:

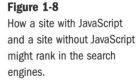

Figure 1-8

How a site with JavaScript and a site without JavaScript might rank in the search engines.

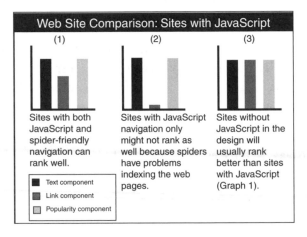

In Figure 1-8, please note that both the text and popularity component levels are equal in all three graphs. A Web page that uses JavaScript in its navigation can rank well in the search engines as long as a spider friendly navigation scheme (text links, for example) is also present on the Web page. However, since JavaScript can "trap" a spider (prevent it from indexing the text on a Web page), the link component level is lower than a site that does not use JavaScript in its navigation.

The link component is not only limited to accessing content, however. One widespread misconception about search engine optimization is that a search engine friendly site is a Web site designed to rank well in the search engines. In reality, a search engine friendly Web site is a user friendly Web site that can be easily found on the crawler-based search engines, human-based search engines (Web directories), and vertical (specialized) search engines.

What is the difference between the first and second definitions? In the second definition, the primary focus is on the end user, not the search engine, because the fact is that Google and Yahoo are not going to spend thousands or millions of dollars on your site's products and services. Your site visitors will.

Search friendliness is not only about being found on Google, Yahoo, MSN Live, Ask, or any other crawler-based search engine. Search friendliness is first and foremost about meeting the expectations of site visitors, accommodating their search behavior. Therefore, always write and design your Web site to meet user expectations. In addition, recognize that your target audience will likely use the commercial Web search engines to find the content available on your site. As a result, your Web site must also meet search engine guidelines for high-quality "findability."

The link component does not only address accessibility. The link component must provide:

- Access
- Relevancy
- Sense of place
- Scent of information

In other words, a site's information architecture and corresponding interface is crucial for long-term, effective search engine visibility. When all of these aforementioned characteristics are addressed on a Web page and across an entire site using keywords, a Web site can easily be found via the commercial Web search engines.

Search engine optimization and Web site usability are not at odds with each other. In fact, I believe that search engine optimization is actually a subset of Web site usability. By analyzing and understanding your target audience's search behavior and keyword usage, and by incorporating this information on Web sites, Web site owners can create a user experience that benefits everyone: your business, your prospects, your customers, and the commercial Web search engines.

Popularity Component—An Overview

The popularity component of a search engine algorithm consists of two sub-components:

- Link popularity
- Click-through or click popularity

Attaining an optimal popularity component is not simply obtaining as many links as possible to a Web site. The quality of the sites linking to your site holds more "weight" than the quantity of sites linking to your site. Since the Yahoo directory is one of the most frequently visited sites on the Web, a link from the Yahoo directory to your Web site carries far more "weight" than a link from a smaller, less visited site.

Obtaining links from other sites is not enough to maintain optimal popularity. The major search engines and some Web directories are measuring how often end users are clicking the links to your site and how long they are staying on your site (i.e., reading your Web pages). They are also measuring how often end users return to your site. All of these measurements constitute a site's click-through popularity.

Currently, the major crawler-based search engines use external, third-party link development to measure a site's overall link popularity. At this time, click-through popularity is not used to determine relevancy. One of the reasons that search engines do not use click-through popularity to determine rankings is click fraud. Many clever search engine marketers create clickbot programs that continuously click a link to a Web page in order to increase a Web page's position.

A site's home page is typically considered more important than any other Web page on a site. In all likelihood, a home page is going to be the URL listed in the major Web directories and industry-related sites, and a home page has more links pointing to it from within the Web site.

After a site is launched, search engine optimizers and Web site owners should incorporate link development as a regular part of their online marketing process because all of the major search engines measure popularity as a part of their search engine algorithms.

Many search engine optimization professionals fail to recognize that Web site usability is crucial to successful, long-term link development. Two sites can have similar or nearly identical content. These two sites might even appear close to each other in search engine results. If two sites contain essentially the same content, the site that is easier to use is going to receive the most link development, specifically the most high-quality link development. When it comes to search engine optimization, usability counts.

Web Design Rules

For optimal Web site usability, all Web sites should follow the Five Basic Rules of Web Design, which state that a Web site should be:

- Easy to read
- Easy to navigate
- Easy to find
- Consistent in layout and design
- Quick to download

In other words, site visitors should find your Web site easy to use. To be honest, I sometimes find that advanced designers and developers tune out when they hear or read the word *basic* because they assume *basic* means *elementary*. The Five Basic Rules of Web Design are elementary in the sense of being straightforward and obvious. However, these rules are crucial for search engine visibility and Web site usability. They are fundamental rules. Besides, if these five rules are so obvious, then why aren't designers and search engine marketers following them?

In order to have a Web site that (a) your target audience will like and use, (b) Web directory editors will approve and list, and (c) objective third parties will link to, all of these rules need to be followed. The most successful Web sites generally follow these Web design guidelines.

It is also important to understand that all of these rules are interrelated. For example, let's say that your home page has a #1 position in one of the major search engines for your targeted keywords, and people click the link to your site. If your site designer has placed a considerable amount of graphic images, animations, and scripting on your home page, causing it to download slowly, most people will not wait for that page to download. So a perfectly good #1 search engine position can be wasted if your site designer does not consider download time, or any of the other design rules.

Rule #1: Easy To Read

I hear people say all the time, "Of course my Web site is easy to read. I'm looking at it right now and I can read it." Which is great if every single person in your target audience is using the exact same computer screen, the exact same browser, the exact same Internet connection, and exact same type of computer you are using. In all likelihood, your target audience is using a variety computers, monitors, Internet connections, and browsers.

In fact, no one knows how site visitors are viewing your Web site. They might be using a notebook computer. They might be using a dial-up connection or a high-speed connection. They might be using a Macintosh computer. Site designers need to accommodate as many platforms, browsers, and Internet connections as possible.

Every single item on your Web pages needs to be legible on the major browsers and on the two types of computers (PC and Macintosh).

All HTML text should be legible with the graphic images turned on and the graphic images turned off (for visually impaired users). That means producing HTML text, background images, and the text in graphic images with the high color contrast. (The highest color contrast comes from using only black and white.) Your site designer should not use backgrounds that obscure your text or use colors that are hard to read.

Your site designer should not set your text size too small (too hard to read) or too large (it will appear to shout at your visitors). If a site is specifically designed for visually impaired users, then the text size should be adjusted accordingly.

All text in graphic images should be legible. High color contrast and font/typeface selection are very important for legibility in graphic images. Generally, producing graphic images that use text in a sans serif ("without feet") typeface has better legibility.

Times and **Times New Roman** are serif typefaces. **Arial** and **Helvetica** are sans-serif typefaces.

Figure 1-9
Serif and sans-serif typefaces.

Animations should not move so quickly that site visitors are unable to read them. If site visitors must watch an animation loop three or more times to view the full message, then the animation is moving too quickly.

Knowing whether content is easy to read is part objective and part subjective, part art and part science. Web site owners can determine the subjective part through focus groups, usability testing, and Web analytics tools.

Color science and research can help Web site owners determine which color palettes to use. For optimal legibility usability experts recommend a color contrast of 90% or more, especially for sites that target an older demographic. For example, yellow is one of the first colors that the human eye registers. Therefore, yellow should be used as a highlight color (a) because it is one of the first colors the eye sees, and (b) because it contrasts well against navy, dark gray, and black.

When your site design or redesign is in the template stage, view it on different browsers, platforms, and Internet connections. Go to a library or a store (such as Kinkos) that has different computers than you have and view your site.

One legibility issue involves XHTML strict and CSS (Cascading Style Sheet) compliance. Personally, I have designed and viewed many sites that adhere to these standards; however, when we view these sites on multiple browsers and platforms, usability test participants often have a difficult time reading a page's content or using the site's navigation scheme. One reason is overlapping CSS layers, layers that overlap each other so badly that words often appear on top of each other.

Better yet, have actual end users who fit your target audience profile view your Web pages and tell you whether everything is legible. Do not rely on your singular, personal perspective to determine your site's legibility. Do not rely on your designer, developer, or IT department staff to determine your site's legibility. Do not rely on your marketing department's opinion, either. The people who count are your site's visitors. If your site visitors have a difficult time reading your site's content, they will click the "Back" button and return to search engine results pages without taking your desired call to action.

Legibility is crucial. If searchers click a link from a search engine to your Web page and if they cannot read your content, they will leave your site with a very poor impression. That poor impression will not help with branding and future link development campaign.

Rule #2: Easy To Navigate

"Easy to navigate" means your target audience should know where they are at all times when they visit your Web site. If they get lost, they should be able to go to a site map, a help section, a site search, or a home page from any page on your site to determine (a) where they are, (b) where they might want to go, and (c) where they have been. Interestingly, effective Web site usability is mostly due to navigational elements.

Web pages should always provide a sense of place and a scent of information. Sense of place is very important in the search engine optimization process. When people click a link from a search engine results page, they do not always go to a site's home page. They most likely land directly on a page that contains the information they are searching for, or they land on a page that will lead them to the desired information. For searchers to feel confident that a site offers the product, service, or information they desire, Web pages should present clear "you are here" cues.

Additionally, searchers should be able to query commercial Web search engines and be delivered to pages that contain the exact information they desire. For example, if a searcher wants to determine the cost of a 42-inch flat-screen television at a variety of online stores, that searcher generally wants to arrive at product pages that show the price and a photo of the available flat-screen televisions.

Information retrieval systems are far from perfect, however, and most content providers do not necessarily understand search engine friendly copywriting. The result? Searchers do not always land on the page that contains the information they desire. They might, however, land on a page that can *lead* them to the information they desire, such as a category or an FAQs (frequently asked questions) page. Providing an information scent on a Web site, therefore, is important not only for closing a sale but also for information retrieval.

To provide an effective information scent, searchers must feel comfortable navigating a Web site. Using important keywords in navigational elements (primary and secondary navigation schemes, breadcrumb links, related cross-links) is critical for providing this scent.

All of your hyperlinks should be clear to all site visitors. Graphic images, such as navigation buttons or file tabs, should be clearly labeled and easy to read. Just as indicated in the First Rule of Web Design, your site designer should select the colors, backgrounds, textures, and special effects on your Web graphics so that they are legible on the major browsers, computer screens, and platforms.

Colors in your text links should be familiar to your target audience. Blue, underlined text usually indicates an unvisited link, and purple/maroon, underlined text usually indicates a visited link. If you elect not to use these default colors, your text links should be emphasized in some other way (bold, a different color, different size, set between small vertical lines, or a combination of these effects). Your hyperlink colors and effects should always be unique—they should not look the same as any other text in your Web pages.

Many site designers like to take the underline out of hyperlinked text to be more creative. If you are designing a site that targets the more experienced Web user, then this design technique should not be problematic as long as the hyperlinked text is unique. However, if your target audience is not very Web savvy, then it is best to keep the underline on the hyperlinked text.

Always determine your navigation elements with great care. Site visitors should find your site navigation to be intuitive, and navigational elements should contain keywords, when appropriate. Navigational elements must also be easily crawled and indexed by the major search engines if you want your site to be easily found via the commercial Web search engines.

Rule #3: Easy To Find

Rule #3 has multiple meanings. Your Web site should be easy to find via the commercial Web search engines. Additionally, the individual products, services, and information that your site offers should be easy to find once your target audience arrives at your site.

For maximum online visibility, your Web site should be easy to find on the search engines, Web directories, and popular industry-specific Web sites. For example, download.com is an industry-specific site for free software downloads. If your company offers a free demo of a 30-day trial of your software, having a link to your site from download.com can significantly increase your site's traffic. There are other popular, industry-specific sites that link for healthcare, finance, manufacturing, etc. that will link to your site.

Internally (within your Web site), the products, services, and information you offer should be easy to find once your target audience arrives at your site. Generally speaking, your target audience does not want to land on your home page and hunt around for information. People prefer to go directly to the Web page that contains the information they are searching for. And if they cannot go directly to the Web page(s) containing the specific information, they need to find that information within three to five clicks, preferably less, before they get frustrated and leave your Web site.

Once your target audience finds the page that contains the information they are searching for, they need to see that information "above the fold," or at the top part of the screen. Even if people can't immediately see your product/service on top of the screen, they need to know that what they are searching for is on a particular Web page. People should not have to scroll to see that the information they desire is available on a Web page.

An FAQs (Frequently Asked Questions) page is a good example of Web site designers not using the "above the fold" strategy particularly well (see Figure 1-10). Let's say you place ten questions on your FAQs page, and the information that your target audience is looking for is the answer to Question #4. Suppose your site designer formats your FAQs pages in a Question1–Answer 1, Question 2–Answer 2 format, as shown in Figure 1-10:

Figure 1-10
FAQs page with a Question1–Answer1, Question2–Answer2 format.

Let's assume that the person viewing this page is a domestic violence victim with children. By looking at the top of this screen, this person is not able to determine whether parent/child interaction is allowed at the shelter. In other words, an answer to an important question might not be available on that Web page or site because the above-the-fold content is not providing a strong sense of place and scent of information that uses the user's language.

However, if all of your important questions are placed at the top of your screen, then your target audience will know that the answer to their question is available on that Web page or site, as shown in Figure 1-11:

Figure 1-11

FAQs page that is formatted for search engine visibility and site usability. The target audience now can see that important information is available on that Web page or site.

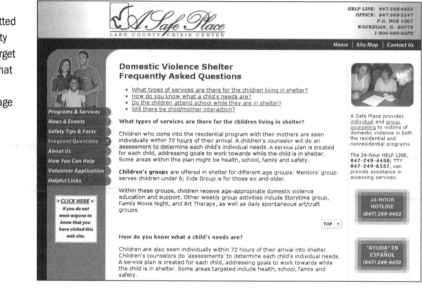

All of your FAQs pages should be formatted in this manner. Not only is this strategy beneficial for reaching your end users, it is also beneficial because this format is a search engine friendly layout.

Making your main products and services easy to find is very important for link development purposes. As stated previously, if your home page states that your firm specializes in three particular services, those three services need to be obvious on your home page, in terms of graphic images and HTML text. If Web directory editors, and ultimately your end users, have to hunt around too much to determine what your company specializes in, you did not make your services easy to find.

If the information on your site is password protected or requires some kind of plug-in to get the information, Web directory editors and site visitors might be unable to determine whether your site delivers the information you claim it does. Make sure some of the information available on your Web site is not password protected so that people can see that your site delivers the content that you claim it does without having to provide private, confidential information or downloading a plug-in.

The last item that should be easy to find is your company's contact information (mailing or physical address, telephone number, fax number, contact person's email address).

In general, your contact information should be in one of four places:

- A header or footer
- The About Us page or section
- The Contact Us page or section
- A Locations page or section

The place Web directory editors are most likely to look for your contact information and the correct spelling of your company name is your About Us page. So even if you do provide contact information in other places, it is still a good idea to place that information in your About Us section. Especially if you place your contact information in a footer because many end users do not scroll to the bottom of a Web page to view information.

Rule #4: Consistent in Layout and Design

Layout means the use of HTML code, scripting, and use of white space on your site. Another way of stating this is screen "real estate," i.e., where you place your text, graphic images, and navigation schemes on your site. Consistency in layout design helps your target audience navigate your site and feel comfortable doing business with you.

Design means the use of graphic images, the special effects on your graphic images, fonts/typefaces, and color. Many aspects of the design should be repeated throughout a Web site. The fonts/typefaces and colors used in the main body text, hyperlinks, and headings should be the same on every page.

If you are showing photos of the products you offer, the photo dimensions (length and width) should fall within a short range. Horizontal photos should have the same dimensions and vertical photos should have the same dimensions. If you use a drop shadow on your product photos, you should use drop shadows on all your product photos.

Graphic images and text should never be placed on a Web page randomly or arbitrarily. Everything should have a visual connection with other items on a Web page. Related items, such as a main navigation scheme and a secondary navigation scheme, should be grouped together so that they are seen as a cohesive group rather than unrelated items.

Making two navigation schemes visually different creates visual contrast but also shows how they are interrelated. For example, a main navigation scheme can be shown at the top of a page using a set of specific colors, and the secondary navigation scheme can open up on the left side of the screen with a different set of colors that blend well with the main navigation.

Figure 1-12 shows an example of a Web page that shows visual contrast and connectivity. This is also a well-constructed Web page for search engines, directories, and the target audience:

1. File tab graphic images that link to home page and site map, in the event the target audience gets lost or needs to re-orient themselves. This set of navigation images is in the same place on every Web page.

2. Main navigation buttons. Button changes color when end users are visiting that section of the Web site.

3. A secondary navigation scheme, or subnavigation, opens up when target audience clicks the link from the main navigation. Text in the subnavigation repeats the text in the main navigation to further indicate that the navigation buttons on the left are a subset of the main navigation.

4. "Breadcrumbs" indicate which page the end users are currently visiting.

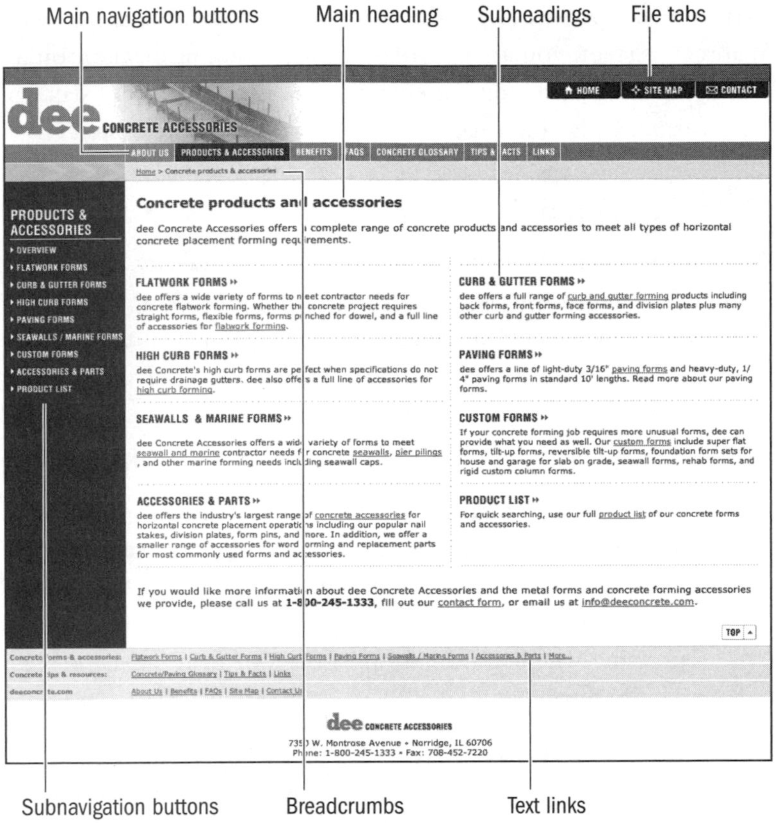

Main navigation buttons   Main heading   Subheadings   File tabs

Figure 1-12
Sample of an "ideal"
Web page.

Subnavigation buttons   Breadcrumbs   Text links

5. Main heading (can also be a graphic image) indicates which page the end users are currently visiting.

6. Subheadings (graphic images) highlight the main features of this section of the Web site. Arrows on the subheadings give a subtle hint that they are hyperlinks.

7. Text links at the bottom of the page correspond to the main navigation buttons. These links indicate which pages the target audience has already visited. The hypertext link colors remain similar to a browser's default colors because the target audience is not considered to be 100 percent "Web savvy."

Consistency in layout and design communicates credibility, trust, dependability, and reliability. Every Web site needs to communicate these sentiments in order to encourage site visitors to take a desired call to action. Additionally, if you make it easy for site visitors to form a mental model of your site by making your page design templates consistent, you are providing a clear sense of place throughout your site. By providing a keyword-focused, consistent sense of place, you are also increasing your site's search engine visibility.

Rule #5: Quick To Download

Site visitors want Web pages that download quickly, preferably within 30 seconds on a standard dial-up connection. Of course, there are a few exceptions, such as pages that specialize in online video games with plug-ins such as Flash or Shockwave that must download first. Below are some general guidelines that will decrease your pages' download time.

- **Use animation sparingly.** Animation should only be used to call attention to important sections of your Web site. Graphic artists who specialize in animation can safely use animation on their pages as long as they are useful. The best way to determine whether animation attracts or distracts is through usability testing.

- **Follow the KISS rule:** Keep it simple, stupid. You want site visitors to notice the products, services, and information you offer on your Web site, not your pretty site design. If site visitors like your site design without taking desired calls to action (Add to Cart, Enroll in Class, Sign Up for Newsletter), then the design is not an effective one, even if it is pretty.

  A person searching for "accounting software" does not type the words "pretty site design" in a search box when looking for information about accounting software.

- **Use smaller graphic images, called thumbnails, for product photos.** On your Products pages, a gallery of small photos will download more quickly than full-size photos. Give site visitors the option to view the larger photos.

  To get a faster download time, always create separate, unique thumbnail-size graphic images from their larger versions. All graphic images should be resized in graphic image software, not with HTML.

- **Use the same graphic images on multiple pages of your site whenever possible.** Using graphic images consistently also lends continuity to your presentation.

  For example, placing your logo on every page of your site (with a hyperlink to your home page) helps with both navigation and branding, and it helps your target audience know whose site they are visiting at all times.

  The logo image will only download once because it will be saved in the browser's cache. Introducing new graphic images on each page requires time-consuming downloading as a visitor moves around your site.

- **Understand the variety of customers in your target audience.** Different customers will tolerate different download times. If you have graphic design or an online game site, your customers are more likely to wait for pages to download in order to experience your creative flair. However, if you are selling machine parts to busy manufacturers, ease of access to valuable information should be your primary concern.

Conclusion

To get the best overall, long-term search engine visibility, Web designers should follow the Five Basic Rules of Web Design, which state that a Web site should be:

- Easy to read

- Easy to navigate

- Easy to find

- Consistent in layout and design

- Quick to download

By following these rules, you are building your Web site to satisfy your target audience. The added benefit of following these rules is that both directory editors and search engines are looking for these same characteristics. These design rules also help form the foundation of effective, long-term search engine optimization:

- Text component

- Link component

- Popularity component

Web pages that contain the words that your target audience is typing into search queries generally have greater search engine visibility than pages that contain few if any keywords.

The way your Web pages are linked to each other also affects your site's search engine visibility. If search engine spiders can find your pages quickly and easily, your site has a much better chance of appearing at the top of search results.

If two Web sites have the same text component and link component weights, the site with the higher-quality link development will usually rank higher and more consistently over time. Sometimes, a popular Web site with little keyword focus will consistently rank higher than sites that use plenty of keywords. Therefore, building a site that satisfies user expectations, achieves business goals, and meets the terms and conditions set forth by the search engines will generate long-term search engine visibility.

Part 2:

How To Build Better Web Pages— Text Files

The foundation of successful search engine optimization consists of three fundamental building blocks: the text component, link component, and popularity component. Web sites that use this core in synergy gain far more search engine visibility over time.

This chapter provides details for creating and maintaining these fundamental building blocks in text-based files. The result? A Web site that meets user expectations, accomplishes business goals, and meets all the terms and conditions set forth by the commercial Web search engines.

Text Component

To obtain maximum search engine visibility, it is essential to understand how your target audience is searching for information on your Web site. When your target audience uses a Web search engine to find the products and services you offer, they type a set of words or phrases into the search box. These word sets are commonly called your site's *keywords* or *keyword phrases*.

In order for your target audience to find your site on the search engines, your site's most important pages *must* contain keyword phrases that match the phrases your target audience is typing into search queries. Web pages can contain sales and marketing language as well, because a Web site needs to accomplish business goals in order to sustain itself. Nevertheless, targeted Web pages should appear to be more focused on the keyword phrases that your target audience types into search queries, not sales and marketing language.

When a search engine spider analyzes a Web page, it determines keyword relevancy based on an algorithm, which is a rather large and complex formula that calculates how Web pages are ranked. The most important text for a search engine is the most important text for your target audience—the text it sees first when it arrives at your Web site.

The most important places to put keywords are:

- The HTML title tag
- Visible body text that can be copied and pasted directly from a Web browser into text editor (such as NotePad or SimpleText)
- Text in and around hypertext links
- Visible body text that is above the fold (text that can be seen on a standard Web browser without having to scroll).

Title-tag text and visible body text are considered primary text by the search engines because all the search engines index this text and place significant weight on it. In other words, all the commercial Web search engines use this text to determine how a Web page will rank. Most of your copywriting efforts should focus predominantly on this text. In fact, very few Web pages receive qualified search engine traffic over time without keyword placement in primary text.

Meta-tag content, alternative text, and text contained in domain and file names are considered secondary text by the search engines because not all search engines index this type of text and use it to determine relevancy.

As a general guideline, I like the Five-Second Usability Test to determine whether a page is keyword focused. Noted usability professional Jared Spool is the originator of this test. For the Five-Second Usability Test, show participants a Web page for five seconds. Then, have participants write down everything they remember about the page on a sheet of paper. If participants do not write down any (or few) keywords, then the page clearly is not keyword focused.

A modification of this test is to show a Web page to usability participants for eight to 12 seconds. After removing the page from their view, ask them if the page was focused on one or more topics. If the answer is yes, then ask participants to name the topic(s). If participants mention keyword phrases, then the page is probably keyword focused.

As an example, using the aforementioned usability tests, your target audience must perform an action (View Source) in order to see meta-tag content (see Figure 2-1). Therefore, meta-tag content is not used, or is rarely used, to determine relevancy on text-based Web documents.

Note

These types of usability tests should generally be given to one participant at a time, not as a group. One of the problems with focus groups is herd mentality. Some participants are too intimidated to give a different answer than the rest of the group.

Figure 2-1

In order to view the meta-tag content on this Web page, end users must perform an action. They must select "View" on the drop-down menu in their browsers, and then select "Source."

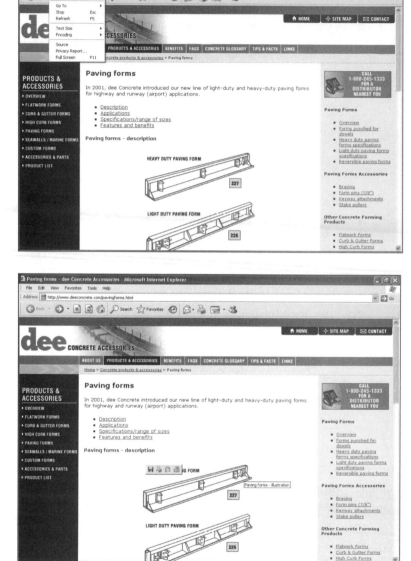

Figure 2-2

Alternative text can be viewed by placing the pointer (in Internet Explorer) over a graphic image. Note that the HTML title-tag content can be viewed without having to perform an action.

However, I highly recommend writing effective copy for meta-tag descriptions for search engines that do use this text to determine relevancy. In addition, many search engines display meta-tag descriptions in search engine results. Thus, it is important to write a meta-tag description that accomplishes two goals:

- Obtaining a good ranking in search engines that use meta-tag descriptions to determine relevancy.

- Eliciting a call to action, that is, encouraging searchers to click the link from the search engine results page to your Web page.

For long-term, effective search engine visibility, far more time and effort must be spent on optimizing primary text than on secondary text. Very few pages receive search engine visibility by modifying secondary text only.

Keyword Selection

The foundation of an effective search engine marketing campaign is selecting the best keywords that your potential customers will use to find your site. Selecting the right keywords requires constant research and maintenance.

Some of the goals of keyword research are to:

- Discover new keyword opportunities

- Fix missed keyword opportunities

- Generate a calendar of keyword phrases (some keyword phrases are more popular at different times of the year)

- Increase the number of clicks from search engine results pages to your Web pages

- Increase the relevancy of Web pages to attain and maintain long-term search engine visibility

I always begin the keyword research process by brainstorming. Pretend that no one has ever heard of your business but is looking for your type of product or service. Remember, you must determine the keywords that your potential *customers* will type in a search query, not the words that you, your boss, your boss's spouse, marketing staff, IT staff, a family member, or your best friend might type in a search query. For long-term, successful search engine visibility, Web pages must use the users' language.

You probably have a decent list of keywords already. Review your company's printed materials. What words are used over and over

Tip

Keeping and maintaining a list of popular, seasonal keyword phrases is a crucial search engine optimization strategy. For example, on a health publisher site, keyword phrases related to allergies are more popular in the spring and summer months, and keyword phrases related to cold and flu are more popular during the winter months.

again? Remove all words used for sales and marketing "hype" from your printed materials. Many of the remaining words are possible keywords and keyword phrases.

When you speak to new and current customers on the phone, what questions do they frequently ask and what words do they use? Do they mention a specific product or service? Do they frequently ask for a specific department? Ask your current customers how they would find you on the Web. You might discover that your current customers use terms you haven't even thought to use. Consider including these unexpected terms in your keyword list.

Usability tests are also a great way to determine targeted keyword phrases. Since usability participants are encouraged to think aloud during a variety of tests (expectancy, card sort and reverse card sort, performance, free exploration, and so forth), and since tests are usually recorded, Web site owners can often identify targeted keyword phrases by listening to recordings of test results. All Web sites should use the users' language in both navigational elements and main content areas of a site.

When you prepare a potential list of keywords, you must determine the various word combinations your target audience is most likely to type in a search query. Singular and plural versions of your most important keywords, synonyms, misspellings, acronyms, and abbreviations (with and without periods) are all potential keywords. As I mentioned previously, I like to begin the keyword research process with brainstorming.

For example, let's use a fictitious company called TranquiliTeas Organic Teas, Inc., which sells organic teas and tea sets. The TranquiliTeas site might have the following keyword list:

organic teas	iced tea recipes
oolong teas	tea spoons
organic oolong tea tea sets	tea kettles
tea recipes	tea bags
herbal tea	specialty teas
decaffeinated tea	tea gifts
whole leaf tea	chinese tea

chinese oolong tea

japanese tea ceremony

oolong tea

green teas

tea set

teacups

herbal teas

black teas

decaffeinated teas

india tea

indian black tea

herbal tea recipes

organic tea

green tea

organic green tea

tea cups

organic tea recipes

black teas

decaffeinated teas

whole leaf teas

loose leaf teas

tea pots

tea kettle

jasmine tea

tea ceremony

tea mugs

japanese tea

japanese green tea

whole leaf tea accessories

tea drinks

tea accessories

tea pot

what is organic tea

gourmet tea

china tea sets

porcelain tea sets

You might have noticed that all the keywords listed above are in lowercase. Generally, when people type in words in a search box, they tend to type in the words all in lowercase. Initially creating your keyword list in lowercase will make this task easier.

When you create your keyword list, think up as many combinations as possible. When people are searching for something specific, they tend to use more than one word. For example, if a person is looking for "software," he might find a variety of software listed in the search results. He might be looking for accounting software, not graphic design software. If he is running a small business, a more accurate search phrase might be "small business accounting software" or "accounting software for small businesses."

It is usually better to target longer keyword phrases because the people who type in specific keyword phrases are more likely to be converted into customers. Three-, four-, or five-word keyword phrases often yield more accurate results in the search engines.

Targeting longer keyword phrases does not mean that you give up the chance to rank well for other keyword phrases or a single word. When you target the keyword phrase "organic herbal tea recipes," you are concurrently targeting all of following words and phrases:

Organic tea recipes	Tea recipes
Herbal tea recipes	Herbal recipes
Organic herbal tea	Tea
Herbal tea	Recipes
Organic tea	

Once you determine your initial keyword list, you can begin to narrow it by using many of the available tools online.

Tools, Techniques, and Tips

When you begin to analyze your keyword list, you are looking for trends. When I prepare a keyword list, I always put the list into a spreadsheet. A spreadsheet helps spot trends quickly and easily.

The first set of data is your initial keyword list. Once you have this keyword list, you need to determine which keyword combinations your target audience is most likely to type into search engine queries. Questions you need to ask yourself are:

- Did people tend to use the singular or plural version of a word?

- What three or four words appeared together most often?

- What was the word order?

If you have a new Web site and do not have any statistics on keywords, the major search engines and Web directories can assist you.

Related searches

Many search engines and directories offer a "Related searches" or "Others searched for" or "Narrow your search" feature in their search results pages. For instance, after searching for "organic tea" at Microsoft's Live, the search box on the results page displays "Related searches" as shown in Figure 2-3.

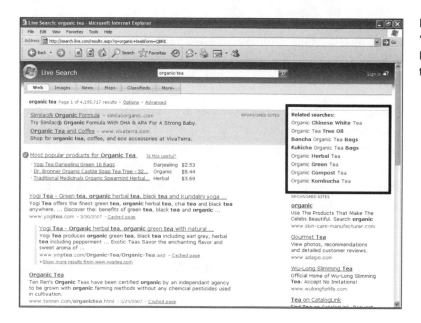

Figure 2-3

"Related searches" for the keyword phrase "organic tea" at Microsoft's Live.

The keyword phrases listed under the "Narrow Your Search" heading are some of the most popular searches conducted by Ask's users that contain the word "tea" as shown in Figure 2-4.

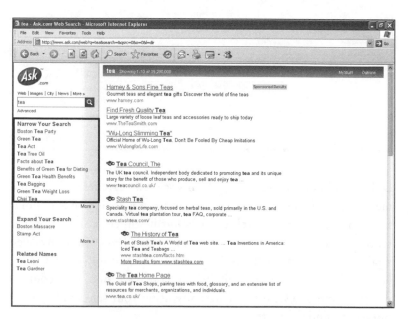

Figure 2-4

"Narrow Your Search" results for the keyword "tea" at Ask.

In this instance, you can see that "facts about tea" is a popular keyword phrase along with the phrases "green tea" and "chai tea." Likewise, if you perform the same search on Yahoo, you might get a different set of popular keyword phrases, as shown in Figure 2-5.

Notice some of the keyword phrases are on your initial keyword list (chai tea, herbal tea, green tea) and a phrase that you might not have thought to target (tea history). What we are beginning to see is a possible pattern. Both "green tea" and "white tea" are popular searches. Therefore, when you are designing and writing your Web site, you might want to have pages dedicated to green teas and white teas.

Figure 2-5

"Also try" search results for the keyword "tea" at Yahoo.

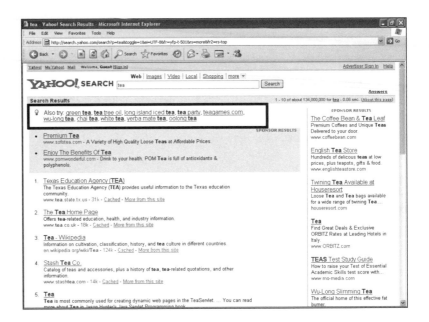

Did some keyword phrases yield no related searches? This could mean that your targeted keyword phrase might not be a popular search phrase on the search engines *but* it still could be a popular search phrase used by your target audience. Data from any Web analytics program (such as WebTrends, Omniture, ClickTracks, etc.) and your site search engine, if you have one, can confirm whether your site visitors are actually using your selected keyword phrases to find your site.

Free and low-cost keyword research tools

In addition to related searches, some search engines offer free or low-cost keyword research tools.

Yahoo Search Marketing

Yahoo Search Marketing is a pay-per-click search engine advertising program that allows you to easily determine the keyword phrases Yahoo searchers are typing into Yahoo queries. The Keyword Selector Tool feature is excellent for refining your keyword list.

The current URL for this tool is:

http://inventory.overture.com/d/searchinventory/suggestion/

Enter one of your keywords into the search box. The search results will be a list of the most popular search terms containing your keyword. For instance, entering "herbal tea" generated the list of matches shown in Figure 2-6:

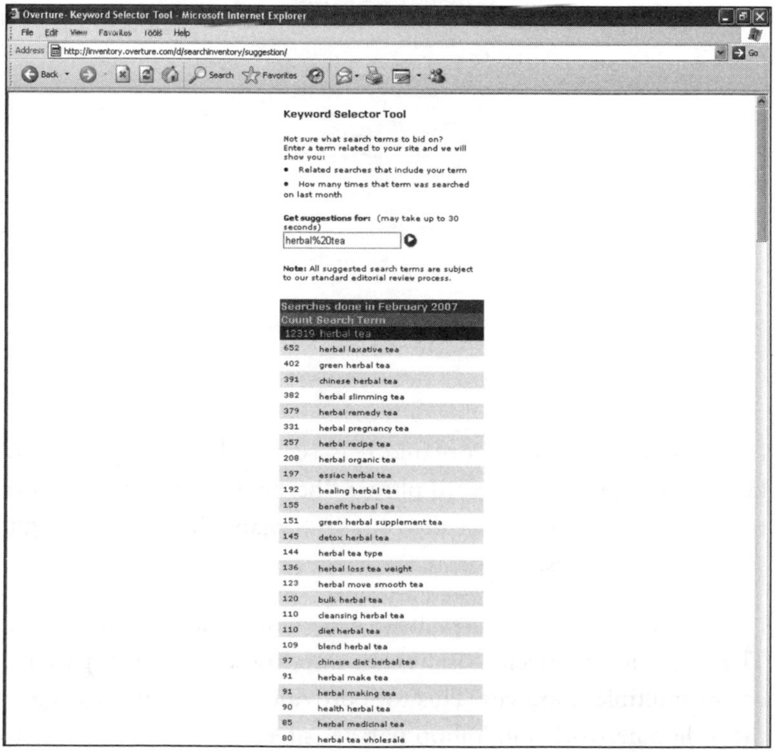

Figure 2-6

Search results for the keyword phrase "herbal tea" at Yahoo Search Marketing.

This list shows how many times people searched for the keyword phrase "herbal tea" in February 2007. That month 12,319 people searched for "herbal tea"; "herbal laxative tea" was the second most popular keyword phrase and "green herbal tea" was third.

Perform as many searches as possible to get a thorough picture of what your target audience is searching for. Since the fictional tea site we are working on sells organic teas, we can query Yahoo Search Marketing for "organic tea" (see Figure 2-7).

Figure 2-7

Search results for the keyword phrase "organic tea" at Yahoo Search Marketing.

Notice that the types of organic teas searched for are green and kombucha teas. The keyword phrase "herbal tea" might be a more popular search phrase, but the phrase "organic herbal tea" might yield better conversions.

Keep track of your search results in a keyword analysis spreadsheet. The number of searches is not as important as search patterns across multiple resources. This tool provides search patterns across the Yahoo network and Yahoo partner sites.

Google AdWords

Google has its own keyword research tool for its pay-per-click AdWords program. The current URL is:

https://adwords.google.com/select/KeywordToolExternal

For this tool, you can enter one keyword or keyword phrase per line in the query box, and Google will present you with a list of keyword phrases. For example, in Figure 2-8, if you enter the single keyword phrase "herbal tea" in the query box, a large number of more specific keyword phrases display. Notice that the keyword phrase "herbal tea benefit(s)" appeared in both Google and Yahoo Search Marketing. Therefore, the TranquiliTeas Organic company might want to create sections on its site about herbal tea benefits, herbal tea and pregnancy, and herbal tea recipes.

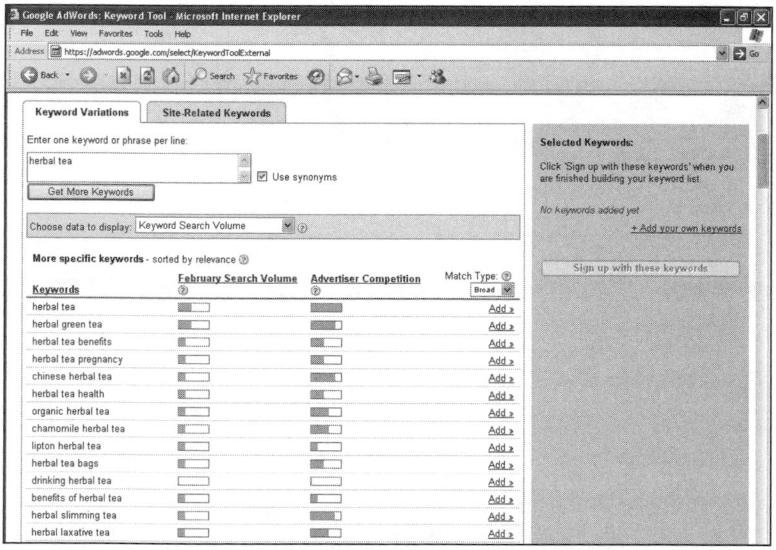

Figure 2-8

Search results for the keyword phrase "herbal tea" at Google AdWords.

Both Google and Yahoo Search Marketing have created these tools for their advertisers. To keep these services free, do not perform exhaustive amounts of searches daily to determine your keyword list. Generally, most companies and organizations can determine a comprehensive keyword list within 40 searches or less on each engine. Once you determine your keyword list from free resources, you can rely on other paid tools to further refine your list.

Microsoft adCenter

Google and Yahoo offer free keyword research tools for their search advertising programs. Microsoft's adCenter requires a small payment for use of its keyword research tool, though some of the nifty tools available in its labs (http://adlab.msn.com/default.aspx) are free.

Figure 2-9

Log in screen for Microsoft adCenter.

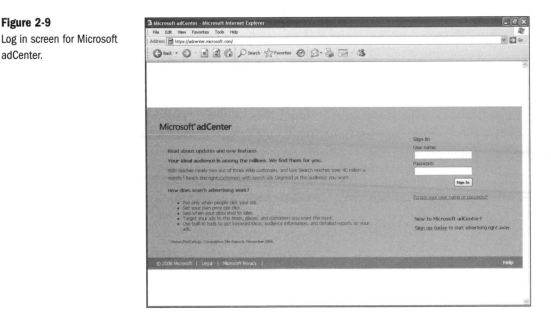

Figure 2-10

Free keyword research tools are also available at Microsoft adCenter Labs.

What I find to be particularly useful about the adCenter keyword research tool is the ability to see variations within similar languages. For example, American English is quite different from Canadian English. And both are different from British English. The drop-down menu in Figure 2-11 shows how keyword researchers can examine the variations among countries.

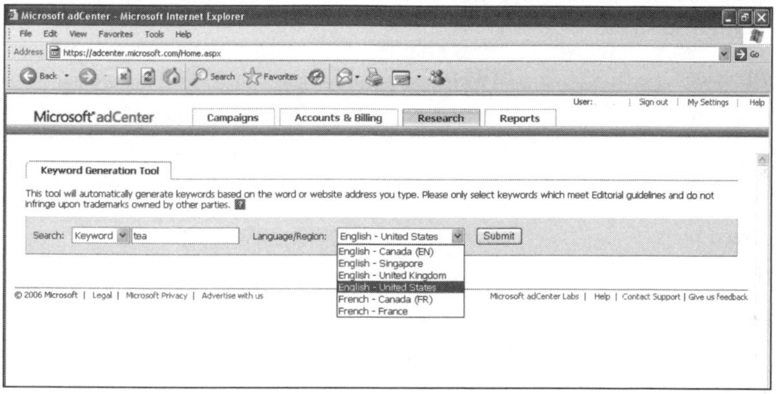

Figure 2-11
To examine the types of keyword phrases that searchers type into search queries at Microsoft's Live in the United States, select the "English—United States" option in the drop-down menu.

I like to export the keyword research results to a spreadsheet so I can compare them side by side.

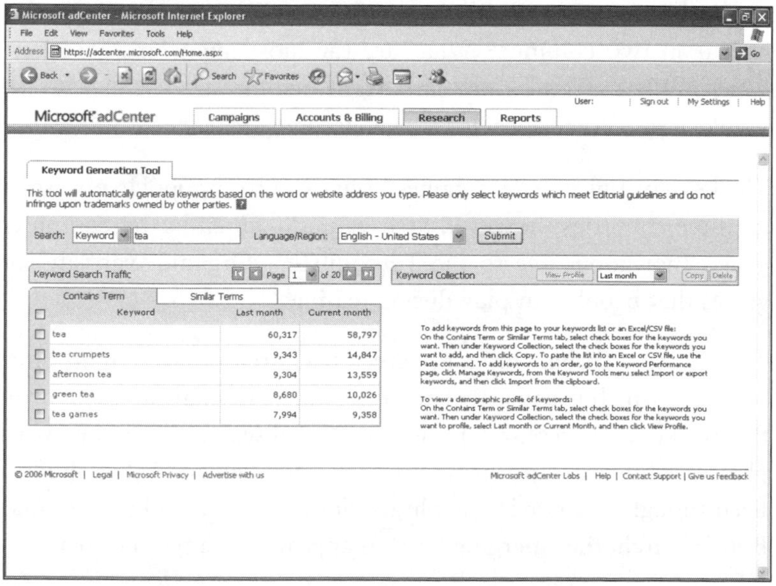

Figure 2-12
Keyword research results for "tea" in American English. You can also research this same keyword in British and Canadian English.

Below is a simple table that shows the differences in keyword popularity among different English-speaking countries. For now, I ignored the number of searches since I was trying to identify patterns and commonalities for use in navigational elements and site categorization.

Table 2-1 Comparison of popular English-language keyword phrases containing the word "tea" in the United States, Britain, and Canada.

American	British	Canadian
Tea	Tea games	Tea games
Tea crumpets	Tea	Green tea
Afternoon tea	Green tea	Tea
Green tea	Tea ritz	White tea
Tea games	Yorkshire tea	Tea biscuits
Scones tea	Tea game	Bubble tea
Hoodia tea	Herbal tea	Oolong tea
High tea	Afternoon tea	Tea party
Herbal tea	Tea rooms	Herbal tea
White tea	Spearmint tea	Tetley tea

What patterns do you see when you look at this table? What keyword phrases appear in all three columns? What keyword phrases appear in two columns? What are the most important core keywords? What are the most important qualifier keywords? Which words appear to be specific to a geographic area?

The keyword phrase "tea games" seems to be a popular phrase in all three countries; however, "tea games" can either be computer games (not applicable to the TranquiliTeas Organic Web site) or games that people can play during teatime.

The phrases "herbal tea" and "green tea" are displayed in all three columns, which is consistent with the keyword analysis we saw on the free keyword research tools and related searches. The keyword phrase "white tea" appears in both the Canadian and U.S. columns. Even though this particular phrase does not seem to be a popular British search, the emerging pattern appears to be types of tea.

Likewise, the keyword phrase "afternoon tea" appears in both the U.S. and the British columns. Perhaps the product descriptions for the teas sold on the TranquiliTeas Organic Web site can include, "Perfect for afternoon tea," or "Our organic green teas are perfect for afternoon tea."

Product pages are not the only page types to utilize important keyword phrases on an ecommerce site. For example, afternoon tea is quite different from high tea. The TranquiliTeas Organic Web site can offer supplementary content about (1) the different types of teatimes, (2) the types of foods and teas commonly served during these times, and (3) recipes. Result? The additional content is an outstanding resource for future link development, and more pages will be available to rank well in the search engines.

Paid keyword research tools

Even though free and low-cost keyword research tools provide researchers with a general idea of core keywords (tea, teas) and important qualifier keywords (organic, green, black, white, herbal, etc.), paid keyword research tools can provide deeper refinement. Trend analysis and seasonal search behavior are some of the further refinements that make paid keyword research tools worth the investment. Two of my favorite paid keyword research tools are Trellian (www.keyworddiscovery.com) and Wordtracker (www.wordtracker.com).

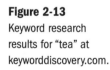

Figure 2-13
Keyword research results for "tea" at keyworddiscovery.com.

Figure 2-14

Keyword research results for "tea" at Wordtracker.com.

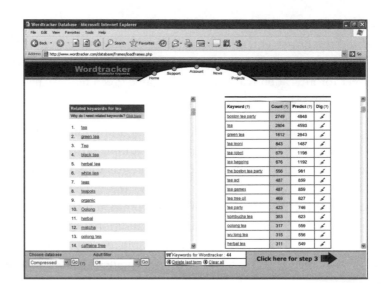

Users of paid keyword research tools often uncover keyword patterns that might not be available on unpaid keyword research tools. For example, I discovered that a considerable number of searchers type reverse word order. Instead of typing "auto loan" (without the quotation marks) in the search box, many searchers type "loan auto" in the search box. The number of searchers who search with reverse word order is too high to ignore. As a copywriter and content provider, I know that the primary text on the page should accommodate this common searcher behavior. How can I easily put reverse word order on a page without sacrificing legibility and the marketing message?

The truth about misspelled words

Many search engine marketers recommend using misspelled words as part of a keyword list. Sometimes misspellings are a good keyword strategy and sometimes they are not a good strategy. The situation depends on the word(s) you are targeting.

For example, "oolong" is a commonly misspelled word. When you perform a search for the misspelled "olong" on Yahoo Search Marketing, only one keyword phrase each appears in the search results:

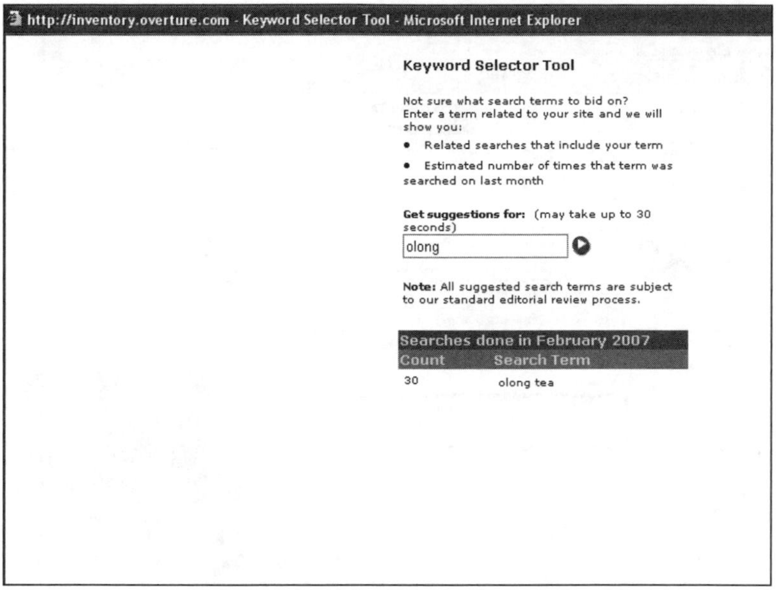

Figure 2-15
Search results for the misspelled version of the word "oolong" at Yahoo Search Marketing.

Since this word does not appear to be a popular search, I would not be overly concerned with the misspelling. To minimally compensate for a misspelled keyword phrase, put the misspelling in the meta-tag keywords attribute.

If a commonly misspelled, targeted keyword phrase is genuinely popular, how might a Web site owner include the most common misspellings in primary text rather than secondary text? One way to compensate for common misspellings is to create useful reference pages, a glossary or dictionary for example.

Many industries have their own lingo, words that the average person might not be familiar with. Additionally, people in your target audience demographic might actually use "lingo" in search queries. Reference pages, as well as product and service pages, can all be available for search engine visibility.

In the health industry, two commonly misspelled words are "hemorrhoids" and "diarrhea." The folks at MedicineNet.com are aware of these common misspellings have incorporated them into their medical dictionary.

Tip

The meta-tag keywords attribute is considered secondary text. In other words, the commercial Web search engines rarely use content contained in the meta-tag keywords attribute to determine relevancy.

Remember, in order for the search engines to consider a word important, the word must be placed within a page's primary text: the HTML title tag and visible body text. In all likelihood, you will not need to create a Web page specifically for a misspelled word unless that word is a popular misspelling.

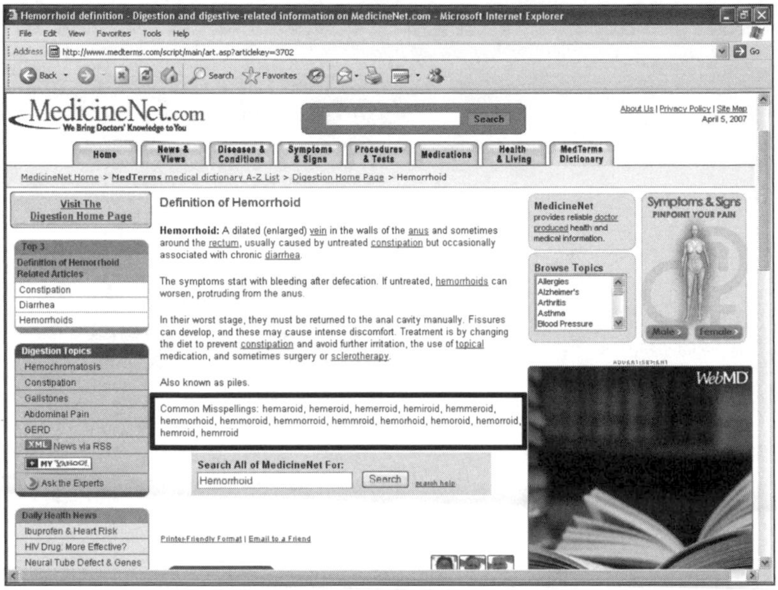

Figure 2-16

The MedicineNet.com Web site targets consumers who are probably not familiar with medical terminology, especially medication names and their proper spellings. Since the word "hemorrhoids" is commonly misspelled, as is a variety of medical terms, the site's medical dictionary incorporates the most common misspellings into reference pages.

Word stemming

Word stemming is the ability of a search to include the "root" or "stem" of words for multiple search results. For example, stemming allows a searcher to enter "marketing" in a search query and get search results for the stem word "market."

Not all search engines have stemming capabilities. Therefore, whenever possible, determine the most popular, targeted variation of a specific keyword. Quite often, the plural version of a keyword is more popular than the singular version. If you believe multiple versions of a word (such as "market" and "marketing") are important, then leave all versions in your keyword list.

Stop words and filter words

Filter words are common words (a, an, but, or, nor, for, the) that the search engines ignore during a search. Search engines filter out these words because the use of them can slow search results without improving accuracy. Filtering out common words can save search engines enormous amounts of space in their indices.

When preparing your keyword list, eliminate all filter words when applicable, since they will be ignored. If you would like to determine whether a word is a filter word, perform a search on a search engine, such as Google. In the search results, Google will tell you which words it ignores:

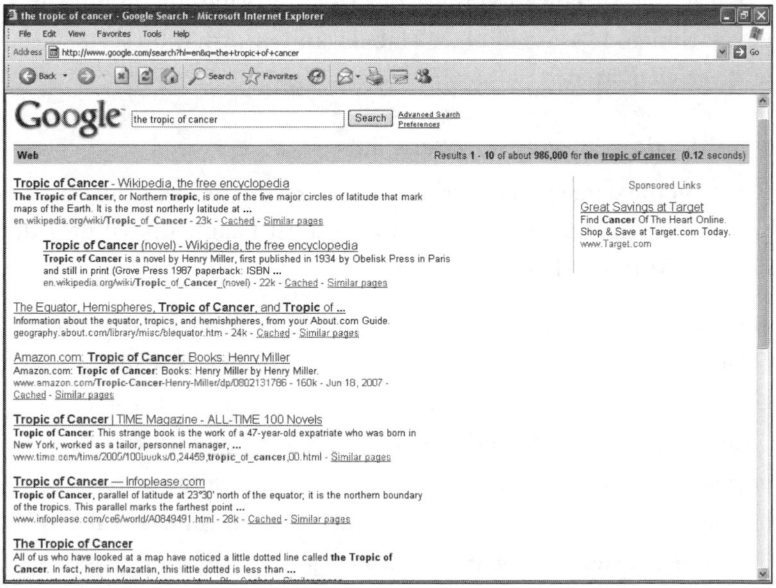

Figure 2-17
Google will ignore the word "the" because it is a common word and filter it out of search queries.

Web site search engines

If you have a search engine on your own Web site, the words entered into site search queries can also be potential words for your keyword list.

Generally, when your target audience arrives at your site via a commercial Web search engine, they want to find the information they are searching for within three to five clicks. The best-case scenario for potential customers would be to go from the search engine results page directly to the page on your site that contains the exact information that they desire. However, this scenario is not always realistic. In all likelihood, your potential customers will browse your site if they do not see the information immediately available. If your visitors cannot find the relevant information by browsing, then they might use your site's internal search engine.

Many usability experts have determined that people prefer to browse for information rather than use a site search engine. Therefore, when you gather potential keywords from your site search engine, keep in mind that your potential customers probably cannot find that information from browsing your site. If site visitors are unable to find desired information on your Web site via browsing, it is a clear indication that your site's information architecture, navigation and "sense of place" labels, and information scents need to be re-evaluated.

What to do with your keyword list

Based on the data gathered from various resources, you can narrow your keyword list. Below is the keyword list I came up with for the fictional TranquiliTeas company:

organic teas	organic green tea	herbal tea recipes
oolong teas	black teas	Japanese teas
green tea	herbal tea	Indian black tea
organic green teas	herbal teas	gourmet teas
organic black tea	tea recipes	tea accessories
organic tea	decaffeinated teas	organic herbal teas
organic oolong tea	whole leaf teas	decaffeinated tea
green teas	English tea sets	loose leaf teas
black tea	porcelain tea sets	Chinese teas
organic black teas	Japanese tea sets	Indian teas
oolong tea	organic herbal tea	tea sets
organic oolong tea	organic tea recipes	

Now the TranquiliTeas company knows how to build part of its Web site based on this keyword list. The Web site owner should create category pages about organic green, oolong, herbal, black, English, Chinese, and Indian teas.

The Web site owner can also create a section of tea recipes, since "tea recipes" appears to be a popular search. Are black tea recipes different from oolong tea recipes? Probably so, since they have different flavors. Maybe they can have seasonal tea recipes: hot tea recipes for winter and cold tea recipes for summer.

This keyword list also sets up some possible Frequently Asked Questions (FAQs) pages. Many people do not know what organic tea is. So some possible questions on an FAQs page might be:

- What is organic tea?

- What is the difference between organic and nonorganic teas?

- What types of organic teas do you offer?

- Are your organic teas available as both loose leaf and whole leaf varieties?

If you look at the short set of questions above, how many times was the word "tea" or "teas" mentioned? How many times was the keyword phrase "organic tea" or "organic teas" mentioned? Creating keyword-rich FAQs pages based on your audience keyword preferences is a way to generate search engine traffic, a strategy that both search engines and directory editors approve.

Listing 2-1 shows a possible layout of the TranquiliTeas Web site based on the keyword list:

Listing 2-1 Possible hierarchical information architecture for the TranquiliTeas Organic Web site.

Home Page
Organic Teas
    Organic green teas
        Asian blend green tea
        Jasmine green tea
        Green Moroccan mint tea
        Decaffeinated green tea with peach
        Roasted green tea (bancha)
    Organic black teas
        Darjeeling tea
        Earl Gray tea
        Orange pekoe tea
        Celtic breakfast tea
        Mango Ceylon with vanilla tea
        Lapsang souchong

(continued on next page)

Listing 2-1 (continued)

Organic oolong teas
    Hunan red oolong tea
    Oolong orange blossom tea
    Oolong tea
Organic herbal teas
    Peppermint herbal tea
    Chamomile herbal tea
    Roseberry herbal tea
    Orange herbal tea
    Ginger herbal tea
    Licorice tea
Loose leaf teas
    English breakfast
    Irish breakfast
    Earl Grey
    Jasmine green tea
Tea Sets & Accessories
    Japanese tea sets and accessories
    Chinese tea sets and accessories
    English tea sets and accessories
    Porcelain tea sets and accessories
    Tea pots
    Tea infusers
    Tea spoons
    Tea bag holders
Special Offers
    Tea samplers
    Loose leaf teas
    Whole leaf teas
    Tea bags
Gift baskets
Frequently Asked Questions
    Questions about organic tea
    Questions about Japanese or green tea
    Questions about Chinese or oolong tea
    Questions about Indian or black tea

Listing 2-1 (continued)

Questions about herbal tea
How to order
Tea Facts
Japanese teas
Chinese teas
Indian teas
English teas
History of tea
Japanese tea ceremony
Tea Recipes
Hot tea recipes
Green tea
Black tea
Oolong tea
Herbal tea
Iced tea recipes
Chai tea
Herbal tea
About TranquiliTeas Organic Tea
Company history
In the news
Location(s)
Money back guarantee
Return policy
Privacy policy
Links & Resources
Contact Us
Thank you page
Request Catalog
Thank you page
Site Map

Although this TranquiliTeas possible site architecture is by no means complete, you can see how all the keywords naturally appear in the site architecture. The site architecture in Listing 2-1 is commonly referred to as a hierarchical information architecture.

Important

If you plan to sell products and services directly on your Web site, create additional pages with a return policy, money-back guarantee, and a privacy policy, when applicable. Web directory editors will be looking for this information on ecommerce sites.

Important

It is not necessary to build a Frequently Asked Questions page for every product or service you offer, just the main categories. All FAQ pages should contain unique content and provide information that your target audience is generally interested in reading. A rule of thumb is to have four to 15 questions and answers on each FAQ page. Three or fewer questions and answers usually is not sufficient content to warrant a single FAQ page. More than 16 questions is too much, and the download time can significantly increase. Between 200–800 words per FAQ are a good benchmark for a single question-and-answer page.

Natural themes

Themes are recurrent and consistent ideas presented throughout a Web site. By narrowing your keyword list to 20 to 50 targeted phrases, natural themes will begin to emerge.

For example, with our fictional TranquiliTeas Web site, theme keywords consistently used throughout the site are "teas," and more specifically "organic teas." Visitors know that on any page of the TranquiliTeas Web site, they will be reading information about organic teas.

The secondary themes might be green teas, oolong teas, black teas, and herbal teas. Various pages can be created around these secondary themes. For example, a set of pages about "green teas" might be:

Green teas (products) > Loose-leaf green teas

Green teas (products) > Green tea in tea bags

Green teas > Japanese tea sets and accessories

Green teas > Recipes

Green teas > History of green teas

Green teas > Frequently asked questions about green teas

Likewise, a natural theme might emerge about oolong teas:

Oolong teas (products) > Loose-leaf oolong tea

Oolong teas (products) > Oolong tea in tea bags

Oolong teas > Chinese tea sets and accessories

Oolong teas > Recipes

Oolong teas > History of oolong tea

Oolong teas > Frequently asked questions about oolong teas

Based on these natural themes, the TranquiliTeas Web site owner now knows how to horizontally and vertically cross-link related pages based on keywords.

A simple way to create natural themes on your site is to create a corresponding set of FAQs pages for each category of products or services. For the fictional TranquiliTeas site, the Web site owner can create an FAQ for each main tea category: organic teas, green tea, oolong tea, black tea, and herbal teas. Likewise, since "tea recipes" is a popular search phrase, the TranquiliTeas Web site owner can create various recipe pages for the different types of teas.

Whenever you create an FAQ page, make sure you link to the related products or services page. If the FAQ page ranks well in the search engines, you will want to encourage site visitors to view your products and services, not only to read your FAQ page.

Likewise, in terms of sales, if a potential customer is interested in purchasing loose leaf green tea, for example, maybe that customer might need a loose leaf tea spoon (to measure the loose tea) or a tea infuser. Maybe a customer interested in Japanese tea sets might also be interested in purchasing green tea. Carefully planned cross-linking encourages your site visitors to make more purchases and communicates to the search engines which pages are important on your Web site.

Therefore, building your Web pages based on keyword research and natural theming makes your content easier to find on the search engines because:

- Most Web pages contain very specific content, keeping your pages focused.

- Important pages are linked to each other, making it easier for your site visitors to look for and to purchase related products and services.

Effective cross-linking will be discussed later in this section.

Keyword Placement

Once you have gathered a list of your 20 to 50 most popular keyword phrases, you can build Web pages and an information architecture based on what your target audience searches for. The next step in the optimization process is to place keywords in important HTML tags on your pages.

Writing effective HTML title tags

An HTML title tag has a specific meaning when it comes to Web site design and the search engines. A title tag is the text placed inside of the <title> and </title> tags.

<title>Plastic Surgery of Southern Connecticut—plastic, aesthetic, and cosmetic surgery</title>

On an actual Web page in a Web browser, the title tag looks like what is shown in Figure 2-18.

Figure 2-18

The title-tag content displays on browsers at the top of the screen. Notice the company name on this page (Plastic Surgery of Southern Connecticut) comes first because a popular keyword phrase is a part of the company name.

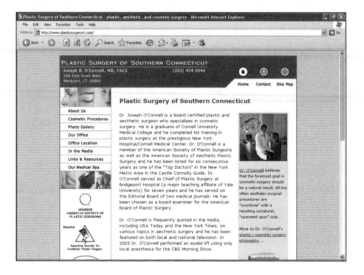

The title tag is very important in terms of search engine visibility because it serves multiple functions:

- Title-tag text is considered primary text by all the search engines, meaning that all the search engines index this text and use it to determine relevancy.

- Title-tag text is the first text shown in individual listings on search results pages. Title-tag content is highlighted as a hyperlink to your Web site. This hyperlink is the call to action—it's letting your target audience know there is a link to information pertaining to the words they entered in a search query.

- Title-tag text is the text shown in Bookmarks and Favorites.

Thus, a title tag serves three main functions. The first function is for search engine visibility. All the search engines consider title-tag text when calculating relevancy. The second function is a search usability reason: user confidence. Searchers are more confident that search engines have delivered the best results when they see their query words displayed in a hyperlink. The third title-tag function is a call to action. Your title-tag content should encourage your target audience to click the link to your site.

All title-tag text should be unique because every page of your Web site contains unique content. Does your About Us page contain the same information as your Products pages? Probably not, and your title tag content needs to reflect the differences in page content.

Unless your company name is well known and has excellent branding, it is best not to place your company name in the title tag. To get or maintain branding and to modify your site to accommodate your target audience, do *not* put your company name in the beginning of the title tag unless you have a keyword in your company name.

For example, the company name TranquiliTeas Organic Teas is a good company name for the search engines because the keyword phrase "organic teas" is part of the company name. Therefore, a good title tag for a page that sells organic green tea might be:

<title> TranquiliTeas Organic Teas: green tea</title>

Some search engine marketers change an official company name to artificially inflate the keyword density inside a title tag. They might separate words that are normally put together. In the following example, a search engine marketer wanted the word "teas" to be more prominent in the title tag. So the company name was misspelled on purpose in the title tag:

<title> Tranquili Teas Organic Teas: green tea</title>

Rather than ruin some otherwise excellent branding, it would be better to put the singular version of the word "tea" at the end of the title tag since the plural version is already a part of the company name:

<title> TranquiliTeas Organic Teas: green tea</title>

Tip

As a rule, write a unique, descriptive title for each page of five to 10 words, or 60 to 69 characters. Remove as many filler words from the title as possible, such as and, a, an, the, and so forth. Titles should contain your most important keyword phrases and accurately reflect the content of your Web pages.

An alternative title that can be equally effective for both branding and search engine visibility is:

<title> Green tea from TranquiliTeas Organic Teas</title>

Notice that I didn't include the abbreviations Inc. or Ltd. or Co. Why? These are words that the target audience is not likely to type into a search engine query.

Power combination strategy

The best way to write a title with targeted keywords is utilizing a strategy called the power combination strategy or a *power combo*. Whenever possible, the first three words in your title tag should consist of words that, when typed in any combination in a search query, will be a keyword phrase. For example:

<title> Organic green teas from TranquiliTeas Organic Teas</title>

The targeted keyword phrases are contained in this title tag are:

- organic green teas
- organic teas
- green teas

Tip

It is not always possible to create your title tags using the power combo strategy. If a three-word phrase seems very unnatural, don't use it.

Remember, your target audience is going to see your title-tag content in the search results. They don't want to see a list of keywords. They want to see a short phrase that clearly and accurately describes the contents of the Web page they will be viewing.

The reason that you should place related keywords close to each other, whenever possible, is that search engines also measure keyword proximity. Keyword proximity is not only measured in the title tags. It is also measured throughout the primary text in an entire Web page.

Singular and plural strategy

Many businesses find that because their target audiences use both the singular and plural version of a word to find their Web sites, using both versions of a keyword can be a good title-tag strategy.

The following title tag contains the singular and plural version of "tea":

<title> Green tea from TranquiliTeas Organic Teas </title>

Keep a list of various titles so when it comes time to build another Web page targeting the same keywords, you will have a database of effective title-tag text. Test title-tag content and measure your audience's response to those titles. Use the titles and keywords that get the best response, and rewrite other Web page titles based on your testing results.

Below is a title-tags list that can go on the organic tea site for a page with content about green tea:

Green tea

Green teas

Organic green tea

Organic green teas

Organic green tea from TranquiliTeas Organic Teas

Organic green teas from TranquiliTeas Organic Teas

Green tea from TranquiliTeas Organic Teas

Green teas from TranquiliTeas Organic Teas

TranquiliTeas Organic Teas: green tea

TranquiliTeas Organic Teas: green teas

TranquiliTeas Organic Teas: organic green tea

TranquiliTeas Organic Teas: organic green teas

Body Text

The visible body text on a Web page is the HTML text contained between the <body> and </body> tags that you can copy and paste directly from a Web browser to a text editor. Text inside of headings, paragraphs, ordered lists, unordered lists, and tables are examples of visible body text.

Due to misuse of various tags and attributes such as the meta-tag description and alternative text, search engines modified the content they use to determine rankings. One aspect about the search engine spiders will not change: They will always index title tags and visible body text to determine relevancy. For this reason, it is important to place keywords throughout the visible body text in your Web pages to guarantee search engines will be able to find and index all of your relevant keywords.

Keyword Prominence

All the search engines consider the words at the top of a Web page, commonly referred to as above the fold, more important than the words on the rest of the Web page. How high up a keyword is on a Web page is called *keyword prominence*.

For example, the Elgin Area Chamber wanted an aesthetically pleasing home page that would help the Elgin community find the site. To be sure that the home page could be found in the search engines, the most important keywords were placed prominently as shown in Figure 2-19.

Figure 2-19

The Elgin Area Chamber made sure the most important text and features on its Web site are visible at the top of the screen ("above the fold").

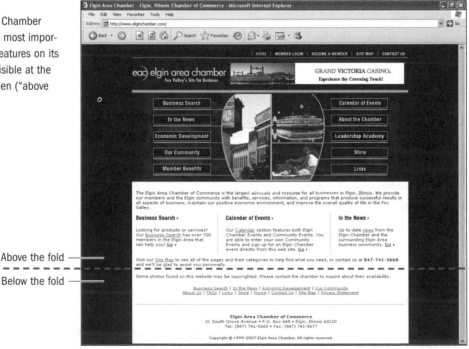

One simple way to include your important keywords at the top of your Web pages is to always include a heading or headline that contains keywords. Use a variation of the title-tag text for a headline. For example, the title tag might state:

<title> Green teas from TranquiliTeas Organic Teas</title>

A simple headline might state:

<h1>Organic green tea</h1>

If you want your headline to contain a call to action, you can change your headline to contain an action verb, such as:

<h1>Order our organic green tea gift set</h1>

The first paragraph on your Web page should accurately describe the contents of that page, using your most targeted keywords. If your Web page contains content that falls "below the fold," then the first set of text on your page should let your target audience know that the information they are searching for is available on that Web page.

An effective way to optimize a long Web page is to write multiple headlines using keywords (as shown in Figure 2-20). At the top of the Web page, make sure there are hyperlinks leading to those headlines. Below is an example of a long Web page with headlines:

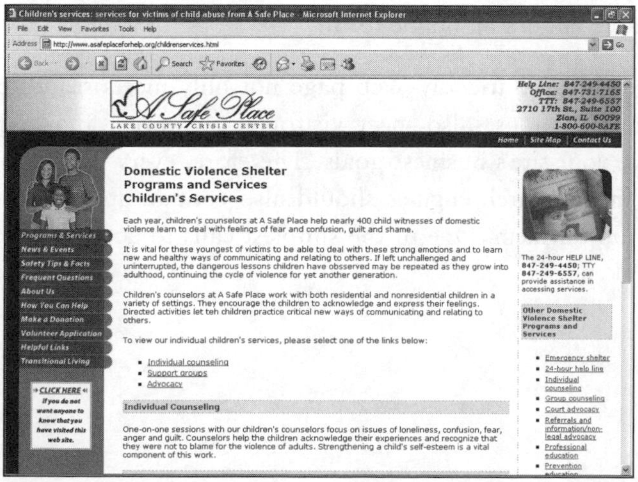

Figure 2-20
A Safe Place offers multiple services for children. To be sure their target audience knows of the different services, they placed hyperlinks to each children's service at the top of the screen.

Although using keywords in your introductory paragraph is very important, Web pages that contain keyword phrases used consistently throughout the body text often have greater search engine visibility.

Another way to increase keyword focus is to write conclusion paragraphs or sentences that can go on almost every page of a site. Every conclusion sentence contains keywords and an appropriate call to action. For example:

<p>If you would like more information about our organic green teas, please email John Smith in our Japanese tea division.</p>

Or if you prefer that your target audience phones you instead of emailing:

<p>If you would like more information about our organic green teas and the other organic teas we provide, please call John Smith at 1-800-XXX-XXXX.</p>

Calls to Action

Obtaining top search engine visibility is only half the battle. To be victorious, you need to persuade potential customers to click the link to your site and purchase the items for sale, or perform whatever call to action you desire. What do you want people to do once they visit your site? Do you want them to subscribe to a newsletter? Pick up the phone and call you? Place an order using shopping cart software? Fill out an online form?

A search engine friendly Web page not only meets search engine standards, it must also meet visitor expectations and help you achieve your site's business goals. Therefore, every page you want listed in the search engines should also contain appropriate calls to action on them. One of the simplest calls to action is a hypertext link.

The benefits of hypertext links are:

- Many search engines consider the text in and around the anchor tag to be important because you do not link to pages that are not important.

- Site visitors automatically understand that the blue, underlined word (or just the underlined word) should link directly to the information contained in that word. In other words, a hypertext link is a natural call to action.

For example, suppose you have a Web page that summarizes the main types of products you have. Many Web copywriters use the phrase "learn more" to indicate that there is more detailed information about a product. If there is more information about a specific product, why not add a specific keyword phrase to highlight it?

So instead of this text:

<a href="greenteas.html">Learn more</a>

Write this anchor text:

<a href="greenteas.html">Learn more about our green teas</a>

Or:

Learn more about our <a href="greenteas.html">green teas</a>

One way I like to remind myself to use more keywords is to ask the question:

What kind of _____ ?

If you offer services, what kind of services do you offer? If you offer products, what kind of products do you offer? If you want your site visitors to read more, what should they read more about? About your products? What kind of products do you want them to read more about?

By answering the question, "What kind of _____," you can naturally come up with your own set of keywords to place within the body of your Web pages.

Meta Tags

A meta tag is an HTML tag that gives information about the content of a Web page, such as what HTML specifications a Web page follows or description of a Web page's content. A meta tag, however, usually does not affect how a Web page is displayed on a browser. For search engine visibility, the most common uses for meta tags are the keyword, description, and robots exclusion attributes.

One of the most widespread beliefs about meta tags is that they are the "secret ingredient" to obtaining optimal search engine rankings. In fact, only some major search engines use meta-tag content for relevancy. Many search engines use meta-tag content when they display the results of a search query. And many search engines (and almost all Web directories) do not use meta-tag content to determine relevancy. So meta tags are not a "secret ingredient" at all. Rather, meta-tag descriptions are considered secondary text that is meant to enhance your site in the search engines.

The meta-tag description attribute

When writing meta-tag content, spend more time writing a good description than writing a keyword list. In terms of search engine visibility, the description is far more important than the keyword list.

Because many major search engines use meta-tag descriptions when displaying the results of a search query, the meta-tag description must accomplish two goals:

- Helping to obtain a good search engine ranking in the search engines that use the meta-tag description for relevancy.

- Eliciting a call to action, such as encouraging people to click the link to your Web site.

A meta-tag description is placed between the <head> and </head> tags. The HTML code for a meta-tag description looks like this:

```
<meta name="description" content="Page description goes here." />
```

When writing your meta-tag descriptions, select the most important four to five keywords per page based on your keyword research. Write careful 200- to 250-character sentences and phrases, targeting the most important words on your Web pages. When you are writing meta-tag descriptions, eliminate as many filler words as you can to make room for the keywords.

Some general guidelines to writing meta-tag descriptions are:

- Do not repeat your exact title-tag content in the meta-tag description. This raises a red flag to the search engine spiders that you might be keyword stacking.

- Place the most important keyword phrases at the beginning of your meta-tag description.

- Use the singular and plural version of your most important keywords, when applicable.

- Try not to separate important keyword phrases.

- Keep keyword repetition to a minimum. Although the search engines do not give specific guidelines for repetition, generally stop at three to four repetitions to avoid keyword-stacking problems.

- Be aware that some search engines treat different words, such as the singular and plural version, as the same word.

- Separate repeated words with important qualifier words.

- Build in a call to action by encouraging your target audience to click the link to your site and "read more about" or "learn more about" your targeted keywords.

- Placing a list of keywords in your meta-tag description is not an effective way of encouraging your target audience to click the links to your site. It also raises a red flag to the search engine spiders for potential spam.

- Make sure your meta-tag contains sentences or long phrases whenever possible.

Tip

If you use words in your meta-tag description that you do not use on your Web pages, most of the search engines consider it spam. As a rather extreme example, it is the equivalent of an adult pornography site using the word "Disney" in the meta tag.

Here is an example of a simple but effective meta-tag description:

```
<meta name="description" content="Get gourmet herbal teas at whole-
sale prices from TranquiliTeas. Organic tea importer offers decaffeinated
herbal teas and other herbal blends. Black, oolong, green, and iced teas
available as loose tea or in tea bags." />
```

The above meta-tag description contains 183 characters without spaces and 217 characters with spaces. You can determine this in Microsoft Word using the Tools > Word Count function.

Simple ways to create similar meta-tag descriptions are:

Change the verb

In the aforementioned meta-tag description, you can remove the word "Get":

```
<meta name="description" content="Gourmet herbal teas at wholesale
prices from TranquiliTeas. Organic tea importer offers decaffeinated
herbal teas and other herbal blends. Black, oolong, green, and iced teas
available as loose tea or in tea bags." />
```

You can also change the word "get" to:

... Providing gourmet herbal teas at wholesale prices ....

... Offers gourmet herbal teas at wholesale prices ....

... Select gourmet herbal teas at wholesale prices ....

... Buy gourmet herbal teas at wholesale prices ....

... Your online resource for gourmet herbal teas ....

Add a call to action at the end of the meta tag

Another way to add quality keywords to your meta-tag content is to add the phrase "Learn more about ... (keyword)." Other ways of stating this phrase are:

... Read details about our gourmet herbal teas ....
... Contact us for more information about our gourmet herbal teas ....

You can also change the verb to a different form. In the example below, we used the word "offers" instead of the "offering."

<meta name="description" content="Gourmet herbal teas at wholesale prices from TranquiliTeas. Organic tea importer offering decaffeinated herbal teas and other herbal blends. Available as loose tea or in tea bags. Also offering black, oolong, green, and iced teas." />

Change the word order or phrase order

<meta name="description" content="Gourmet herbal teas at wholesale prices. Also offering black, oolong, green, and iced teas. Organic tea importer offering decaffeinated herbal teas and other herbal blends. Available as loose tea or in tea bags." />

When you adjust phrases, be careful so that you are not keyword stacking. Remember, all meta-tag descriptions should accurately reflect the body-text content of the Web page.

If you do not place text in the meta-tag description, the search engines that use meta-tag descriptions will come up with their own description based on the content of your Web page. That description probably will not showcase your Web pages in the best light, as shown in Figure 2-21.

Tip

If you do not have the time to write unique meta-tag descriptions for your Web pages, copy and paste the first two sentences of your main HTML text into the meta-tag description.

---

5. **16 ct Tea Shop Irish Breakfast (closeout)**
   (Please turn on JavaScript in your web browser for Quicklinks) Stash Tea Quicklinks: *** Select Category *** Stash Tea online shopping home page A World of Tea home page Order by item number Accessori

---

Figure 2-21

A Web page obtained a top position in a major search engine, but its descriptions begins, "(Please turn on JavaScript in your Web browser for Quicklinks)…" A meta-tag description with keywords and a call to action could yield more clicks.

Many search engine marketers like to use the list of keywords in the meta-tag description. Not only is this search engine marketing strategy borderline spam, it is also a poor way of encouraging visitors to click the link to your site. Would you click this in a search result?

---

5.   **Green tea,Sencha,Black tea,Kukicha,hot tea,Assam,iced tea,Ceylon tea,chai,herbal…**
   656 - TeaTeaTea triple the flavor. Selection of teas from green **tea** to oolong to **black tea**. Single estate,blended,**organic**,decaffeinated,flavored and scented.

Figure 2-22

Top search result from another commercial Web search engine. Keywords are stuffed in the title and meta-tag description. This search result is difficult to read and contains no call to action.

Using a company name in a meta-tag description

Just as with the title tag, unless an official company name contains keywords, do not use it in a meta-tag description. Or move it to the end of the description. For example, "Inc." really is not a keyword unless the site is Inc. magazine.

The meta-tag keywords attribute

When selecting words to place in the meta-tag keywords attribute, it is best to select keywords that you actually use on the content of the Web page. If a word appears in your meta tags that does not appear in your main body content, then it raises a red flag that you are not accurately communicating page content to the search engines and site visitors. As a result, the page can receive a lower relevancy score.

When selecting keywords and keyword phrases for this meta-tag attribute, consider the following variations:

- Singular vs. plural: When creating your keywords list, place the version of the keyword that your site visitors use the most at the beginning of your keyword list.

- Uppercase vs. lowercase: Most search engines do not use case sensitivity as an element of their algorithms. Thus, using all versions (all uppercase, all lowercase, initial capitalization) of keywords and keyword phrases is probably a waste of time and can result in a spam penalty for keyword stacking. Consider this as well: When people type in words and phrases in a search engine query, they tend to type words very quickly. The quickest way to type in words is not to use any capitalization.

- Commas vs. no commas: It makes no difference to the search engines that use the meta-tag keywords attribute whether you use commas or spaces to separate your keywords and keyword phrases. If it is easier for you to view your keyword phrases with commas, then use them. Using commas will not affect your Web page's relevancy.

- Misspelled keywords: Since some keywords are commonly misspelled (such as the word "millennium"), you might want to put a misspelled keyword in your meta-keywords tag. If that misspelled word does not appear in your main body text, this strategy is a generally waste of time.

The meta-revisit tag

The meta-revisit tag supposedly instructs a search engine spider to revisit a Web page within a specified period. The HTML code for this tag looks like this:

```
<meta name="revisit-after" content="14 days" />
```

According to the instructions in this meta tag, the search engine spiders are instructed to revisit this Web page every 14 days.

I like to use this meta tag to quiz potential search engine marketers to see how knowledgeable they really are.

No one can tell a search engine spider what to do. You cannot tell a search engine to revisit your site every 14 days. You cannot tell a search engine what language to index your site in. In fact, on their submission forms, search engines do not even guarantee that your Web pages will be listed.

So don't use this meta tag for commercial Web search engine visibility. It is useless.

The meta-robots tag

Some Web site owners do not want search engine spiders to index the content of a specific Web page. So they use the meta-tag robots exclusion attribute to accomplish this. The following shows the proper HTML coding for this meta tag:

```
<html>
<head>
<title>Green tea from TranquiliTeas Organic Teas</title>
<meta name="robots" content="noindex" />
</head>
```

Not all search engines will honor this type of meta tag. They have indicated that you should use the robots.txt file, which is discussed on page 118.

Many search engine marketers like to instruct the search engines to index a page using this meta tag:

```
<html>
<head>
<title>Green tea from TranquiliTeas Organic Teas</title>
<meta name="robots" content="index, follow" />
</head>
```

According to this meta tag, the search engines are supposed to index the text on the page that contains this tag, and the search engines are supposed to follow the links on this page. This is another useless meta tag. Search engines automatically index the text and follow links on a Web page unless specifically told not to.

Alternative Text

Alternative text is the text that is placed inside graphic images in HTML code. Alternative text instructs a browser, "If this graphic image is not downloaded, show this text in its place."

The HTML code for alternative text looks like this:

```
<img src="images/home.gif" height="25" width="60" alt="TranquiliTeas Organic Teas home" />
```

- **IMG:** This is the HTML coding that tells the browser to insert a graphic image into a Web page.

- **SRC:** This is the attribute that indicates which file name or URL of the graphic image you want to place on the page. In this example, the image name is a GIF called home.gif, which is stored in the directory called images on a Web site. The file name or URL must be enclosed in quotation marks.

- **WIDTH / HEIGHT:** These tags are your graphic image's dimensions, measured in pixels. Using the WIDTH and HEIGHT attributes in your IMG SRC tag preserves the layout of your pages. Also, pages using the WIDTH and HEIGHT attributes in their IMG SRC tags download faster than pages not using these attributes.

- **ALT:** Stands for the alternative text attribute. Alternative text must also be enclosed in quotation marks.

Alternative text will appear in the place of graphic images if your visitors are using a text-only browser. Furthermore, people with disabilities (particularly the visually impaired) may use devices such as screen readers. These devices translate the contents of a page into Braille or into speech. Therefore, the only way that graphic images can be "read" is by placing alternative text inside your site's graphic images.

Search engine marketers and Web designers often overlook this attribute. Many graphic image search engines index alternative text, thus making your graphic images another place to strategically place keywords.

Also, if you are using Explorer as your browser, when you position your pointer over a graphic image, Explorer will display the alternative text message in a little box next to the cursor (similar to pop-ups).

For example, let's say you have a Web site that offers graphic design services. One of your navigation buttons has the word "Services" on it. The alternative text for that graphic image can be:

```
<img src="images/services.gif" width="120" height="20"
alt="Services" />
```

The word "services" is not very descriptive of the type of services your site offers. Remember the question, "What kind of _____?" Fill in the blank. What kind of services does your Web site offer? If your site offers graphic design services, for example, a better phrase for the alternative text would be:

```
<img src="images/services.gif" width="120" height="20" alt="Graphic
design services" />
```

Many unethical search engine marketers stuff as many keywords as they can into a graphic image, a spam tactic called keyword stuffing. The following alternative text is an example of keyword stuffing:

```
<img src="images/services.gif" width="120" height="20"
alt="Graphic design—graphic designer—graphic designs—graphic
designing services" />
```

The keywords and phrases must be relevant and accurately describe the graphic image.

Important

Keyword prominence also applies to graphic images. In other words, the graphic images (containing alternative text) that your target audience views at the top of the screen are more important than the graphic images at the bottom of a screen.

Transparent images

Many Web designers use a transparent 1 pixel x 1 pixel image, commonly called a blank.gif or a clear.gif, to get elements on a page to line up correctly. Because of current browser incompatibilities, there is still a need for these images.

However, according to the search engines, when you place alternative text inside a graphic image, that text must be relevant (a) to the actual graphic image and (b) to the Web page the image is placed on. Hiding keywords or links inside a graphic image is considered spam.

So if you must use transparent images, do not place any alternative text in the graphic image, or just put a punctuation mark like an asterisk (*) as the alternative text. Search engines do not read punctuation marks.

URL/File Names

Many search engine marketers believe that placing keywords in your domain name and your file names greatly affects search engine positioning. In other words, the domain name:

http://www.tranquiliteasorganic.com/

should get a significant boost in search engine visibility because the word "teas" and "tea" is in the domain name. The domain name:

http://www.tranquiliteasorganictea.com/

should get a stronger boost than the previous domain name because this domain name contains more keyword phrases.

But the best domain name for this site should be:

http://www.tranquili-teas-organic-tea.com/

Therefore, a page on the TranquiliTeas site should name its green tea page greenteas.html, as follows:

http://www.tranquili-teas-organic-tea.com/green-teas.html

Simply placing keywords in a domain name and/or a file name is not going to make or break top search engine visibility. Remember, search engines index text and follow links. If a Web page does not contain keywords and does not have a link architecture for the search engines to find those keywords, a domain name with keywords in it will do no good in obtaining top search engine visibility.

Keywords in the domain names and file names are not as important as people are led to believe. Unfortunately, as soon as people read that an item has an impact on search engine positioning, they place far too much importance on items that really will not make or break positioning. Why focus your energy on a strategy that has minuscule impact rather than strategies that have true impact, such as Web copywriting, site architecture, and popularity?

Plenty of Web pages rank well and receive qualified search engine traffic without having any keywords in the URL structure. Plenty of Web pages do not rank at all and have keywords in the URL structure. Other items on your site are far more important for obtaining long-term search engine visibility.

Keyword Density

Keyword density is a measure of the number of times keywords occur within a Web page's text.

$$\frac{\text{Keyword phrase}}{\text{Total \# of words on a page}} = \text{Keyword density}$$

Search engine marketers calculate keyword density in different ways. Some marketers include all the words on a Web page. Some marketers do not include stop words or filter words in the total word count. Regardless, you will hear many different numbers, depending on the search engine marketer.

A 250- to 800-word page (including stop words, not including meta-tag content and alternative text) is a good benchmark because a page with this amount of text generally contains genuine content on a subject. Once a page contains more than 800 words, your site's visitors will need to scroll many times to view your page's content. In all likelihood, they will not read much farther than the top of the screen.

Tip

Keywords in a domain name give minuscule boost when all other factors (text, link, and popularity components) are equal. A file name for a graphic image is important if you wish your site's graphic images to appear in graphic image searches. Otherwise, do not obsess over file naming for search engine visibility. File naming is important, however, for usability reasons.

Tip

Though it is important to use keywords to show both search engines and site visitors what your pages are about, I do not recommend spending a great deal of time on measuring the keyword density on every page. Do not become obsessed with a number that has little value.

Further, if you cannot present sales copy in less than 800 words, you will probably lose audience interest. So make sure your pages contain quality, relevant content in as few words as possible.

Since keyword density can be artificially generated quite easily, search engines are placing less and less emphasis on it. In fact, many engines have reported that they no longer use keyword density to determine a page's keyword focus.

Term Highlighting

Nonetheless, keyword focus is important from a search usability perspective. Whenever a searcher types a keyword phrase into a search query, keywords are highlighted in various places in the search results. In the main (or organic listings), terms are highlighted in the HTML title-tag content, the meta-tag description or page snippet, and the URL, as shown in Figure 2-23:

Figure 2-23

Term highlighting in Yahoo for the keyword phrase "organic oolong teas." Notice that term highlighting occurs in the HTML title tag, description (from a page snippet or meta-tag description, or both), and the URL.

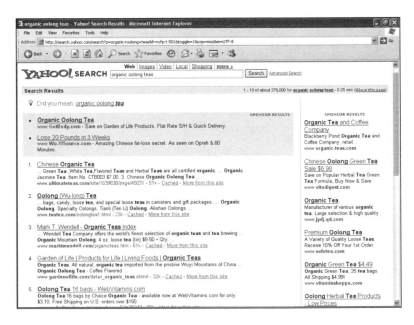

The reason that keywords are highlighted in these various places is to help searchers feel more confident that they are being delivered to the most relevant search results. In other words, if searchers type the keyword phrase "organic oolong teas" (without the quotation marks) into Google, they will feel more confident that they will find desired information because they see the term being highlighted (in bold) in various places. This keyword emphasis in search results is commonly referred to as term highlighting.

After searchers click a link to a Web page, they want to be delivered to a page that contains the keywords they typed in the search box. In other words, if searchers typed organic oolong teas into a search box, they want to see that same keyword phrase appear on the Web page they land on, preferably above the fold.

Foreign Languages

At this time, the major commercial Web search engines tend to be U.S.-centric, dominating search results and highlighted news, even though the search engines do not officially have U.S. editions of their spiders. However, their search interfaces and search results are presented in English.

Generally speaking, if you have a U.S.-based company, then your domain name should end in .com, .net, .edu, .gov, or .org. When you register your domain name, your official contact information should contain a U.S.-based address, phone number, fax number, and email address. In all likelihood, if you have a U.S.-based domain name, then your company has a physical location in the United States.

If your site is written in the English language, it will automatically be crawled by English-language, country-specific search engines. For example, U.S.-based sites will show up in regional search engine results from Australia, United Kingdom (U.K.), and Canada.

If you feel your target audience extends to non-English speaking countries, then you will need to modify your Web site to meet the needs of that target audience. To be successful in non-English search engines, it is best to purchase country-specific domain names and write the Web pages in the appropriate language.

Suppose our fictional TranquiliTeas company has a target audience in the United States, France, Germany, and the United Kingdom.

Tip

Search engines constantly test the term highlighting feature in search results pages so that they can deliver the best search experience. Too much term highlighting often negates the search experience. The search results pages might look too busy. On the flip side, too little term highlighting also negates the search experience because user confidence decreases. User confidence is important for providing a strong information scent, which is crucial for a Web site's success.

Tip

Having a domain name for a specific country is a key indicator that your site belongs in non-U.S. search engines. If it is within your budget, I recommend creating unique Web sites for each targeted country. If you do not wish to create an entirely new Web site for each country, you can create subdomains or subdirectories on a single main site.

This company will want to register the following domain names:

www.tranquiliteasorganic.com	(U.S.)
www.tranquiliteas.fr	(France)
www.tranquiliteas.de	(Germany)
www.tranquiliteas.co.uk	(United Kingdom)

These four domain names can all point to the same Web site. On the home pages for each site, ask visitors to select a preferred language. When the appropriate language is selected, the link will go to an appropriate URL that is written in the selected language.

Country-specific Web pages should always be written in the official language of the targeted country. So if you are targeting France, your Web pages should be written in French. Web pages presented in French can be located in a subdirectory called France or français, as shown below:

http://www.tranquiliteasorganic.com/francais/

Or you can create a subdomain with pages only written in French. The subdomain can have the URL:

http://francais.tranquiliteasorganic.com/

When you submit your site to foreign search engines and Web directories, be sure to submit the appropriate domain name. For example, one of the most popular search engines in France is called Voilá. The TranquiliTeas company will want to submit www.tranquiliteas.fr to Voilá and any French-language Web directory. Likewise, www.tranquiliteas.co.uk will be submitted to U.K.-based search engines and Web directories.

Special Characters

When writing for non-U.S. search engines, you will often find that you use specialized HTML code to specify a letter in an alphabet. For example, in Spanish, if you want to write the word "Olé" in HTML, the code might look like:

Olé

Or it might look like:

Olé

Currently, the crawler-based search engines do not translate many foreign-language characters neatly into search results. Until the search engines become more effective with languages other than English, do not use any special characters in your title tags and meta tags. If you are using Olé in your title tag, you want it to appear in the search results:

Olé

You do not want the word to appear in search results as:

Olé

If you plan to target non-U.S. search engines, then you will have to write up a set of targeted keywords and keyword phrases for each language, even English-language search engines. For example, in this country we commonly refer to wireless telephones as "cellular phones" or "cell phones." In the United Kingdom and most of Europe, these phones are referred to as "mobile phones."

Therefore, if you know you are targeting different countries, all keyword research should be country-specific.

Link Component

One of the most important building blocks of a successful search engine marketing campaign is the link component, also referred to as a site's information architecture and corresponding interface. Some search engine optimization professionals commonly label the link component as site architecture. Regardless of the label, the link component consists of the following elements:

- Web site's navigation scheme(s)
- Relevant cross-linking (vertical and horizontal)
- "You are here" cues
- Calls to action and information scent
- Page layout
- URL structure

Site architecture is very important because the search engine spiders must be given access to all elements on your Web pages, including keyword-rich text, graphic images, and multimedia files. Therefore, the way your pages are linked to each other, and the way your Web site is linked to other Web sites, have a major impact your site's search engine visibility.

Whenever possible, link component elements should communicate the following information:

- Access
- Keyword relevancy
- Sense of place
- Scent of information
- Context

Without an effective information architecture and corresponding page layout, Web site owners must often pay for search engine visibility via paid inclusion or pay-per-click programs, or they often resort to search engine spam techniques.

Search engine optimization and Web site usability are not at odds with each other. Most of the time, user-centered interface design and search optimization are intricately related. By analyzing and understanding your target audience's search behavior and keyword usage, and by incorporating this information into your Web site, you can create a search experience that benefits everyone: your business, site visitors, current customers, and the commercial Web search engines.

Navigation Schemes

Web site designers should always consider their site visitors' preferences before creating a site's navigation scheme. Navigation schemes should allow visitors to find what they desire as quickly and easily as possible.

Many Web sites use multiple navigation schemes. For example, a site might have a series of navigation buttons down the screen's left side and have corresponding text links at the bottom of the screen (see Figure 2-24).

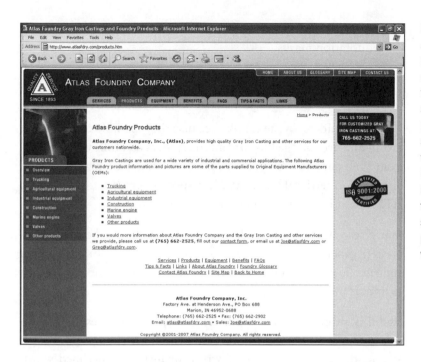

Figure 2-24
Atlas Foundry has multiple navigation schemes to ensure that site visitors can find the foundry they are searching for. Text links are placed at the bottom of the screen in the event that site visitors scroll to read or scan long pages, and navigation buttons are located at the top and the left side of the screen. For usability purposes, embedded text links within the body content.

Types of common navigation schemes are hypertext links, navigation buttons, image maps, drop-down/pull-down menus, Flash.

In the following sections, I will discuss each type of navigation scheme, its advantages and disadvantages, and how the navigation scheme you select can impact your site's search engine visibility.

Hypertext links

A hypertext link is a word or set of words placed inside of an anchor tag. Anchor text is placed between the <a> and </a> tags. The HTML code for a simple hypertext link is shown below:

```
<a href="oolongtea.html">Oolong tea</a>
```

- <a begins the anchor tag.

- href is the attribute of this anchor tag. This stands for *hypertext reference* and refers to the target location of a Web document. In this example, the location of the Web document is a Web page named oolongtea.html. It is *very* important that the location of the Web page in a hypertext link be enclosed in quotation marks.

- Oolong tea is the anchor text.

- </a> closes the anchor tag and hypertext link.

All engine spiders love text links because they are able to record the text in and around the link *and* all the spiders can follow these links from Web page to Web page. In fact, search engine marketers and information retrieval scientists use a specific term that refers to the HTML text inside of a hyperlink: *anchor text*.

Many search engines consider anchor text relevant because Webmasters generally link to pages that contain information their target audience is interested in reading. Therefore, anchor text is deemed as important.

Usability professionals also like text links because these links provide valuable information about visited and unvisited pages. People assume that a blue, underlined word (or just an underlined word) indicates an unvisited link, and a purple or faded color indicates a visited link.

Furthermore, usability professionals often recommend implementing hierarchical breadcrumb links on a Web page as a secondary navigation element. Breadcrumb links are text link schematics on every Web page that let people know (a) the Web page they are viewing and (b) the Web pages they have already viewed.

Breadcrumb links are commonly placed at the top of a Web page and are hierarchical. Figure 2-25 shows how breadcrumbs are typically formatted on a Web page.

Many Web directories, including Yahoo, use breadcrumbs as a navigation scheme, as shown in Figure 2-26.

Since hierarchical breadcrumb links are generally placed near the top of Web pages, search engines consider the text placed inside the breadcrumb links important. Therefore, if you have a site that uses breadcrumbs as a navigation scheme, use keywords consistently in them.

Tip:

All hypertext links should have a unique appearance. With rare exceptions, hypertext links should not look like any other type of text on a Web page. Site visitors should know that text on a page is clickable without having to place their pointers over the clickable text.

Figure 2-25
Evolution Design Systems uses breadcrumb links as part of their secondary navigation scheme.

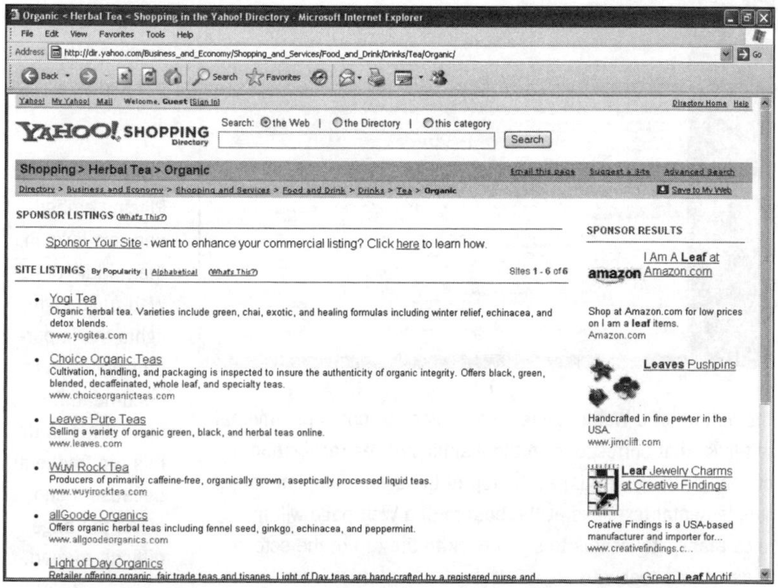

Figure 2-26
The Yahoo Directory's bread-crumb links are shown at the top of the screen. Home > Business and Economy > Shopping and Services > Food and Drink > Drinks > Tea > Organic are all part of the breadcrumb link trail.

Text link placement

Because all search engines can index the text and follow the links in a hypertext link (as long as the URL structure is not problematic), I highly recommend using them as either the primary or secondary navigation for a Web site design.

Figures 2-27 thrugh 2-30 highlight some places to implement text links on a variety of Web sites.

The top of a Web page is not always the best place to put text links because this is often the first text that the search engines will see. As long as the text is short, it should not interfere with search engine visibility.

Locational breadcrumb text links at the top of a Web page generally are not problematic because they tend to be short. In order for this text to be effective for search engine visibility, be sure to use keywords when appropriate.

Figure 2-27
Various places on a business-to-business (B2B) Web page where text links can be used effectively.

The left side of a Web page is not always the best place to put text links because this is also the first text the search engines will see.

If the text inside the text links is too long, the search engines will often use this text in their snippets in the search results. Also, the Web page might not appear to be focused on a specific topic.

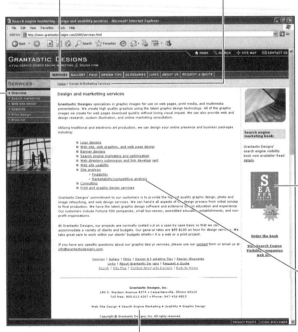

The right side of a Web page is a good place for related text links because site visitors can view important relevant content "above the fold."

Placing embedded text links in the middle of a Web page highlights the important points in the document. Be careful not to do this too frequently because it can make the page difficult to read.

The bottom of a Web page is a good place to put supplemental text links that correspond to the graphic images (navigation buttons or image maps) at the top of the screen. Implementing supplemental text links at the bottom of a Web page will not force many site visitors to scroll back to the top of the screen to navigate a Web site.

Since the amount of anchor text at the top of this B2C category page does not comprise the majority of this page's content, it does not interfere with search engine visibility.

Locational bread-crumb links communicate a sense of place and are keyword focused.

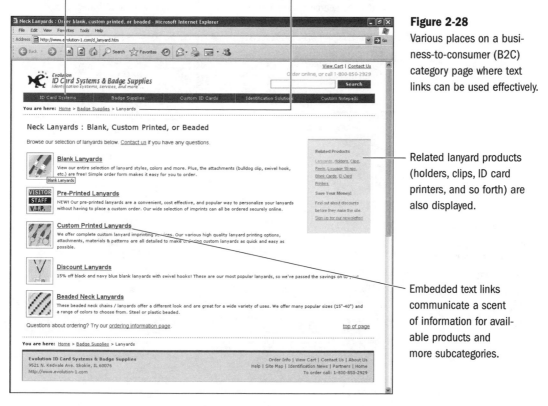

Figure 2-28
Various places on a business-to-consumer (B2C) category page where text links can be used effectively.

Related lanyard products (holders, clips, ID card printers, and so forth) are also displayed.

Embedded text links communicate a scent of information for available products and more subcategories.

Since the amount of anchor text at the top of this reference page does not comprise the majority of this page's content, it does not interfere with search engine visibility. The global link to a site map is both user friendly and search engine friendly.

Locational breadcrumb links communicate a sense of place and are keyword focused, which is extremely helpful on a medical information site with thousands of Web pages.

Figure 2-29
Various places on a reference page where text links can be used effectively.

Many of the available definitions within this online medical dictionary are cross-referenced in the event that site visitors are unfamiliar with a medical term within a definition.

Suggested readings by doctors and latest medical news are all related to the definition. On this particular Web page, all of these related links are keyword focused, relevant, and provide a strong information scent.

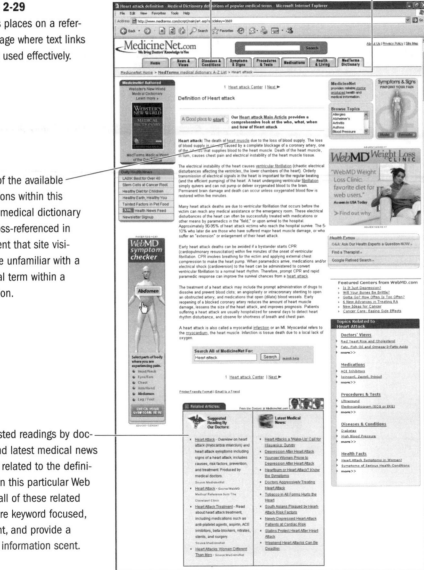

The embedded text link at the top of the page provides a sense of place—the blog entry has been categorized in the Google/SEO category.

The primary navigation scheme consists of keyword-related categories.

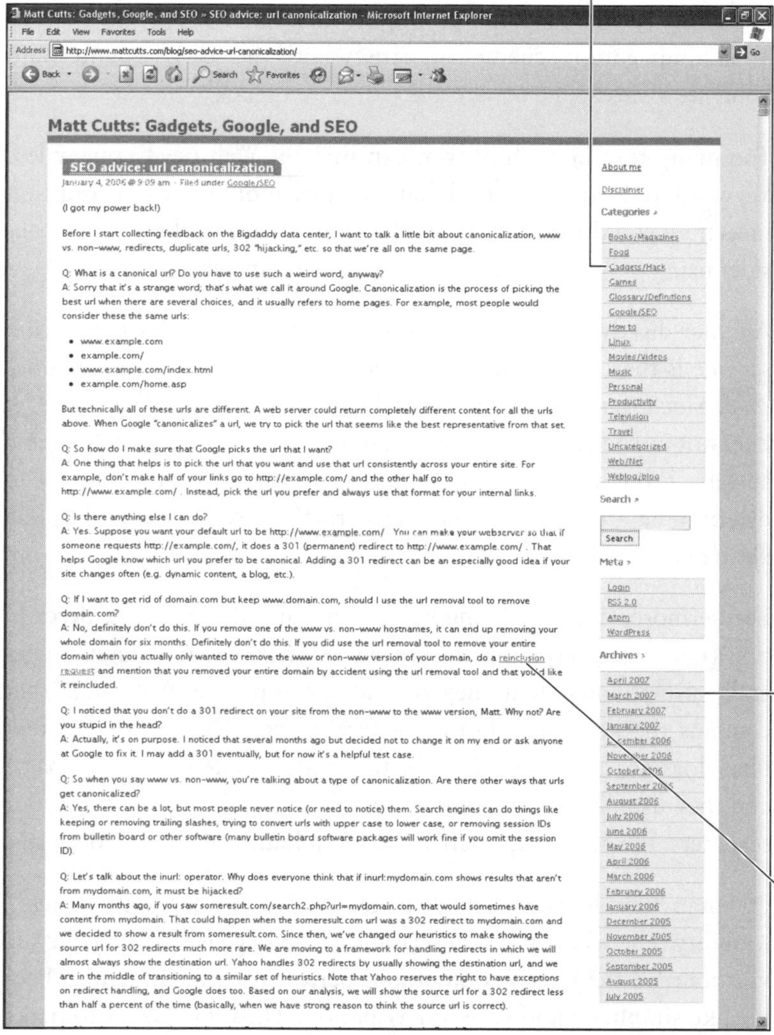

Figure 2-30

Since many bloggers do not have education and experience in user-centered design and search engine optimization, many blogs are not search engine friendly Web sites. This blog site is an exception. Information has been categorized as well as archived, providing a clearer information architecture.

The secondary navigation scheme consists of archival or temporal text links, which are important on news or news-like Web sites.

Embedded text links are used throughout the site to provide a strong scent of information.

Potential problems with hypertext links

On the surface, a text-link navigation scheme may seem like an ideal solution because all of the search engines seem to prefer this type of link. A Web page full of text links tends to download much faster than a Web page full of graphic images. So using text links as a main navigation scheme can satisfy both the search engines and your site visitors.

Too many text links, however, can make a Web page appear less keyword focused. If you find that you have more words in your text links than you do in the main body content, you might want to consider using graphic images as part of your navigation scheme.

Another disadvantage of using text links as the primary navigation scheme is that it is often the first body text that the search engines read. Since this text tends to be the same on many Web pages, it does not introduce unique content immediately to the search engine spiders, though the search engines have made great advances in determining a page's "unique fingerprint" by removing boilerplate elements.

Furthermore, if a search engine does not use the meta-tag description's content to display in the search results, the search engines generally use the first text they find at the top of a Web page that contains the keyword phrase. Generally speaking, a series of text links does not accurately describe the unique content of a Web page, and they usually do not contain an effective call to action. To your searchers, the description can appear as a bunch of unrelated words.

Too many text links on a single page can also interfere with a page's legibility. The whole point of writing a Web page is to have your site visitors read the page's content and perform a desired action. People like simplicity and ease of navigation. Thus, find ways to make your text links more visually distinct, easy to find, and legible, such as placing them in a colored table cell or a colored sidebar.

If you find that your text links are interfering with search engine visibility and page legibility, consider using graphic images as an alternative means of navigation.

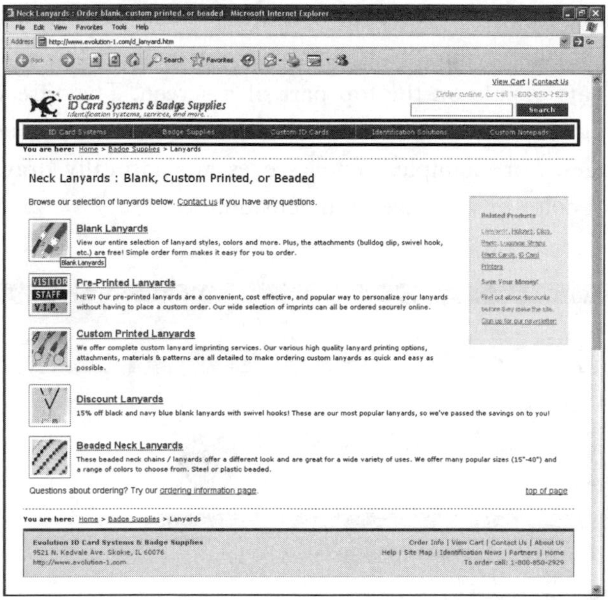

Figure 2-31
Evolution Design Systems
uses text links as the primary means of navigation.
Since the text links do not
dominate the site's main
content and use targeted
keywords, this is an effective, search engine friendly
navigation scheme.

Navigation buttons

A navigation button is a single graphic image, generally in a GIF or
a JPEG format, that links to a single URL.

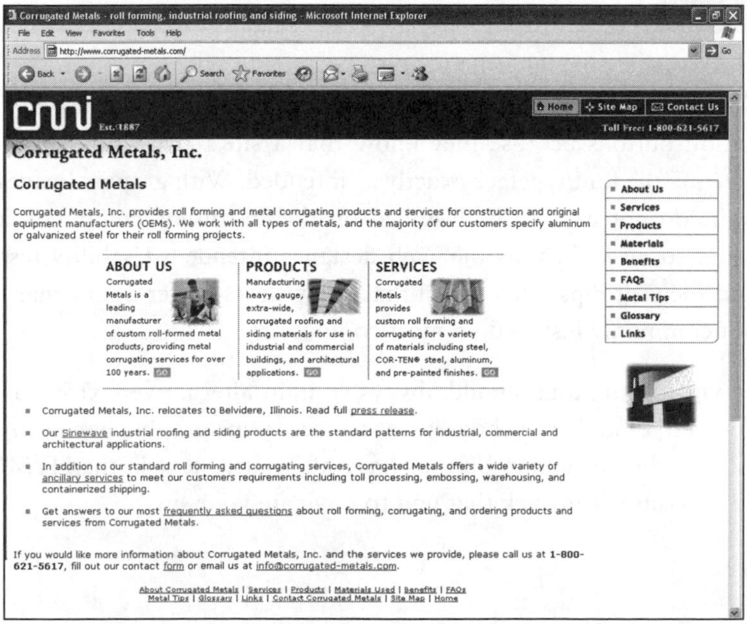

Figure 2-32
Corrugated Metals Inc. uses
navigation buttons as their
main navigation scheme.
They place their navigations
at the top of the screen and
along the right side. Even
though the navigation buttons appear to be a single
graphic image, when you
right-click and select the
Open Image in New Window
option, you will see that
there is one navigation button per link.

Navigation buttons give your visitors a visual representation of how to navigate your site right away, especially if the navigation buttons are visible on the top part of a screen. They are visually appealing and can easily draw attention to important parts of your Web pages. For example, people's eyes are naturally drawn to a splash of color or a change in dimension.

Figure 2-33

ARCH Venture Partners' Web designer used contrasting colors to highlight the "on" and "off" buttons on the site. This use of color draws attention to the navigation scheme and lets site visitors know what page they are on, visually.

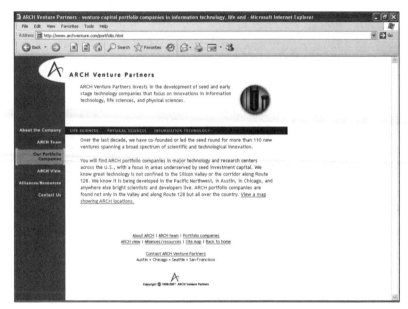

Web designers and graphic designers, in particular, like to use navigation buttons because they know that a site's target audience is viewing the font/typeface exactly as intended. With graphic images, fonts do not need to be installed on the end users' computers in order to view them as the Web designer intended. Usability tests and focus groups often reveal that site visitors prefer a font that is not commonly installed on most computers.

Navigation buttons should always contain alternative text in case your target audience chooses not to view your graphic images. As long as the navigation buttons have alternative text in the HTML code, visitors can click that text to navigate your site.

Figure 2-34
The Corrugated Metals site uses alternative text. In this example, the Materials button is not loading. In its place is the alternative text. Site visitors will still be able to click the alternative text to go to the Materials page.

Potential problems with navigation buttons

All of the search engines can follow the link surrounding a navigation button, as long as the navigation button does not contain some types of JavaScript within the anchor tag. JavaScript can pose problems with search engine spiders; therefore, not all search engines will follow that type of link.

This type of link is search engine friendly:

<a href="oolongteas.html"><img src="images/oolong.gif" width="60" height="20" alt="Oolong organic teas" /></a>

- <a begins the anchor tag.

- href is the attribute of this anchor tag referring to the target location, which is the Web page called oolongteas.html.

- > closes the anchor tag.

- <img begins the image tag.

- src is an attribute of the img tag. This attribute is often called "source." The source of the image tag can be found in a directory called "images." Inside the "images" directory is a GIF image named "oolong.gif."

- The width and height attributes tell the browser the dimensions of the graphic image. Always use the height and width attributes because they greatly decrease the download time of a Web page.

- alt is the alternative text attribute. The alternative text in this example is "Oolong organic teas."

- /> closes the img tag.

- </a> closes the link to the Oolong Teas page.

When you add too many attributes to the anchor tag, such as a rollover script, the attributes can make links less search engine friendly, though some rollover scripts are more search engine friendly than others. Currently, the major search engines prefer straightforward link coding without any type of script. So if you know your site will be using certain rollover effects on navigation buttons, then it is best to include an alternative navigation scheme that the search engine spiders can follow.

However, if navigation buttons without rollovers are used in conjunction with hypertext links, then Web designers can place keywords in multiple places: both within the hypertext links and in alternative text of the navigation buttons. Many search engine marketers recommend this combination because of the dual benefit.

Image maps

An *image map* is a single graphic image that allows users to access different Web pages by clicking on different areas of that image. In other words, an image map is a single graphic image that contains multiple links. Figure 2-35 shows an example of an image map:

Figure 2-35

The Tesko Enterprises Web site uses image maps as a main navigation scheme. On this page, there are two image maps: the side navigation and the graphic image in the middle of the screen.

Many search engines will not follow the links inside an image map because of the possibility of image spam. So if you use an image map as part of your site's navigation scheme, always use text links or navigational buttons elsewhere on your Web pages.

Many search engine marketers automatically think that because many search engines will not follow the links inside image maps they should not use image maps in site navigation. This belief is not always a credible conclusion because in many situations a single graphic image will download much more quickly than multiple graphic images.

For example, if a site has 16 navigation buttons that are 2K each, the total size for these graphic images is 32K. A single image map might only be 8 to 10K, much smaller than the set of navigation buttons. With the image map there will be only one call to the server, as opposed to 16, which will also speed things up regardless of file sizes.

Some search engine optimization professionals make blanket statements regarding image map usage. If an image map is not search engine friendly, then one might assume that image maps should never be used as a navigational element on a Web site. Some image maps are very useful, such as the one shown in Figure 2-36:

The reason a combination of two navigational elements (image map and corresponding text links) works so well is that it accommodates ease of use for most site visitors. For example, a searcher who wants local information from California is more likely to click the link in the image map because California is a large state. Users find it easier to click the state of California rather than to find the word "California" within the text links.

Delaware and Rhode Island, however, are small states. Users find the list of text links more useful than clicking the links in the image map, especially since the state list is presented alphabetically.

The benefit of designing and coding for site visitors resulted in this Web page being more search engine friendly. In the event that crawlers will not follow, or are unable to follow, the links contained in the image map, the corresponding text links provided access to content.

Important

Browsers download graphic images on a Web page. Search engines do not download your graphic images when they request a page from your server. Remember, search engines index text and follow links. They are not looking for graphic images. They are looking for a Web page's HTML text and links to follow within that text. Only search engines that crawl the Web specifically for graphic image searches will store information about your graphic images.

Figure 2-36

Many visitors find it easier to click the state than to search for and click a text link in a long list. Clickstream data confirms that site visitors prefer clicking the image map than clicking the text-link list of states.

Alabama	Illinois	Montana	Puerto Rico
Alaska	Indiana	Nebraska	Rhode Island
Arizona	Iowa	Nevada	South Carolina
Arkansas	Kansas	New Hampshire	South Dakota
California	Kentucky	New Jersey	Tennessee
Colorado	Louisiana	New Mexico	Texas
Connecticut	Maine	New York	Utah
Delaware	Maryland	North Carolina	Vermont
District of Columbia	Massachusetts	North Dakota	Virgin Islands
Florida	Michigan	Ohio	Virginia
Georgia	Minnesota	Oklahoma	Washington
Hawaii	Mississippi	Oregon	West Virginia
Idaho	Missouri	Pennsylvania	Wisconsin
			Wyoming

Tip

Remember, an image map is a graphic image. Always place alternative text in the HTML code of an image map, especially if the image map is at the top of a Web page.

When is it not a good idea to use an image map? If the only navigation scheme on your Web site is graphic images, then it is best to use navigation buttons because all the search engines can follow the links surrounding navigation buttons. However, if you are using both graphic images and text links as a navigation scheme, consider the pages' download time. If the image map downloads more quickly than a set of navigation buttons, then the image map might be a better choice.

Drop-down/pull-down menus

Figure 2-37 shows examples of two types of drop-down menus:

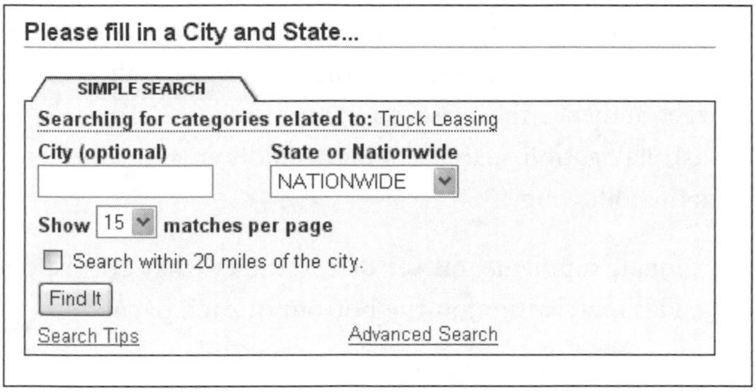

Please fill in a City and State...

SIMPLE SEARCH

Searching for categories related to: Truck Leasing

City (optional)

State or Nationwide

NATIONWIDE

Show 15 matches per page

☐ Search within 20 miles of the city.

Find It

Search Tips   Advanced Search

Figure 2-37
Examples of two drop-down menus. The first type of drop-down menu is not search engine friendly because search engines do not fill out forms. The second drop-down menu is more search engine friendly because it uses DHTML and invisible CSS layers that are meant to be seen and used by site visitors. Most HTML editing software can automatically generate drop-down menus.

The main advantage of using drop-down menus in a navigation scheme is screen real estate. Drop-down menus do not initially take up as much screen space as a series of navigation buttons or text links. Furthermore, by freeing up screen space, Web site owners are able to place more content that their target audience wishes to read above the fold.

Potential problems with menus

Many drop-down menus are generally not search engine friendly because they require either JavaScript or a CGI program to work. Since search engines generally do not follow these types of links, always have an alternative form of navigation for the search engines to follow.

Usability experts do not always recommend drop-down menus as a navigation scheme because people decide what they are going to click before they place their pointers over a navigational element. Additionally, menu items often hide important text and graphic images in the main content area of a screen, making it more difficult for site visitors to see important items and to take a desired action.

As long as menu items do not contain long lists of items, Web designers can combine drop-down menus with corresponding text links at the bottom of a Web page for search engine visibility.

Tip

Always test and measure the effectiveness of drop-down menus. Do not assume that your site visitors use them, even technically savvy users. One might believe that since most computer users understand how to use drop-down menus, they would have no problems navigating a site with them. User data, however, shows that site visitors prefer to browse sites via embedded text links and site search engines.

Flash navigation

At this time, some search engines are able to follow links embedded in Flash elements, but their success rate is hit or miss.

If you have determined that potential and current site visitors prefer navigating a site using Flash elements, then, by all means, give your target audience the Flash navigation scheme. To make pages with Flash navigation search engine friendly, make sure your site contains the following:

- A global, supplemental set of text links (that correspond to the Flash navigation) at the bottom of each page.
- A site map or a site index.
- Relevant horizontal and vertical cross-linking.

Almost all Web sites should contain some sort of text-link navigational element, such as locational breadcrumb links and embedded text links.

Relevant Cross-Linking

Many search engine optimization professionals confuse cross-linking with link development. Cross-linking is internal. It is a link from one page on your site to another page on your site. Link development is external. Link development is the quality and quantity of external, third-party Web sites (such as a Web directory) linking to your site.

There are two types of internal cross-links: vertical and horizontal. Both cross-link types need to be consistently present on a Web site to communicate the importance of content on all Web pages.

One example of a vertical cross-link is a locational breadcrumb trail, which follows the format below:

<u>Home</u> > <u>Category</u> > Product name

The problem with most Web sites' information architecture is that it is primarily hierarchical in nature. This hierarchy is precisely the reason search engines will not deep crawl a Web site. The cross-linking communicates that deep-level pages are not important.

Even though all sites should have clear categorization, another problem with having vertical-only cross-linking is that it communicates to the search engines that the home page is the most important page on the site as shown in Figure 2-38:

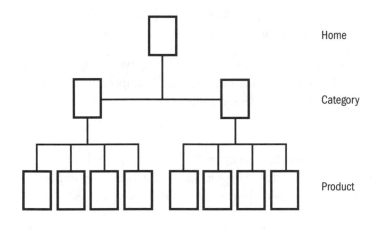

Home

Category

Product

Figure 2-38

Using only vertical cross-links communicates to both search engines and site visitors that the home page is the most important page on a Web site.

When searchers arrive on your site from a search engine results page, they usually do not want to land on the home page. They would prefer to land on the page that contains the exact information they desire. Therefore, the home page should not receive the most emphasis. Category and product pages are more important to searchers.

This is what searchers want:

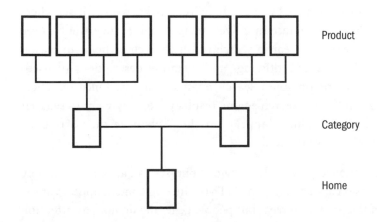

Product

Category

Home

Figure 2-39

Using a combination of keyword-focused horizontal and vertical cross-links communicates to both search engines and site visitors that category and product pages contain important information.

I am not saying to randomly throw cross-links on a page purely for search engine visibility. Instead, implement the cross-links that are most appropriate for every page type on your site. For example, a glossary page will probably contain alphabetical cross-linking, embedded text links, primary and secondary navigation schemes, and breadcrumb links. A product or article page is not likely to contain alphabetical cross-linking but will have the others.

Relevant cross-linking also minimizes negative pogo-sticking behavior. Therefore, cross-linking is equally important for search engine visibility as well as site usability.

"You are here" cues

Providing a sense of place on every Web page is not only an important part of the Web development process, it is also an important part of the search engine optimization and sales processes.

When searchers click a link from a search engine results page, they do not always arrive on a site's home page. In all likelihood, they arrive on a page somewhere within a Web site. Searchers usually land on a page that contains desired information, or they land on a page that should easily lead them to desired information. For searchers to feel confident that a site offers the product, service, or information they desire, Web pages should present clear "you are here" cues.

The most important "you are here" cue is keywords. If searchers type a keyword phrase in a Web search engine, they want to see those keywords appear in search results, which is the main reason keywords in HTML title tags and meta-tag descriptions (if used) are crucial for optimum search engine visibility. Once searchers click a link from a search engine results page, they want to see that same keyword phrase appear on the Web page they arrive at, preferably above the fold.

As I mentioned previously, keyword phrases can appear in a variety of places on a Web page. The HTML title-tag content appears at the top of the browser screen, but people generally do not pay attention to that part of the screen due to "banner blindness." People do, however, tend to focus on the center of the screen, three to four inches from the top of the screen. Web designers commonly place HTML headings in that area.

Locational breadcrumb links are also frequently placed in that key area of screen real estate. Even though site visitors typically do not use breadcrumb links to navigate a Web site, these links are important because they provide both keyword focus and a sense of place on a Web page.

Interestingly, using Jared Spool's Five-Second Usability Test for the past few years, I determined that site visitors mostly recall the heading content. I attributed this recollection to screen real estate allocation, extra white space surrounding the heading, color, and font size. Some questions I ask during the usability test are:

- What Web page are you viewing?

- Whose Web site are you viewing?

- What information is presented on this Web page (or what content is available on this page)?

- What section, if any, of the site are you viewing?

- How confident are you that you will see desired information on this page?

Providing a sense of place consistently throughout a Web site makes a site more search engine friendly if the "you are here" cues are keyword focused and used appropriately. In addition, this consistency increases user confidence, making it more likely that site visitors will take a desired call to action, such as "Add to Cart" or "Sign up for newsletter."

Scent of information

Ideally, searchers should be able to query commercial Web search engines and be delivered to pages that contain the exact information they desire. For example, if a searcher wants to determine the cost of a navy cashmere scarf at a variety of online stores, that searcher generally wants to arrive at product pages that show the price and a photo of the scarf.

Tip

During the interview process, I found that participants mention many "you are here" cues including headings and subheadings, locational breadcrumb links, global navigational elements, and main-content area text. If important keywords are used in all or most of these places, site visitors feel more confident the Web page contains the information they desire. This confidence transfers to the entire site if the cues are used consistently.

Figure 2-40

The MedicineNet Web site has outstanding search engine visibility due to pages providing clear "you are here" cues and a strong information scent. On this reference page, the file tab for the medical dictionary is highlighted, and the bread-crumb link uses an important keyword phrase: medical dictionary.

Information retrieval systems are not perfect, however, and most content providers do not necessarily implement keyword-focused copywriting. As a result, searchers do not always land on the page that contains the information they desire after they click a link from a search engine results page. Searchers might, however, land on a page that can lead them to the information they desire, such as a category or FAQ page. Providing an information scent on a Web site, therefore, is important not only for closing a sale but also for search engine visibility.

To provide an effective information scent, searchers must feel comfortable navigating a Web site. Using important keywords in navigational elements (primary and secondary navigation schemes, breadcrumb links, other related cross-links) is crucial for providing this scent. Some of the questions I often ask during the five-second usability test include:

- Is the information you wanted available on this page?

- If not, where can you go to find this information?

- How can you get to that information?

- What pages have you visited? What pages haven't you visited? How did you determine this?

- How can you go back to pages you have viewed previously (if applicable)?

- How confident are you that you will see desired information on this page if you click this link?

- After clicking a link, do you see the desired information on the following Web page?

Providing a keyword-focused information scent can make a site search engine friendly as well as user friendly.

URL structure

The URL structure is part of the Web interface. In an ideal situation, domain and file names can provide useful information about a page's information architecture. For example, if participants are only shown the following static-looking URL during a usability test:

www.tranquiliteasorganic.com/oolongtea.html

They assume that the Web page's content is about oolong tea available at the TranquiliTeas Organic Web site. Dynamically generated URLs, or URLs that contain problematic characters, often pose indexing problems for the search engines.

Dynamically generated URLs

Dynamically generated URLs are usually created using a technology such as Active Server Pages (.aspx), Cold Fusion (.cfm), Hypertext PreProcessor (.php), Java Server Pages (.jsp), or Perl. Often, search engine optimization professionals state that search engines cannot follow dynamically generated URLs. This statement is partly true. A more accurate statement is that search engines may not be able to crawl the URL used in order to retrieve Web pages. Or search engines will not crawl a particular URL structure because search data indicates that a certain URL structure tends to deliver redundant and/or poor content.

Let's compare a static Web page URL and a dynamic Web page URL. A typical static Web site is comprised of a series of Web pages that end in an .html or .htm extension. Each page is a unique file and has unique content, and the URL has no "stop" symbols such as a ?, &,

$, =, +, or %. For example, on the fictional TranquiliTeas Web site, a static Web page for the oolong tea page will have the following URL:

http://www.tranquiliteasorganic.com/oolongteas.html

In contrast, a dynamic Web site has very few files that contain original content. The files from a dynamic Web site are comprised of templates that give instructions on how to present content, but the templates contain little or no unique content. The main content of dynamic Web sites is stored in a database. When a page is viewed on a dynamic Web site, the template will load content from the database. In order to tell the template to load specific content, parameters (or variables) are added to the URL.

For example, if the Tranquiliteas site uses a database to showcase different products, the URL might look like the following:

http://www.tranquiliteasorganic.com/products.aspx?product_no=25

The name of the template page is products.aspx, the question mark (?) communicates to the search engines that the URL is dynamic, the product_no is the name of a variable or parameter, and 25 is the value assigned to the variable. In this example, the number 25 will correspond to the oolong tea content in the database.

The above URL is generally search engine friendly because there is only one parameter in the URL, and many search engines do not have any problems indexing dynamic URLs with a single parameter. Once the URL contains multiple parameters, however, it becomes increasingly difficult for the search engines to determine if the resulting Web page contains unique content. Furthermore, search data indicates that redundant content is more likely to be delivered when URLs contain many parameters.

If a URL contains a question mark (?), search engines do not automatically reject the URL. Rather, the question mark is seen as an indicator of dynamic content. Other symbols also act as indicators of dynamically delivered content such as &, $, =, +, or %.

Why don't search engines like to crawl URLs that contain these characters? Basically, there are three reasons:

1. **Search engines do not want the same content delivered to them over and over, which is often a problem with dynamic URLs.**

   Also, end users do not want to see identical pages dominating search results. By stopping at the question mark or one or two parameters following a question mark, search engines can prevent some identical content from being listed in search results.

   Sites that generate session IDs in the URLs also have the same problem. For example, if the TranquiliTeas Web site had the following URL:

   http://www.tranquiliteasorganic.com/products.jsp?BV_SessionID=0532038767

   http://www.tranquiliteasorganic.com/products.jsp?BV_SessionID=0235426067

   These pages might not be considered search engine friendly due to the question mark (?) and the equals sign (=). These URLs have the same content but different URLs. But if the following URL loads in a browser:

   http://www.tranquiliteasorganic.com/products.jsp

   The search engines should be able to list this page.

2. **Search engines want their search results to be accurate.**

   Search engines regularly update their indexes every two to four weeks. If they include dynamically generated URLs in their search results, the content might change between the time they recorded the URL and the time the URL appears in the search results. The possible outcome? Information in search results pages might not be accurate.

3. **Some dynamically generated URLs can "trap" a search engine spider and cause it to crash.**

   In some situations, a search engine spider may encounter a dynamic Web page where the database program or CGI process feeds it an infinite number of URLs. Programmers who fail to close their "if" or "while" statements on Web pages can crash a search engine spider.

Search engines have made great progress in their ability to spider dynamic URLs. In the meantime, Web developers should focus their efforts on delivering Web pages to the search engines that are more user friendly, minimizing the appearance of "stop" characters in their URLs.

For example, in a dynamic URL, one way to display a single Web page with multiple parameters, separate each parameter with an ampersand (&). So a URL with two parameters can look like the following:

http://www.tranquiliteasorganic.com/products.asp?product_no=25 &product_sortorder=asc

This URL is much more difficult for the search engines to index because they have no way of knowing what parameters identify a new Web page and what parameters are just a means of sorting content, a navigation scheme, or anything that just does not justify indexing the URL as a new and unique Web page.

Thus, one way to make dynamic sites more search engine friendly is to minimize the number of parameters in the URL. Other ways to make dynamic sites search engine friendly are adding static information pages, modifying the stop characters in the URL, using pay-for-inclusion (PFI) programs, and participating in pay-for-placement (PFP) advertising.

Absolute and relative links

In general, there are two types of links: absolute and relative. An absolute link defines a specific location of the Web file or document including (a) the protocol to use to get the document, (b) the server to get it from, (c) the directory it is located in, and (d) the name of the document itself.

Below is an example of an absolute link:

```
<a href="http://www.tranquiliteasorganic.com/oolongtea.html">
Oolong tea</a>
```

- <a begins the anchor tag.

- href is the attribute of this anchor tag referring to the target location. The URL enclosed in quotation marks will give the location of the Web file once you click the link. In this example, if you click the text link, you will go to the Oolong Tea page on the TranquiliTeas Web site.

- http:// is the protocol (hypertext transfer protocol).

- www.tranquiliteasorganic.com is the domain name, which has a specific address on a Web server.

- oolongtea.html is the name of the HTML document on TranquiliTeas' Web server.

- Oolong tea is the anchor text.

- </a> closes the anchor tag and hypertext link.

With a relative link, the search engine spider or browser already knows where the current document is. Thus, if you link to another document in the same directory, you do not need to write out the full URL. Only the file name is necessary. Below is HTML code for a relative link:

```
<a href="oolongtea.html">Oolong tea</a>
```

Nevertheless, make sure that your site has all of its canonical ducks in a row, so to speak. Have the appropriate 301 redirects for www vs. non-www (and http vs. https) URLs in place. Additionally, in the very unfortunate event that your site has been set up to accept wild card subdomains, using relative links might be more trouble than using absolute links.

The title attribute

Many search engine optimization professionals mistakenly believe that placing keywords in a hyperlink's title attribute (if used) will help a page rank. Below is a hypertext link with the title attribute:

```
<a href="http://www.tranquiliteasorganic.com/greentea.html"
title="Green teas from TranquiliTeas Organic Teas">Green tea</a>
```

- <a begins the anchor tag.

- href is the attribute of this anchor tag referring to the target location. In this example, if you click the text link, you will go to the Green Tea page on the TranquiliTeas Web site.

- http:// is the protocol (hypertext transfer protocol).

- www.tranquiliteasorganic.com is the domain name, which has a specific address on a Web server.

Tip

Since it makes no difference to the search engine spiders whether you use an absolute or a relative link, use the one you are most comfortable using. Search engine spiders automatically convert relative links into absolute links. Therefore, it is not necessary for Web developers to convert all links on a Web site to absolute links.

- greentea.html is the name of the HTML document on Tranquiliteas' Web server.

- Green teas from TranquiliTeas Organic Teas is the title attribute text.

- Green tea is the anchor text.

- </a> closes the anchor tag and hypertext link.

Search engines do not use the text in the title attribute to determine relevancy. However, if you have the time to implement this text, it can help provide a stronger scent of information on browsers that display the title attribute when a pointer is placed over the link.

General tips for dynamic URLs

Search engines are becoming increasingly adept at spidering dynamic Web pages. If you view the search results in many search engines, you can see URLs appearing with question marks (?) and equal signs (=).

One way to increase the search engine visibility of dynamic URLs is to convert the troublesome symbols in the URL into symbols that are more search engine friendly, such as a comma or a forward slash.

If modifying the URL is not an option, other solutions exist to increase search engine visibility: static information pages, limiting the number of parameters in the URLs, pay-for-inclusion programs, and pay-for-placement search engine advertising.

Static information pages

One of the simplest solutions for dynamic Web sites is to create static HTML pages that the search engines are able to index. Not all Web pages on a site need to be dynamically generated, especially pages whose content does not need to be updated frequently. In fact, many Web sites naturally contain information pages. Does your site have an FAQ section, a glossary of industry-related terms, tips or facts related to your products and services? These are all examples of content that can be included on information pages. Figures 2-41 and 2-42 are excellent examples of information pages.

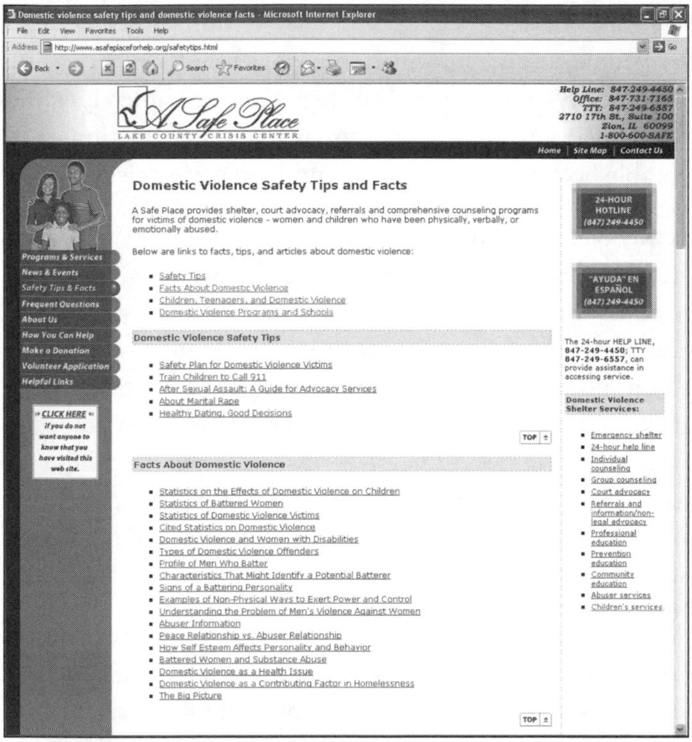

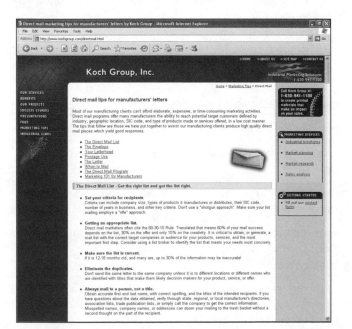

Figure 2-41
A Safe Place has a large set of information pages containing quality information about domestic violence safety tips and facts.

Figure 2-42
Koch Group, Inc. provides industrial marketing solutions for manufacturers, also has a set of tips tailored for manufacturers. One of their most popular pages has information on direct mail tips.

Information pages vs. doorway pages

Many people confuse information pages with doorway pages. The two types of search engine strategies are completely different. Doorway pages are a form of spam, whereas information pages are acceptable both to search engines and Web directories.

Doorway pages are Web pages created specifically for search engine positions. They are not created to benefit end users. Typically, the copy on doorway pages is computer-generated, not written by professional copywriters or content providers. Doorway page companies typically create thousands of computer-generated pages for a single keyword or keyword phrase. All of these pages are fed to the search engines via free Add URL forms, polluting their indexes with unnecessary and repetitive information. Doorway pages are not pleasant to look at, and they often contain so much gibberish they must be cloaked. End users would not continue visiting a Web site if they viewed these types of pages.

Information pages, on the other hand, are specifically created to benefit site visitors because they provide information of interest. Because information pages are always a part of a Web site, they can help a site gain more popularity in the search engines *and* the Web directories.

Table 2-2 compares the characteristics of information and doorway pages:

Table 2-2 Characteristics of Information and Doorway Pages

Information page characteristics	Doorway page characteristics
Designed and written primarily for site visitors.	Designed and written for positioning only.
Visually match the appearance of your Web site.	Are typically text-only pages.
Are never computer-generated Web pages; always designed for human viewing.	Are typically computer-generated Web pages.
Always hosted on the same server as the main Web site to help boost popularity.	Often hosted on a server separate from the main Web site.

Table 2-2 (continued)

Information page characteristics	Doorway page characteristics
Pages with extraordinary content can be submitted and accepted into Web directories.	Are never accepted in major, reputable directories.
Site visitors and search engine spiders always view the same page.	Site visitors and search engine spiders generally do not view the same page.
Contain no spam techniques (redirects, hidden text, keyword stacking, and so forth).	Often contain spam techniques, especially redirects, which is why many doorway pages must be cloaked.

Modifying stop characters in the URL

Another way to increase the search engine visibility of dynamic URLs is to modify the stop characters in the query string to search engine friendly characters, such as a forward slash (/) or a comma (,). For example, this dynamic URL:

http://www.tranquiliteasorganic.com/products.asp?product_no=25

can be modified to be this URL:

http://www.tranquiliteasorganic.com/products.asp/product_no/25

so that the search engines will include the pages in their indexes.

Software and workarounds exist on the Web that will present your Web developers with solutions for Active Server Pages, Cold Fusion pages, CGI/Perl, and sites on Apache servers. The most updated information is available on the subscribers-only section Search Engine Watch at:

http://www.searchenginewatch.com/subscribers/more/dynamic.html

This information will also be available on the companion Web site.

Pay-for-inclusion (PFI) programs

One strategy to consider for dynamic Web sites is pay-for-inclusion (PFI) programs. With a PFI model, a search engine will guarantee that pages from a Web site will be included in its index in exchange for payment. The PFI model is beneficial to search engine marketers and Web site owners because:

- They know their Web pages will not be dropped from a search engine index.

- The pages will be re-spidered very quickly.

This type of program guarantees that your submitted Web pages will not be dropped from the search engine index for a specified period, generally six months or a year. To keep your guaranteed inclusion in the search engine's index, you must renew your payment. This guarantee saves Web site owners considerable time and expenses. With a PFI program, Web site owners will not need to continually monitor each search engine to see whether a page has been dropped from an index and resubmit.

A PFI program does *not* guarantee that the pages will appear in top positions. Thus, all pages submitted through paid inclusion programs should be optimized.

Search engine marketers find paid inclusion programs save them considerable time and expense because a Web page cannot rank if it is not included in the search engine index. Furthermore, PFI programs allow dynamic Web pages to be included in the search engine index without having to implement costly redesigns and workarounds.

Session IDs and the Search Engines

Unfortunately, URLs that contain session IDs are often the kiss of death in the search engines. The problem with session IDs is that the same content is delivered over and over in the search results with a different URL. To counter mirror content being displayed in search results, many search engines simply will not include Web pages with session IDs.

If a Web site owner finds that session IDs are essential for delivering timely, quality content to site visitors, search engines offer pay-for-placement advertising programs.

Pay-for-placement (PFP) search engine advertising

Many Web site owners find that it saves considerable time to participate in pay-for-placement search engine programs, such as those
offered by Yahoo Search Marketing, rather than deal with poten-
tially costly workarounds. PFP search engine programs guarantee
something that paid inclusion programs do not guarantee: top positions. As long as you bid the top two or three positions, your advertisement will receive guaranteed display in the top of the search
engine and its partners. The guarantee has exceptions, such as a low
click-through rate in AdWords forcing an ad further down the
page, even if the advertiser has the highest bid.

Robots Exclusion Protocol

The robots exclusion protocol is a text file that you place on your
server instructing search engine spiders *not* to crawl and index the
information in specified areas on your Web site. In other words, the
protocol tells the search engine spiders which sections of your site
are off limits.

With the robots exclusion protocol, Web site owners can instruct
search engine spiders to not index individual Web pages, subdirectories, or even an entire site. Instructions can also be tailored for
individual search engines.

For example, Google is currently the only search engine that
indexes Flash sites reasonably well. A Web site owner can use the
robots exclusion protocol to instruct Google to index the Flash site
and tell the other search engines not to index the Flash site.

When to use robots exclusion protocol

Some Web files are not important to the search engines, such as
items in a CGI-BIN directory. When your target audience searches
for information, they are not interested in your site's programs that
generate your forms or your drop-down menus. They are not interested in a Web page that states "Under Construction." Your target
audience is interested in the products and services you are offering
on your Web site.

Using the robots exclusion protocol ensures that unnecessary information is not shown in search results, such as pages that are under construction. Be sure that the robots exclusion protocol is placed on your server *first*, before placing any excluded content on your server. Why? Sometimes, the search engine spiders will come to your Web server before you have had a chance to place the robots exclusion on your server. It only takes seconds for a search engine to gather information about your Web pages.

Other situations where robots exclusion might be necessary are dynamically generated pages that could present a spider trap, printer-friendly pages, and pages that contain identical data but sorted in different ways.

The meta-tag robots exclusion

One way to instruct the search engines not to index the content of a specific Web page and not to follow the links on a specific Web page is to use the meta-tag robots exclusion on every page you do not want the search engine to crawl. The proper HTML coding for this meta-tag is:

```
<html>
<head>
<title>Page title goes here.</title>
<meta name="robots" content="noindex, nofollow" />
</head>
```

The robots.txt file

The robots.txt file is a simple text document that instructs the search engines not to index parts of your Web site. You can easily build this file in NotePad (PC) or SimpleText (Mac).

The robots.txt standard should be placed in your server's root directory. In other words, put your robots.txt file in the same place that you put your home page, as shown in Figure 2-43. The URL for all robots.txt files looks like the following:

http://www.companyname.com/robots.txt

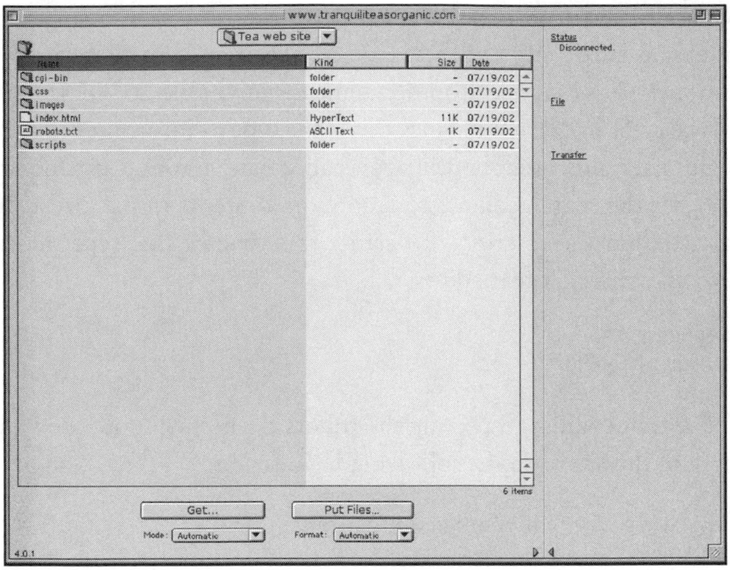

Figure 2-43
The robots.txt file is always placed in the same directory as your site's home page. In this example, the home page is named index.html.

A search engine respecting the robots.txt file will ask for the file before trying to crawl any page within your site. For example, if your entire Web site is under construction and you do not want the search engines to record any of the information on the site until you are finished, type the following text into a text editor:

User-agent: *
Disallow: /

Be sure to name the file robots.txt and to not use any other file extension. If you save the file as a Word document and call it robots.doc, the search engines will ignore that file.

In the above example, user-agent allows you to specify the search engine engines or browsers that should follow the directions on the second line. The way to exclude all search engines is to use the asterisk symbol shown above.

The disallow portion lets specify the directories and file names on your server that you do not want the search engines to index. In the example above, the forward slash instructs the search engines to ignore everything in your root directory. In other words, the search engines will not index the pages in your entire Web site.

Generally, most Web site owners do not want the search engines to ignore an entire site but rather specific sections of a Web site. For example, sites that use drop-down menus might use a CGI-script or a JavaScript in the menu. Since this is the type of information search engines are not interested in, you can create a robots.txt file that instructs the search engines to ignore the contents of the directories that contain these scripts. To create this type of file, type the following text into a text editor:

```
User-agent: *
Disallow: /cgi-bin/
```

The search engines respecting the robots.txt file will not index anything in the site with the following URL string:

http://www.companyname.com/cgi-bin/

Pages that are under construction or pages that might present spider traps to the search engines, such as a Calendar page, are also good pages to place in the robots.txt file. To exclude an individual Web page, type the following text into a text editor:

```
User-agent: *
Disallow: /calendar.html
```

In this example, search engines respecting the robots.txt file will not index anything in the site with the URL:

http://www.companyname.com/calendar.html

Server-Side Include

A server-side include (SSI) is a type of HTML comment that instructs a Web server to dynamically generate elements of a Web page before it sends the Web page to a browser or a search engine spider. The key item to remember is that a Web server constructs a Web page before it sends the Web page to the search engines. Therefore, any page built with server-side includes must contain the most important elements of a search engine friendly page: keyword-rich text and a navigation scheme that the search engine spiders can follow.

Figure 2-44 outlines how Web pages with SSI comments are presented to the search engines:

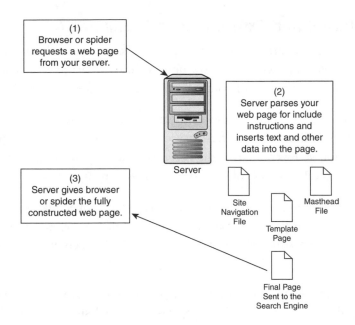

Figure 2-44
Web pages that are con-
structed using SSIs are created in the Web server first,
and then they are presented
to the search engines. As
long as the fully constructed
pages are optimized, they
can appear at the top of
search engine results.

Web designers can place any type of element inside an include file. The most common items to use as include files are mastheads, navigation elements, and content.

In order to make SSI Web pages search engine friendly, the fully constructed pages should contain keyword rich text in the title tags, meta tags, visible body text, and alternative text. If a Web developer inserts a navigation scheme via SSI, make sure the navigation scheme is spider friendly. When in doubt, create two forms of navigation: one for your target audience and one that the search engine spiders can follow. A set of text links at the bottom of every page can increase a site's search engine visibility.

Web pages that use server-side includes generally have a file extension of .shtml or .shtm. For example, if the fictional TranquiliTeas site used a server-side include as part of its design, the oolong tea page URL would look like the following:

http://www.tranquiliteasorganic.com/oolongtea.shtml

Since this URL contains none of the stop characters that a typical dynamic URL contains (?, &, $, =, +, or %), the URL is search engine friendly.

Warning

One of the main problems with a Web page that uses multiple SSIs is download time. When a search engine spider requests a page from a server, the server should be able to present the spider with a fully constructed Web page as quickly as possible. Quite often, a server can take a considerable amount of time to construct a page. As a result, a spider might "time out" and leave without recording the information on a Web page. This is one of the technical reasons that search engines do not include all Web pages in their indexes.

Internal and External Search Engines

If you have a site search engine or some kind of search function, how well your own pages show up in your own search results indicate the effectiveness of your internal search engine optimization.

How well your pages show up in the commercial Web site search engines indicates how effective your external search engine optimization is. By comparing the two sets of data, you can determine the total effectiveness of your site optimization strategies.

Site search engines are a valuable place to be collecting keyword data because you can compare what people are typing into the search engines to find your type of site and what people are typing into your site search engine after they have arrived.

For example, if you determine that your end users are able to find a popular product or service using your internal site search engine but are not able to find that information using the major search engines, then it might be a good idea to place a dynamic URL into a paid inclusion program.

Some data to monitor with your internal site search engine include:

- Most popular searches (top search words)
- Least popular searches
- Searches that yielded no results (top not found words)
- Percentage of searches that yielded no results
- Searches that yielded results but no click-throughs (top not clicked words)

If you find that your most popular searches on your site search engine yield little or no results, then you know you should be adding Web pages that give your target audience what they are searching for. In fact, according to User Interface Engineering in a report titled "Getting Them to What They Want," top usability experts Erik Ojakaar and Jared Spool determined that users who found content were far more successful when they navigated by using categories and text links than by using a site search engine. Users were far more likely to find their target content when they didn't use the site's search engine than when they did use it. So if your site's visitors are using your site search engine too much, it might be an indication that they are having difficulty finding information using the site's normal navigation scheme.

Another good item to check is your meta-tag description. If the meta-tag description is displayed in Yahoo, for example, and your site ranks well, then you know you probably have written an effective meta-tag description for the commercial Web search engines.

Compare that data to your site search engine data. Many site search engines use the meta-tag description for display on search results. If a site search yields targeted pages in the search results but very few people click those links in the search results, the meta-tag description and the title tag content might not be effective for your target audience once they arrive at your site.

Popularity Component

Popularity has become increasingly important among the search engines. A Web site's popularity component provides the search engines with feedback about a site's usefulness to a target audience. In other words, more useful Web sites are more relevant to a particular search.

If two Web sites have similar text and spider-friendly link architectures, the site with greater popularity will consistently rank higher over time because: (a) credible Web sites usually link to pages with valuable information, and (b) site visitors tend to use the same Web site over and over because the information it contains is relevant.

Therefore, building a site that appeals to both directory editors and your target audience is important for getting and maintaining maximum search engine visibility.

As mentioned in Part 1, the popularity component of a search engine algorithm consists of multiple subcomponents:

- Link popularity
- Click-through popularity

Link Popularity

The *link popularity* of a Web page can be defined as the number and quality of links pointing to that Web page. Link popularity is not as simple as obtaining as many links as possible to a Web page. The quality of the sites linking to a Web page holds far more weight than the quantity of sites linking to a Web page.

The major search engines have gone beyond measuring the number of links to a Web site. Some links are more credible than others, especially since many unethical search engine marketers have created free-for-all link farms in attempts to boost link popularity. For this reason, sites with high-quality, credible links pointing to them gain more popularity than sites with low-quality links pointing to them.

Therefore, sites with three high-quality links pointing to them will often rank higher than sites with hundreds of low-quality links pointing to them. So before beginning a link-building campaign, carefully select the places you wish to obtain links from, beginning with the most credible Web sites.

Web directories

Suppose you created an online store that sells organic teas. On this site, you might sell organic teas and you also might have a series of Web pages providing recipes for spiced tea. To get maximum link popularity from the major Web directories, it is possible to have the site listed in multiple categories. On one directory, for example, the home page can be submitted to the category:

Shopping > Online Stores > Food & Wine > Beverages > Tea > Specialty Teas

The page that shows the various spiced tea recipes can be submitted to a completely different category:

Lifestyle > Food/Wine > Beverages > Tea > Tea Recipes > Spiced Tea

Furthermore, if your online store has a physical address where shoppers can go to purchase your tea products offline, then your site might be relevant for a regional category in the same directory.

Not all Web sites can have multiple pages listed in the major Web directories. However, if a Web page's individual content offers unique, substantial information such as tips, advice, definitions (a glossary or dictionary), how-to articles, *and* the individual page is submitted to a completely different branch of the directory structure, then chances are favorable for getting multiple directory listings.

Industry-specific Web sites

Some credible Web sites offer information on very specific topics. For example, if you were looking for information on health-related issues, WebMd.com might be a good place to search for information. A link from WebMd.com to a health-related site can increase the site's link popularity. If you offer a free software demo on your Web site, you can request a link from shareware.com or download.com. If you offer marketing tips, find a Web site that publishes marketing tips and offer to write an article for them.

Professional associations

Many professional associations offer links to member Web sites. This is another way to help your site gain link popularity because professional associations are generally considered credible sources of information. A Chamber of Commerce site can be a good place to obtain additional listings.

Educational institutions

Many grade schools, colleges, and universities look for Web sites that relate to the specific subjects they teach. A religion professor might look for a site about the history of Japanese Buddhism. An art professor might look for sites that discuss the psychology of color. Links from educational institutions are valuable not only for popularity but also for branding purposes. Many students will remember your site once they become professionals.

Requesting Links

To find credible, industry-specific Web sites, use the major search engines and directories. If sites are consistently appearing at the top of the search results and are listed in the major directories, the search engines consider those sites important.

Go to the search engines and type in your major keyword phrases and analyze the search results. Determine the best noncompeting sites (i.e. sites that are not your direct competitors) and see if they have a Links or a Resources page. These are sites you can request links from.

To get the best popularity boost, make sure the sites linking to you are also listed in the three major directories.

When requesting that your site be added to an industry-specific or a noncompeting site, do not waste the Web site owner's time. Make your link request as easy as possible for the Web site owner to process. Send the Web site owner a polite email, complimenting the site characteristics or specific pages with excellent content (to make sure the owner knows you have read the site), the exact URL and description that you would like added to the Links page, and why you believe your Web page is beneficial to the particular Web site.

Even better, add the Web site that you would like to link to your site to your Links or Resources page. When you email the Web site owner, you can tell him or her that you have linked to the site and would like them to review the title and description you have written on your Links page. Give the Web site owner the opportunity to edit their own title and description. If the Web site owner likes your site, he or she may be very likely to provide a reciprocal link.

Be Careful Whom You Link To!

All the search engines make it clear that linking to "bad neighborhoods" can get your site penalized. Though no one can control which Web sites link to you, you have total control over which sites you link to. So do not participate in any free-for-all (FFA) Web sites or participate in Web rings to artificially boost your site's link popularity.

Always make sure your Links page is a part of your Web site, is featured as either a primary- or secondary-level global navigation link, and is hosted on your Web server. If your Links page is not a part of your Web site, then, in all likelihood, your site will be penalized for artificial link building. For example, one of the best URLs for the TranquiliTeas site will look like the following:

http://www.tranquiliteasorganic.com/links.html

So it is best to link to credible sites.

Click-Through Popularity

Getting other Web sites to link to your Web site is not enough to obtain long-term search engine visibility. Your target audience must be able to find the information they are searching for once they arrive at your Web site. Hopefully, your target audience is able to perform a search on a search engine, click the link to your site and go directly to the Web page with the exact information they are searching for. But this often is not the case. Sometimes, your target audience will navigate your site a bit to be sure the information on your site is credible, usually three to five clicks.

If your target audience cannot find the information they are searching for on your Web site, they will hit the "Back" button on their browser to return to the search results. The search engines are able to measure whether your end users are returning to the search results or staying on your Web site. This measurement constitutes a page's click-through popularity.

Many search engines can measure:

- Number of times end users click links to your site.
- How long end users visit your site.
- How often end users return to your site.

If your target audience continually clicks the links from the search engines to your site *and* they stay on your site to gather information, your site popularity increases. If your target audience clicks links to your site and does not find the information they are searching for, your site's popularity decreases. In other words, your target audience influences how visible your site is among the search engines.

Off-the-Page Criteria

Some aspects of link popularity are an example of *off-the-page criteria*, which are factors that Web site owners cannot influence to increase search engine visibility.

Web designers have complete control over what words they place on their pages and where they place these words. They have control over how pages link to each other. In fact, on-the-page factors can be computer-generated for search engine visibility, which is one reason why doorway pages came to be a popular search engine marketing strategy.

Because items such as keyword density and keyword prominence can easily be reproduced, search engines are relying more and more on off-the-page criteria to determine relevancy. Link popularity and click-through popularity are just two types of off-the-page criteria. However, unethical search engine marketers have discovered ways to artificially generate popularity through free-for-all (FFA) link farms, affiliate programs, and domain spamming. Therefore, search engines are continuing to find other off-the-page criteria to determine which Web pages will receive top positions.

Other Design Considerations

Some of the most beautiful Web pages are created entirely in Flash or with graphic images to preserve the aesthetics of the colors, uncommon typefaces, and movement. These Web pages, by virtue of effective offline and online advertising campaigns, might get plenty of traffic and sales conversions.

To make pages like these more search engine friendly, search engine marketers might recommend that visible HTML text be added. They might recommend placing text links at the bottom of the screen or using a series of breadcrumb links at the top of the screen. They might recommend placing a 250-word paragraph on each page. These items, though essential for search engine visibility, can interfere with the overall look and feel of a Web site. What should a Web site owner do when faced with this dilemma?

Web sites should be constructed primarily for your target audience. Your customers are the ones who purchase your products and services, not the search engines. So if your target audience prefers a Flash site and your other marketing efforts are providing effective sales leads and conversions, then maybe a pay-for-placement search engine strategy is the best solution. Always build a site based on what your target audience prefers. Testing your audience preferences is imperative for a successful Web site.

You might find that your target audience does not mind a set of text links at the bottom of your Web pages, especially if those links fall below the fold. Those text links can help increase your site's search engine visibility. Higher search engine visibility can increase sales.

Search engines will not change their rules based on a designer or marketer's personal preferences. Sometimes, aesthetic preferences conflict with search engine visibility. Ultimately, Web site owners must decide which is more important: personal aesthetics or increased search engine visibility?

Bells and Whistles

Flash, DHTML, JavaScript rollovers, style sheets, AJAX, and animation can add style and pizzazz to any Web site. Additionally, some bells and whistles can make site navigation easier to understand and make a site easier to read. So bells and whistles are not necessarily bad items to add to a site if they enhance the user experience.

Nevertheless, bells and whistles can interfere with a search engine optimization campaign. Search engines always look for text on a Web page, and some Web site designs present the search engines with no text to index, as is the case with many Flash designs. Some site designs contain keyword-rich text, but some design and navigation choices do not allow the search engine spiders to access to that text.

Technical choices or methods for building a Web site can also interfere with how well a search engine can crawl a site. In other words, the design of Flash navigation buttons is not problematic for the search engines, but the Flash technology used to produce the navigation buttons is often problematic for the search engines.

The best design solutions involve planning, testing, and implementation. If you know your company is going to use search engine optimization as part of its online marketing strategy, creating search engine friendly design templates can save your company considerable time and expenses.

JavaScript and Search Engine Visibility

JavaScript is a programming language that allows Web site designers to add flair and interactivity. Some of the most common uses

Tip

Do not assume that marketing departments or design teams know what your target audience prefers without testing the effectiveness of your Web pages. If you have a Flash site, also create an HTML version of your site. Measure the traffic on each of the sites. You might find that your target audience, overall, uses the HTML version of the site more frequently but the Flash version generates more sales leads.

for JavaScript include rollovers/mouseovers, pop-up windows, form validation, and drop-down navigation menus. In fact, the use of JavaScript rollovers has become so widespread that they are now considered a standard part of Web site design packages.

When a Web designer uses JavaScript on a site's navigation scheme, the scripts can greatly decrease the "crawlability" of the links. Currently, most search engines will not follow the links embedded inside JavaScript code (including rollovers and menus), or they will greatly limit the types of JavaScript-embedded links they will crawl.

Some JavaScript code is more search engine friendly than other scripts. Generally, the simpler the script the more likely a search engine spider will be able to crawl the link.

Specifying alternative content with the <noscript> tag

The <noscript> tag provides alternative content for browsers that do not support JavaScript or visitors who have disabled JavaScript while surfing the Web. The <noscript> tag, if used, is placed between the <head> and </head> tags. The HTML code in Listing 2-2 shows the proper coding for the <noscript> tag in the fictional TranquiliTeas Web site:

Listing 2-2 Coding for the <noscript> tag.

```
<noscript>
<h1>Organic green, oolong, and herbal tea</h1>
<p>TranquiliTeas Organic Teas offers a wide range of gourmet organic
teas at wholesale prices.</p>
<p>To view our selection of choice organic teas, please select one of
the links below:</p>
<ul>
<li><a href="herbalteas.html>Herbal teas</a></li>
<li><a href="greenteas.html>Green teas</a></li>
<li><a href="oolongteas.html>Oolong teas</a></li>
<li><a href="blackteas.html>Black teas</a></li>
<li><a href="teasets.html>Tea sets and accessories</a></li>
<li><a href="teas.html>teas</a></li>
</ul>
<p>If you would like more information about our organic teas or
would like to order one of our catalogs, please fill out our <a href=
"contact.html">contact</a> form or call us at 1-800-XXX-XXXX.</p>
</noscript>
```

The <noscript> tag and search engine spam

Unfortunately, many unethical search engine marketers discovered that they could hide text on a Web page by using the <noscript> tag, even though the Web page does not contain any JavaScript. Some search engine optimization professionals abuse the <noscript> tag in an attempt to boost rankings. Never use this tag to hide any unrelated content or links that you would not otherwise show to your end users.

Because of the widespread abuse of this tag, most of the search engines either ignore or decrease the relevancy of the text inside the <noscript> tag. Additionally, most end users will never see the content inside the <noscript> tag. Except for the title tag (that is not really hidden) the search engines ignore all hidden tags, or at least not use them to determine relevancy.

Adding all this extra HTML code inside the <noscript> tags can significantly increase the download time of your Web pages.

Therefore, before adding any type of JavaScript and <noscript> tags to your site, determine whether the extra code is necessary. If a JavaScript is written well, the <noscript> tag is unnecessary. Many sites get plenty of qualified traffic from the search engines without any JavaScript in the site design.

Frames and Search Engine Visibility

Whether Web site designers should use frames in Web site design has been hotly debated since browsers have been able to support them. Usability experts do not recommend the use of frames because people are not able to properly bookmark a framed page, and because the URL appearing in the browser does not match the content. End user opinions are divided as well. They either love them or hate them. Newbie Web users often get confused with the navigation scheme. Savvy Web users will opt to view pages without the frameset. Overall, most people prefer not to navigate a framed site when given the choice.

If you are creating a new Web site or modifying an existing design, I recommend not designing with frames. Search engines do know how to handle content in frames. However, the links in search engine results pages can send visitors to Web pages with no navigation schemes. With proper planning, framed sites can be search engine friendly.

Understanding frames and the search engines

All search engines spiders index text and follow links. The problem with the initial frameset code is that it does not present search engine spiders with keyword-rich text to index and a set of links to follow. Listing 2-3 shows some standard HTML code for a basic frameset page for the fictional TranquiliTeas site:

Listing 2-3 Code for a basic frameset page.

```
<html>
<head>
<title>Organic green, oolong, and herbal tea from TranquiliTeas Organic
Teas</title>
<meta name="description" content="Get gourmet herbal, green, and
oolong teas at wholesale prices from TranquiliTeas. Organic tea importer
offers decaffeinated herbal teas and other herbal blends. Black, oolong,
green, and iced teas available as loose tea or in tea bags." />
<meta name="keywords" content="organic teas green oolong tea herbal
blends TranquiliTeas decaffeinated loose tea bags" />
</head>
<frameset cols="120,*" border="0" framespacing="0"
frameborder="no" marginheight="0" marginwidth="0">
<frame src="buttons.html" name="navigation" noresize scrolling="no"
border="0" marginheight="0" marginwidth="0" />
<frame src ="content.html" name="content" noresize scrolling="auto"
border="0" marginheight="0" marginwidth="0">
</frameset>
<body>
</body>
</html>
```

If you analyze this code, you can see why many framed sites tend not to perform well in the search engines. There is virtually no content on this Web page except for the title-tag and meta-tag content. And if a search engine does not use meta-tag content for relevancy, such as Google, the only content used for ranking purposes on this Web page is the title-tag text. A single keyword phrase hardly indicates quality content to searchers.

The <noframes> tag

Conceptually, with a framed site, the browser will display one of two types of pages. If a browser can read frames, it will be served the frameset content. If a browser cannot read frames, it will display the content between the <noframes> and </noframes> tags.

If your site uses a frames design, always include keyword-rich content and links to the most important pages in your site within these tags. That way, the search engine spiders will record your most important text.

Listing 2-4 is a short example of how to properly code an initial frameset page. (If I were to create content inside the <noframes> tags, I would write 200 to 400 words of quality information to indicate to both the search engines and site visitors that this text is quality content. Also note that in the following code, I added the style sheet inside the <head> and </head> tags so that the <noframes> content will match the site design.)

In the example below, the content within the <noframes> and </noframes> tags is more or less the same used on the content.html page served in the frameset.

Listing 2-4 Sample HTML code illustrating the <noframes> tag.

```
<html>
<head>
<title>Organic green, oolong, and herbal tea from TranquiliTeas Organic
Teas</title>
<meta name="description" content="Get gourmet herbal, green, and
oolong teas at wholesale prices from TranquiliTeas. Organic tea importer
offers decaffeinated herbal teas and other herbal blends. Black, oolong,
green, and iced teas available as loose tea or in tea bags." />
<meta name="keywords" content="organic teas green oolong tea herbal
blends TranquiliTeas decaffeinated loose tea bags" />
<link rel="STYLESHEET" type="text/css" href="css/style1.css"><style
type="text/css"></style>
</head>
<frameset cols="120,*" border="0" framespacing="0"
frameborder="no" marginheight="0" marginwidth="0">
<frame src="buttons.html" name="navigation" noresize scrolling="no"
border="0" marginheight="0" marginwidth="0">
<frame src ="content.html" name="content" noresize scrolling="auto"
border="0" marginheight="0" marginwidth="0">
</frameset>
```

continues

Important

Do not place a second set of meta-tag or title-tag content inside the <noframes> tag. Why? Meta-tag or title-tag content belongs between the <head> and </head> tags, not between the <body> and </body> tags. Placing extra titles and meta tags on your Web pages can result in a spam penalty because this technique is clearly used to artificially inflate keyword density, not to benefit your site visitors.

Listing 2-4 (Continued)

```
<body>
<noframes>
<h1>Organic green, oolong, and herbal tea</h1>
TranquiliTeas Organic Teas offers a wide range of gourmet organic teas
at wholesale prices.
To view our selection of choice organic teas, please select one of the
links below:
<ul>
<li><a href="herbalteas.html>Herbal teas</a></li>
<li><a href="greenteas.html>Green teas</a></li>
<li><a href="oolongteas.html>Oolong teas</a></li>
<li><a href="blackteas.html>Black teas</a></li>
<li><a href="teasets.html>Tea sets and accessories</a></li>
<li><a href="teas.html>teas</a></li>
</ul>
<p>If you would like more information about our organic teas or would
like to order one of our catalogs, please fill out our <a href=
"contact.html">contact</a> form or call us at 1-800-XXX-XXXX.</p>
</noframes>
</body>
</html>
```

The <noframes> tag and search engine spam

Unfortunately, a long time ago, unethical SEO professionals discovered that they could hide text on a Web page by using the <noframes> tag, even though the Web page does not contain a frameset.

Because of the widespread, blatant abuse of this tag, most of the search engines either ignore or decrease the relevancy of the text inside the <noframes> tag.

Navigation and frames

As stated previously, a search- friendly design has at least two forms of navigation: one that site visitors can follow and one that search engines can follow. A framed design is no exception, especially when it comes to search engine visibility.

The simplest way to make the main content of a framed site search engine friendly is to add a set of text links at the bottom of every Web page. For example, in Figure 2-45, the left frame contains navigation buttons and the right frame contains the main content. Site visitors are able to access the Products & Accessories page from the home page, as shown in Figure 2-46:

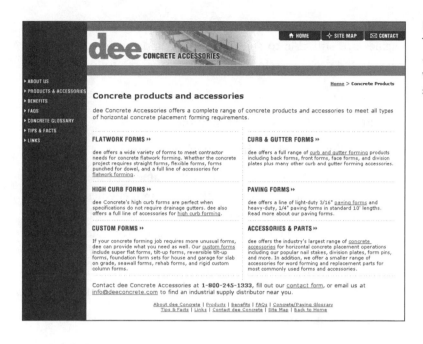

Figure 2-45

The dee Concrete Products & Accessories page as it would appear in a framed site design.

However, if dee's Products & Accessories page appeared in search engine results, and if visitors clicked the link from the search engine results directly to the Products & Accessories page, the page would not appear in the frameset. It would appear as shown in Figure 2-46:

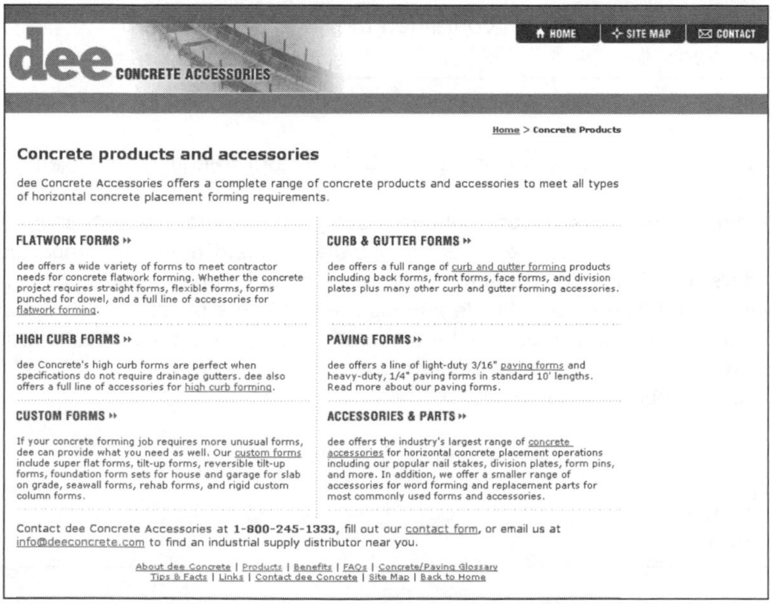

Figure 2-46

The Products and Accessories page as it would appear after clicking a link from the search engines.

Even though this page does not appear within a frameset, the search engines are still able to spider this page and the other important pages in the dee Concrete Web site because of the following:

- Text links at the bottom of the page.

- Breadcrumb links at the top of the page.

- Text links embedded in the main body text.

Therefore, when creating a Web site with frames, always be sure the main content frame has a set of links the search engines can follow. The search engine spiders also have to, somehow, find the interior pages. If there are no links to the internal pages from the frameset, if the interior pages are not submitted to the search engines, and if there are no links from other sites to the interior pages, then the search engines might have a difficult time crawling the interior pages.

Frames and JavaScript

If you prefer that the Web pages on your site always remain within the frames design, you can insert JavaScript on all your pages so that browsers will automatically load the frames design. Place the JavaScript in between the <head> and </head> tags as shown in Listing 2-5 for the fictional TranquiliTeas site:

Listing 2-5 JavaScript contained between <head> and </head> tags.

```
<html>
<head>
<title>Organic green, oolong, and herbal tea from TranquiliTeas Organic
Teas</title>
<meta name="description" content="Get gourmet herbal, green, and
oolong teas at wholesale prices from TranquiliTeas. Organic tea importer
offers decaffeinated herbal teas and other herbal blends. Black, oolong,
green, and iced teas available as loose tea or in tea bags." />
<meta name="keywords" content="organic teas green oolong tea herbal
blends TranquiliTeas decaffeinated loose tea bags" />
<script language="JavaScript">
<!--
if (top == self) self.location.href = "framesetname.html";
// -->
</script>
</head>
```

This script will not load the most appropriate content page in the frameset. The script only loads the frameset you specify, which is generally the home page. Additionally, site visitors will not be able to use the Back button because each page on your site automatically loads the frameset page.

Another solution is to create a home page that gives site visitors the option to view a site both with and without a frames design. After analyzing your site's traffic logs for at least three months, determine which design your visitors prefer. You might find that your site visitors prefer the unframed version of your site since unframed sites are generally easier to navigate. If your visitors prefer the unframed version, use that site design template for future Web site designs. Extra bonus? Qualified search engine traffic tends to increase after frames are no longer a part of a site design.

Note

Although other scripts exist, which allow framed pages to be bookmarked and which can load specific pages within the frameset, it is best to let your site visitors select their preference. Many people just do not like frames designs, and they appreciate the option to turn the frames off.

Optimizing Blogs and Forums

Many Web site owners like blogs because the blog software currently available is preformatted, making it easy for anyone with little or no information architecture and design skills to create a decent, presentable blog. Content developers like the idea of user-generated content because they do not have to take the time to write unique content themselves.

Many search engine optimization firms use blog optimization as the hot buzz phrase and solution for every type of Web site for the same reasons: easy-to-use design templates and user-generated content. Add the supposed link development opportunities from distribution to RSS publishers, and blogs appear to be the perfect search engine optimization solution for every type of Web site.

What all these groups fail to recognize is that the same Web design, usability, and optimization principles that apply to "regular" Web sites also apply to blog sites. The organization of information on blog sites is primarily based on temporal (or time) elements rather than user-centered, keyword-focused information architectures. In addition, many people mistakenly assume that the average blogger automatically writes and formats search-friendly content.

Link development to blog content is not as simple as some search engine professionals claim. For example, with RSS-published links, the links do not typically lead to the same URLs every day. Many bloggers do not write about the same topic every time; therefore, the links' context and relevancy frequently change.

With link development, no one person describes content in exactly the same way as another person. If I gave 1000 people an article to read and asked them to link to that article using a title (as the hyperlink) and a short description or summary of that article, I will likely get 1000 unique responses. RSS-published links and descriptions are identical.

Of course, I am not saying that blogs cannot be search engine friendly. They certainly can be. As long as blog creators keep usability principles and the building blocks of successful search engine optimization in mind, blogs can deliver a great return on investment (ROI).

10 steps to successful blog optimization

Below are some guidelines for optimizing blog sites:

1. **Research targeted keyword phrases before writing blog content.** With blog sites, it almost seems as if the keyword research process is nonexistent. Before you categorize and headline blog content, use the keyword research tools offered at Yahoo, Google, and Live to get a clearer idea of the terminology your site visitors might use to find the product, service, or information your site offers. If you are using a blog for business reasons or want others to read your blog, you should make it easy for site visitors to find information. Using keywords is a part of this process.

2. **Implement keyword phrases in blog pages' HTML title tags.** I know this step seems like a "duh" statement, but optimization guidelines for other Web-page types apply to blog pages as well. Many bloggers forget to implement keyword-rich text into unique title-tag content.

3. **Implement keyword phrases in blog headlines and short descriptions (or snippets).** Blog headlines often serve multiple functions. First, the heading text is considered primary text by all the major search engines. Therefore, this text is used to determine relevancy.

   Second, when we perform eight-second usability tests and eye-tracking analyses, we find that participants tend to remember the headlines due to font/typeface characteristics (change of color, type size, etc.) and white space.

   Third, blog headlines and short descriptions (or snippets, if used) are typically displayed as links to your blog pages in RSS publishers. With RSS publishers, people typically see only the headline, even if snippets are available, and use that content to determine whether to click the link. Keyword-focused headlines can encourage clicks to your blog pages. As a result, the links pointing from objective, third-party sites will use your most important keyword phrases.

   Finally, consistent keyword implementation increases user confidence. When searchers go from search engine results page to your blog page, or from another ranked page (found via search engines) to your blog page, they will see their targeted keyword phrases used continuously, making them more confident that the blog pages contain the information they desire.

4. **Customize blog design templates with a better information architecture.** Categorizing content only by year/date provides very little contextual relevancy. On a blog or news site, a temporal/archival navigation label is an important characteristic that identifies the page type as a blog or news page. Nonetheless, make sure your blog's information architecture provides other contextually relevant means of navigating the site. Keyword-focused navigation makes it easier for site visitors to find information on your Web site.

5. **Implement horizontal and vertical cross-linking.** Remember, providing "You are here" cues and information scents apply to blog pages as well as other types of pages. Locational breadcrumb links and categorization links are important for providing both a sense of place and a scent of information. But

horizontal cross-linking is equally important. Linking to related blog posts via embedded text links provides a strong information scent and communicates relevancy to the search engines.

Do not assume that searchers followed a chronological sequence to your blog content. With search engines, people often arrive in the middle of a blog with no other context than their query words. Relevant cross-linking will provide topic background and context in the event they want to read more about your ideas.

6. **Make the URL structure search engine friendly.** Even though the first part of the optimization process is keyword research, the first part of the search engine process is access. Content will not matter for search engine visibility if the search engines cannot access that content. Many "out-of-the box" blog platforms do not automatically create search friendly URLs. Therefore, be ready to implement URL workarounds, or find a blog platform that does not make the workarounds necessary.

7. **301 redirect or robots exclude redundant blog content.** When bloggers create an information architecture for their blogs, they often use that same content in the archives section and the categorized section, essentially creating two copies of the same content. Be proactive. Select the URL that provides the best access, relevancy, sense of place, and scent of information (usually the categorized content) and use that as the canonical URL.

8. **Be careful whom you link to.** Blog and forum spam is rampant on the Web because sploggers (spam bloggers) found an easy way to get links to their Web sites quickly and easily. Search engines will penalize Web sites that link to poor-quality, spammy Web sites. Tools are available for managing both comment and trackback spam. When in doubt, use the no-follow attribute on questionable links.

9. **Ping other sites, especially news or blog-related sites.** News and blog search engines will index your blog content more quickly if you ping them whenever you add a new blog entry. Though relevancy algorithms apply on these types of search engines, the new blog entry provides a quick ranking opportunity on these types of search engines.

10. **Implement a long-term archiving strategy.** With blog sites, the
    linkage properties will change very quickly. People who find a
    particular blog entry useful will want to link to that specific
    content. Review your Web analytics software and determine
    the blog entries people find most useful. Make sure the URL is
    archived and easy to link to. These entries are perfect for long-
    term link development.

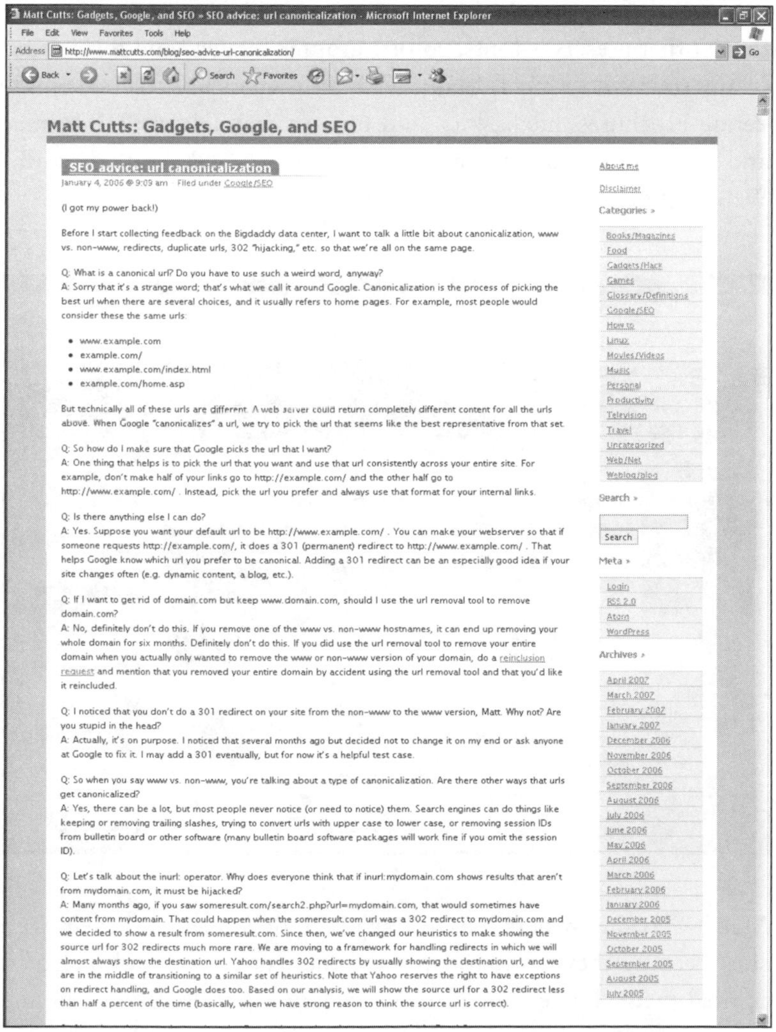

Figure 2-47

Notice that this blog site has categories as well as temporal/archival cross-links. The categorization provides contextual relevancy.

Optimizing PDF Documents

Search engines have become increasingly efficient at indexing different types of documents. Google, for example, can index 13 types of documents (in addition to HTML formatted documents) that include Microsoft Word, Microsoft Excel, Microsoft PowerPoint, rtf (rich text format), and Adobe® PDF documents. Other search engines can index PDF documents as well.

PDF stands for portable document format, which is a universal file format that preserves fonts, colors, graphic images, and formatting of any source document. Many Web site owners like to create marketing brochures, media kits, and how-to manuals in PDF format and make them available on the Web. Figure 2-48 shows a typical Web page brochure formatted as PDF.

Figure 2-48

The Metalith Web site offers a downloadable PDF brochure.

Many Web site owners like to have PDF documents on their Web sites because they want to preserve the exact look and feel of a printed piece. For example, let's say you would like your online brochure text to display in the typeface Avant Garde. In order for the online brochure to appear in this typeface, your site's visitors must have the Avant Garde font installed in their computers. If your visitors do not have this font installed, your online brochure will look different than what you intended. Therefore, many online brochures are formatted as PDF documents.

PDF documents can achieve top search engine visibility when formatted correctly. In fact, some top search engine results are PDF documents as shown in Figure 2-49.

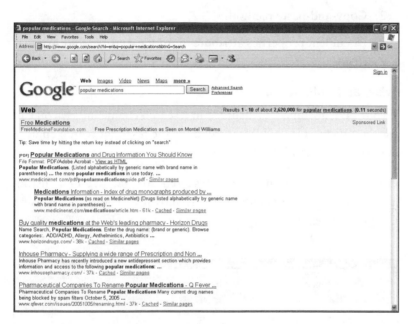

Figure 2-49
A PDF document displays in the top spot in Google for the keyword phrase "popular medications."

The building blocks of successful PDF document optimization are the same ones for HTML file optimization:

1. **Text component.** PDF documents should contain the words and phrases that targeted searchers are likely to type in to search queries. In other words, PDF document text should use the user's language.

2. **Link component.** Search engines and site visitors should have easy access to PDF documents. Additionally, PDF document content should also communicate relevancy, a sense of place, and clear information scents.

3. **Popularity component.** Encouraging external, third-party link development to PDF documents.

Keyword-rich text

In order to make your PDF documents search friendly, the documents must contain actual text, not a picture of text. There are three ways to determine whether a PDF document contains text the search engines can index:

1. "View as HTML" feature in search engine results pages.

2. Copy-and-paste method.

3. Document properties attribute in Adobe Acrobat and Acrobat Reader.

"View as HTML" feature

If your PDF document is included in a search engine index, you can use the "View as HTML" feature to see the text that search engines are using to determine relevancy.

First, perform an inurl: type of search so that the PDF listing appears on a search results page, as shown in Figure 2-50, using Google as an example:

Figure 2-50

How a PDF listing should appear after a URL search. If your PDF document does not appear in a search result after this type of search, the search engine is either having a difficult time accessing the content in the URL, or the information architecture to the PDF document is substandard. You can also refine the search to return only PDF documents.

Google and other commercial Web search engines allow searchers to view PDFs as HTML formatted documents. If you click the "View as HTML" link, you will see the search engine friendly text within a PDF document, as shown in Figure 2-51:

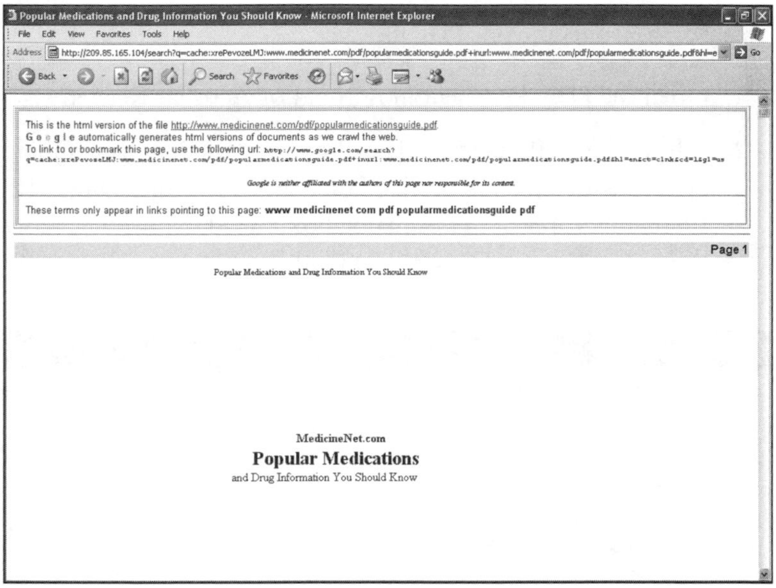

Figure 2-51
This is the text that Google is currently able to extract from the PDF document.

Copy-and-paste method

A simple way of determining the search engine friendly text in a PDF document is to perform the following steps:

1. Open the PDF file in Adobe Acrobat or Acrobat Reader.

2. On a PC, select Control-A. On a Mac, select Command-A (to select all).

3. After the text is highlighted, select Control-C (PC) or Command-C (Mac) to copy.

4. Go to a text editor: Notepad (PC) or SimpleText (Mac).

5. Press Control-V (PC) or Command-V (Mac) to paste the selected text into the text editor. This is the text used to determine relevancy within a PDF document.

Document properties attribute

Another way to determine if a PDF document contains text the search engines can index is to check the Document Properties dialog box. If no fonts are displayed in the Document Properties dialog box, then the PDF document does not contain text.

To check for fonts in your PDF files:

1. Open the PDF document in Acrobat or Acrobat Reader.

2. Select File > Properties. The Properties dialog box should appear with a file tab labeled Fonts, as shown in Figure 2-52. If any fonts appear in this dialog box, the PDF document contains text the search engines can index.

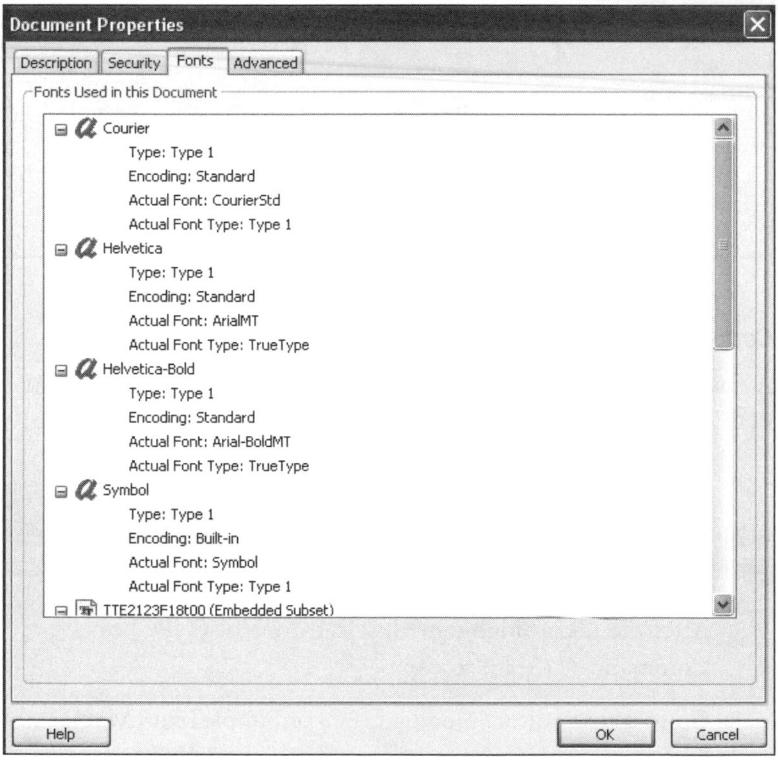

Figure 2-52

The Document Properties > Fonts dialog box for this PDF document displays multiple fonts, which means that the search engines are able to index the text in this document.

To see the specific text the search engines are able to index, use the Select Text tool, which is highlighted in Figure 2-53:

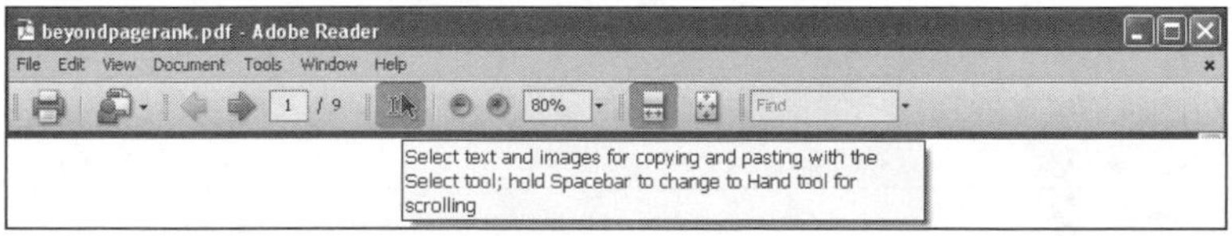

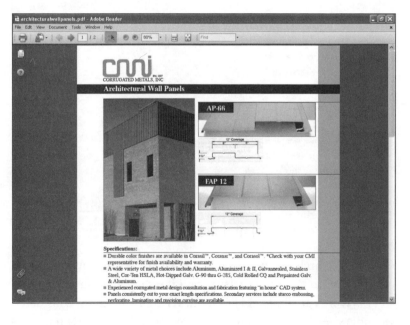

Figure 2-53
The Select Text tool in Acrobat Reader.

Try to highlight the text in the PDF document, as shown in Figure 2-54. The text you are able to highlight is the text that the search engines can index.

Figure 2-54
In this PDF example, the text in the main paragraphs can be highlighted, but the abbreviation in the logo (CMI) cannot. Therefore, the search engines are not able to index the text in this logo.

PDF metadata

Adobe Acrobat does allow PDF creators to add metadata to PDF documents, as shown in Figure 2-55:

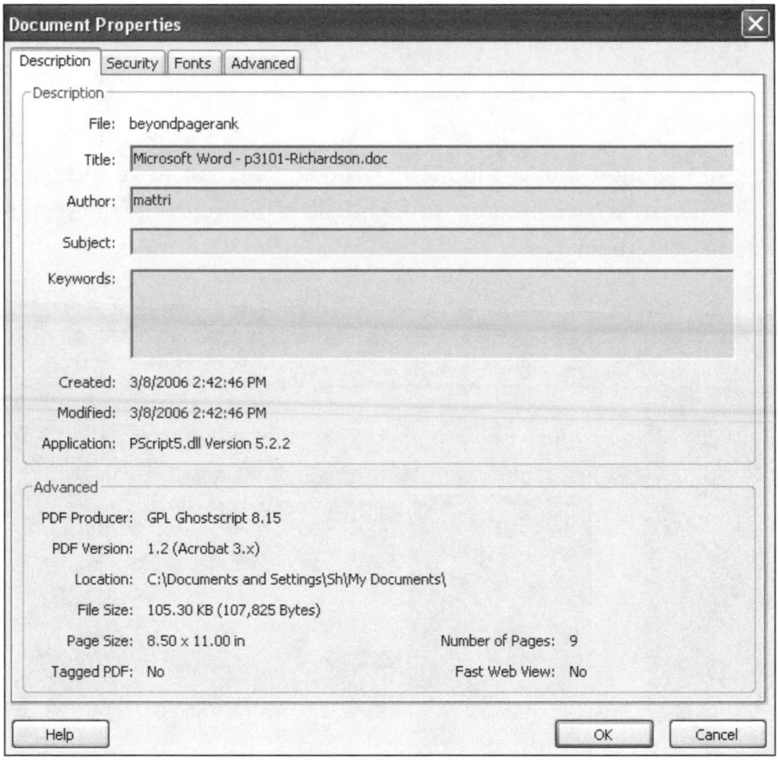

Figure 2-55
Some important metadata fields are title, author, subject, and keywords.

Tip

If you have the time to add useful metadata information to your PDF files, I highly recommend doing so when you create the PDF, making it a normal part of your formatting process. The commercial Web search engines might not use PDF metadata to determine relevancy, but other information retrieval systems (perhaps your own site search engine) might.

Keyword research, search friendly copywriting, and metadata optimization should be a normal part of the Web site optimization process.

Currently, search engines do not use a PDF document's metadata information to determine relevancy. Like the meta-tag description and keywords attribute in HTML files, PDF metadata is considered secondary text because search engines are able to access text content within a PDF document.

Providing access to PDF content

Two reasons many PDF documents with outstanding content do not receive qualified search engine traffic are lack of access and orphaning.

Lack of access

Many Web site owners will only provide access to white papers and brochures after site visitors fill out a form. The reason they do this is lead generation. In exchange for site visitors' personal information (name, email address, address, phone number, etc.), site visitors can download useful and informative white papers, for example.

Search engine spiders do not fill out forms to access Web content. So if the only way to access PDF content is through forms, the PDF document's listing will not appear in search results.

Orphaning

Many Web site owners do provide access to PDF documents. However, they do it in a way that communicates, "I do not believe this content is important."

For example, many Web site owners link to PDF content in the following hierarchical, linear manner:

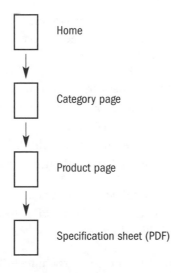

Home

Category page

Product page

Specification sheet (PDF)

Figure 2-56
Many Web sites that contain specification sheets for individual products link to the PDFs in this manner.

All too frequently, the only link on a Web site to a PDF document comes from an individual product or service page, essentially orphaning the PDF document. This one-way information architecture and corresponding interface communicates to the search engines that you (the Web site owner) must not believe the PDF's content contains valuable information. If you believed the content were valuable, then you would link to the URL in more than one place.

One simple way to create additional links to PDF documents is to add them to a site map. Many search engine professionals, and even search engine representatives themselves, often feel a site map is a magic solution for providing access to content. However, as I outlined in previous sections of this book, access is only one part of the link component. Relevancy, a sense of place, and information scent are all equally important. Usability counts with both cross-linking and external, third-party link development.

Always communicate important information to site visitors before they click a link to a PDF document. First, let people know that if they click a link they will be viewing a PDF document. Acrobat Reader (a different application) will be launched if it is installed on end users' computers. Launching a new application when people do not expect it leads to a poor user experience.

Second, because PDF file size tends to be significantly larger than HTML file size, let users know the file size before they click the PDF link. Remember, meeting user expectations leads to a positive search experience.

Finally, link to PDF documents using important keyword phrases in or near anchor text. Including only hypertext links in a site map will help, but it is not an ideal solution for search engine optimization. A better solution is to summarize each PDF document's overall content, using appropriate keyword phrases whenever possible.

For example, on the fictional TranquiliTeas Web site, a simple way to let visitors know they will be viewing a PDF document is to make the hypertext link look like the following:

View the TranquiliTeas Organic Tea Brochure—PDF (360K).

Some Web site owners like to create category pages with summaries to each PDF document. They add the category page links to the site map (or site index) as well as making the category page a part of a site's global navigation scheme.

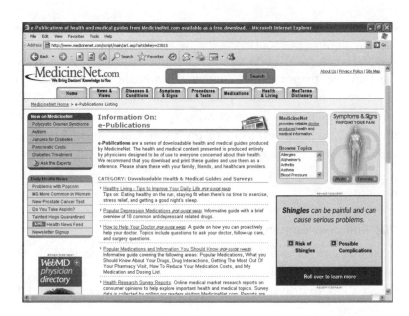

Figure 2-57
MedicineNet has a list of online publications on its Web site.

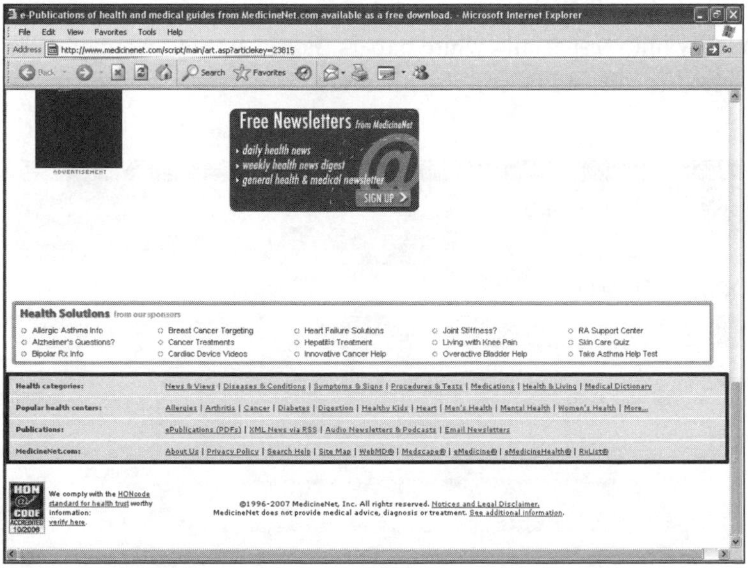

Figure 2-58
The online publications link is located in the global footer.

Robots excluding PDF content

Sometimes, the same content on a Web site is formatted as HTML and as PDF. To avoid duplicate/redundant filtering, use the robots exclusion protocol, the robots.txt file specifically, to let the search engines know not to crawl the redundant content.

One way I implement PDF optimization is to put redundant content PDFs in one directory and original content PDFs in another directory.

For example, the redundant content PDFs might be listed under a directory category labeled "pdfs" and the original content PDFs might be listed under a directory category labeled "pdf." I only apply the robots exclusion protocol to the redundant content PDFs, as shown below:

```
User-agent: *
Disallow: /pdfs/
```

PDF link development

External, third-party link development to PDF documents might be more difficult to implement due to the file format. Most people expect a link to deliver an HTML formatted document, not a PDF document.

Nonetheless, PDF documents with unique content can receive high-quality links, especially white papers. For example, two major Web directories allow PDFs in their listings.

Figure 2-59

Some of the health categories in Yahoo list PDF documents.

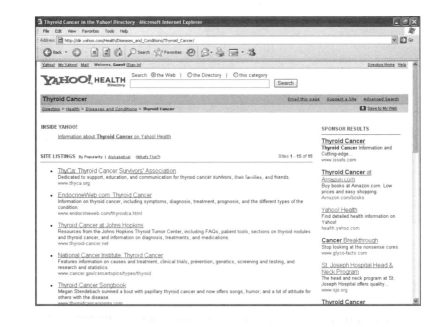

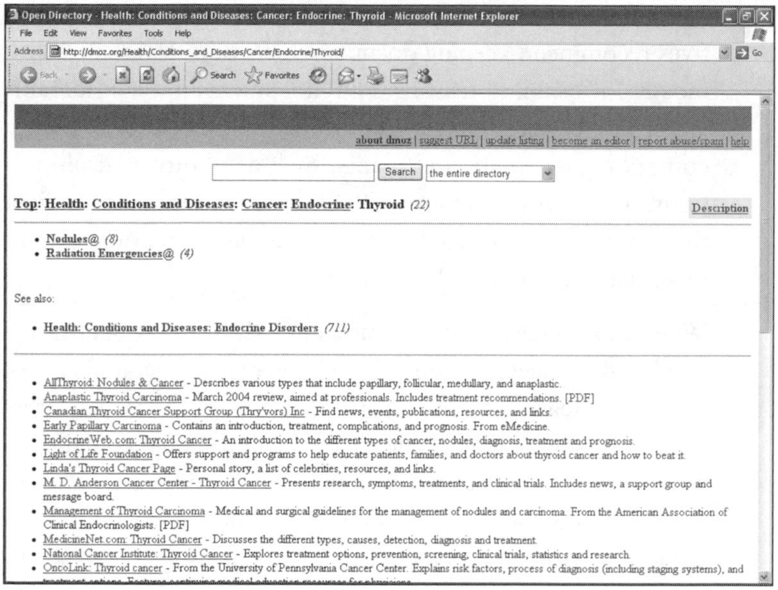

Figure 2-60
The Open Directory will also list useful PDF documents.

Eight steps to successful PDF optimization

The same optimization guidelines apply to PDF documents that apply to HTML documents.

1. **Make sure your PDF documents contain text that the search engines can index.** Search engines are currently unable to index the text inside graphic images in PDF documents. So if you create a PDF document by using a flatbed scanner, making it an image-only PDF, the search engines will not be able to extract that text.

2. **Use keyword-rich text in your PDF documents.** The main advantages of optimizing PDF documents is that they tend to be text-heavy documents, and their URL structures are quite simple. A little bit of keyword research and keyword placement can result in higher PDF visibility.

3. **For PDF documents with multiple pages, ensure that the most important text is on the first page of your PDF document.** Be sure that the titles, headlines, and text on the first page of your PDF documents contain your most important keywords, when appropriate.

4. **Minimize download time.** In general, search engine representatives recommend keeping document file size to less than 100K, mostly for usability reasons. PDF documents are considerably larger files because fonts are embedded in them and they often contain high-resolution elements, such as photos and illustrations. Two ways to minimize PDF download time are to limit the number of fonts used and to use lower resolution graphic images in Web-only PDF documents.

5. **When appropriate, create optimized HTML pages with abstracts of PDF documents.** If your PDF documents are large file sizes, such as manuals or catalogs, consider creating HTML pages that summarize the PDF files. The abstract pages should contain 200 to 250 words of quality content within the <body> and </body> tags. Title tags and meta tags should also contain keywords.

   Additionally, whenever possible, the anchor text leading to the PDF document and words near the anchor text should contain keywords.

6. **Be sure to have links to your PDF documents in multiple places on your Web site.** Do not orphan your PDF documents in the site's link architecture. Add links to PDF documents in your site map or site index. If your Web site contains many PDF documents, categorize them and create a PDF or online publications section with a topical site map. Communicate to both search engines and site visitors that you believe your PDF documents' content contains useful, relevant information.

7. **Robots exclude redundant content.** Since the commercial Web search engines have been able to index PDF documents and many other text-based documents for a long time, formatting the same content in different formats will only lead to duplicate content filtering and a lower index count. Be proactive. Exclude redundant content using the robots.txt file.

8. **Be realistic.** Not all PDF materials (such as trifold marketing brochures and annual reports) can use keyword-focused text. Some PDF documents should not have a table of contents, headers, and footers. Understand which types of PDF documents can easily be optimized and which types cannot. Focus your optimization efforts on the PDF documents that can be optimized.

Conclusion

The foundation of an effective, long-term search engine marketing campaign contains three building blocks:

- Text component
- Link component
- Popularity component

Building a search engine friendly Web site is also building a customer friendly Web site because you are building the site based on words your audience types into search queries. Web pages that contain the words that your target audience is typing into search queries generally have greater search engine visibility than pages that contain few if any keywords.

Pages with dynamic content and visual flair can attain excellent search engine visibility as long as Web designers plan ahead. If a Web site owner expects to use search engine marketing as part of an online marketing strategy, creating search engine friendly design templates can save considerable time and money.

The way your Web pages are linked to each other, the way your Web site is linked to other Web sites, and the way other sites link to your site affects your site's search engine visibility. If search engine spiders can crawl your Web pages quickly and easily, the pages stand a much better chance of appearing at the top of search results. Providing easy access, keyword focus, "You are here" cues, and information scents are important for both search engine visibility and Web site usability. When all these elements are addressed as part of a site's information architecture and corresponding interface, your target audience is more likely to land on the pages that contain the exact information they are searching for.

If two Web sites have similar copywriting, spider-friendly navigation schemes, and site architectures, the site with greater popularity will usually rank higher. Therefore, building a user-friendly site that appeals your target audience is imperative for maximum search engine visibility.

Remember, Web sites should primarily be designed for your site's visitors, not for the search engines. Search engine spiders are not going to spend thousands or millions of dollars purchasing your products and services. Your target audience will. So always design with your target audience in mind.

The search engines offer pay-for-inclusion programs and pay-for-placement advertising programs for sites that are not created with a search engine friendly design template.

Nonetheless, a search engine friendly design can be a more cost-effective use of time and resources than paid advertising. A carefully optimized site with a spider-friendly navigation scheme can deliver long-term results, reaping a return on investment that lasts for years. Search engine advertising results frequently deliver short-term results, resulting in the continual development of new advertisements and destination pages.

Web site owners might also find that a combination of search engine marketing and search engine advertising delivers the best results. Ultimately, Web site owners will have to decide which form of search engine marketing delivers the best return on investment for their businesses.

Part 3:

How To Build Better Web Pages— Nontext Files

Text-file optimization is crucial to overall search engine visibility because it provides contextual information for image- and multimedia-file optimization. In fact, the three principles of text-file search engine optimization (text component, link component, and popularity component) are applicable to nontext files but in slightly different ways.

This chapter provides details for implementing each principle into image, video, and audio files. When text and nontext optimization support each other, everyone benefits: Web site owners, searchers, site visitors, and the commercial Web search engines.

Understanding Nontext File Optimization

Currently, search engines have a difficult time extracting text information from both image and multimedia files—if they can extract it at all. Until search engine technology reaches the point where the engines can successfully identify an image's or a video's true content, they must rely on a variety of direct and indirect information to determine file content. Direct information often comes in the form of metadata and/or a file substitute. Indirect information might come in the form of a file format or text content surrounding an image or multimedia file.

As a result, a number of people with different job responsibilities frequently determine the success or failure of search engine visibility for graphic images and multimedia files. File creators, such as videographers and graphic designers, should ensure that files are formatted and named appropriately. Content providers and copywriters should ensure that the text surrounding graphic images and multimedia files directly supports the content within those file types. And Web developers must ensure easy access to those files.

On the surface, it might seem as if the search engine optimization (SEO) for image and multimedia files is straightforward and easy. In reality, it requires great attention to detail, strong communication among team members, and consistency in file naming, labeling, categorization, and presentation. The final result is a Web site that gains visibility and qualified leads among a variety of search engines.

Image Search Engine Optimization

Approximately 15–20 percent of search engine queries are graphic-image queries. Due to this volume of graphic image queries, the commercial Web search engines created specific databases. In fact, image search is so prevalent that it is the first "file tab" or main navigational/sorting element after the default text-file search (Figure 3-1):

Figure 3-1
The four major search engines currently show image search as the main type of search after text-based searches.

Additionally, image search results have crept into the main search engine results pages. For example, if the search engine data shows that a set of keyword phrases clearly indicates that the searcher desires to see a photograph, the first search results page will include graphic images at the top of the screen.

Figure 3-2

Search results for "frank sinatra pictures" (without the quotation marks) on both Yahoo and Google. Because the searcher used the keyword "pictures" as part of the query, search engines deliver image search results at the top of main search results.

Other places where image search results commonly appear include:

- Shopping search engines

- News search engines

- Photo-sharing sites (such as Flickr)

- Social media sites

Figure 3-3
Shoppers want to see what they are purchasing. Without a product photo, a sales conversion is unlikely.

Therefore, image search optimization should be a part of a site's online marketing efforts, especially for ecommerce sites.

The problem with image search optimization is that graphic images are comprised of bits instead of text. Currently, the major search engines are unable to directly compare keywords with the actual content of a graphic image, although the search engines have made significant advances in recent years. Search engines can identify colors within images, and even differentiate male and female faces.

As mentioned previously, until technology reaches the point where search engines can successfully determine an image's true content, search engines must rely on a number of indirect and direct contextual cues. Therefore, to properly optimize a site's graphic images for search engine visibility, use the following techniques.

Eight Steps to Successful Image Search Optimization

Here are some general guidelines for optimizing graphic images for search engine visibility.

1. **Use the most appropriate image format.** If a graphic image is formatted as a JPEG, search engines usually interpret the image to be a photograph (picture) or a complex illustration. JPEG is the abbreviation for Joint Photographic Experts Group and is the appropriate format for graphic images containing thousands or millions of colors.

   GIF is the abbreviation for Graphics Interchange Format and contains only 256 colors. GIFs are supported by practically all Web browsers, can include transparent backgrounds, and support interlacing (providing a low-resolution preview of the graphic image to site visitors while it downloads).

   Search engines also display PNG (Portable Network Graphics) files in image search results, but this file type is not as commonly used as JPEG and GIF.

   As an example, if a search engine encounters a file named green-tea.jpg, the file format and file name indicate that the graphic image is a photograph of green tea.

2. **Name the image with appropriate keywords, when applicable.** File names are rarely used to determine the content of a text-based file because search engines are able to extract the text content from the actual page. Since the search engines currently are unable to extract text content from a graphic image, file naming is more important for graphics-based optimization than graphics-based optimization.

   Keep in mind: It is best to name files in a manner that makes sense to site visitors. File names should be easy to type and easy to remember. Many image search engines display the file name in search results, and keywords are highlighted in the file name. Do not let software generate file names. It is best for graphic designers to manually name graphic images based on keyword research and actual photo/image content.

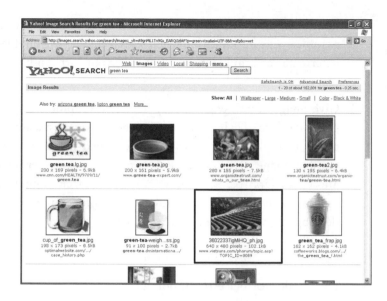

Figure 3-4

A search for "green tea" in Yahoo image search yields over 160,000 results. Which file name do you believe searchers will focus on, green-tea.jpg or a computer-generated number?

Finally, do not keyword-stuff graphic image names. The file name green-tea.jpg makes sense to both searchers and search engines. The file name green-tea-green-teas-loose-leaf-green-tea-bags.jpg does not benefit search engines or searchers.

3. **Give the graphic image keyword-based, textual cues.** Search engines analyze the text surrounding a graphic image to determine its actual content. Therefore, using keyword-rich captions next to graphic images, especially in product photo descriptions, is important for search engine visibility.

It is not always possible to use captions on graphic images. For example, a product photo is a good place to use a caption, but captions on navigation buttons are not practical or useful. Thus, alternative text becomes the natural place to accurately describe an image's content. As described in Part 2, alternative text is the text that is placed inside graphic images in HTML code. Alternative text instructs a browser, "If this graphic image is not downloaded, show this text in its place." Alternative text is also important for accessibility reasons.

In the past, unethical search engine optimization professionals have abused the alternative text attribute so badly that search engines do not use this attribute to determine relevancy for text-based files. Alternative text becomes more important for graphic image optimization when search engines are unable to determine the graphic image's content from surrounding primary text.

4. **Give image search engines easy access to graphic images.** A graphic image's URL structure (Web address) is just as important for graphics-based files as it is for text-based files. If a graphic image's URL structure contains too many problematic characters (&, =, ?, $, +, %), then search engines are unlikely to crawl that URL. Likewise, another mistake Web developers make is putting the "Click to see larger image" hyperlink inside a JavaScript. When they do that, they limit search engines' access to that image file.

   Finally, do not place the robots exclusion protocol on your graphic-image URLs if you want your graphic images to appear in image search results.

5. **Create unique and original graphic images.** All too often, identical or nearly identical graphic images appear next to each other in image search results and shopping search results (Figure 3-5). Once searchers have clicked one product image, they are unlikely to click an identical or nearly identical product, making it less likely to convert a searcher into a buyer.

Figure 3-5

Once searchers have already viewed a product photo, they are unlikely to click subsequent hyperlinks surrounding identical or very similar photos.

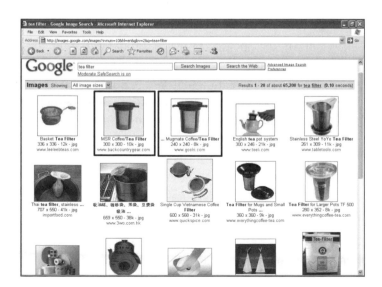

For that reason, try to use as many original photos and other graphic images as you can on your site. Even if you are a retailer or distributor who receives product photos from a manufacturer or other supplier, you can make the product photos unique by putting your logo or trademark on them.

6. **Improve image quality.** Another way to differentiate graphic image conversions in search results pages is to have better image quality than competitor sites.

For example, on an ecommerce site, Web designers should create three different sizes for products: thumbnails (for display on category pages), medium photos (for product pages), and large photos (for "View detailed image" in pop-up windows). Since search engines resize graphic images to fit their search results pages, have your design team view each targeted graphic image on an actual image search results page. How does the photo look? Is it difficult to see important details? If the targeted graphic image contains text, is the text legible in image search results? Have your design team adjust image quality so that the image displays well on both the Web site and image search results.

7. **Make sure Web pages containing targeted graphic images are fully optimized.** Optimizing the page for contextual search improves the search engine visibility for graphic images. Important keyword phrases should appear in primary text (titles, paragraphs, locational breadcrumb links, and other anchor text, headings, and so forth) as well as secondary text (meta tags, alternative text, etc.). Text-file optimization provides context for graphic images. Optimizing the page the graphic image appears on can be just as important as optimizing the image itself, including tagging on photo-sharing sites.

8. **Give objective third parties a reason to link to graphic-related content.** Not all graphic images are linkworthy, nor are pages that contain graphic images. Nevertheless, unique graphic images (such as maps and news photos) are linkworthy. Pages with outstanding internal cross-linking and external link development tend to get more search engine visibility than

pages without these characteristics. This link weight carries over to graphic images contained on a page.

Since people are always looking for noncompetitive sites with unique content, consider how a unique illustration or photo might supplement content.

Flash and Search Engine Visibility

Flash is a wonderful way to create Web sites with visual flair and interactivity. Web designers love to use Flash because it provides an effective way to deliver vector images over the Web, as opposed to bitmap images. Vector graphics are scalable, which means that when site visitors resize a browser window, Web pages designed in Flash will stay in proportion no matter how large or small the browser window becomes. Furthermore, Flash movies stream, meaning that once part of a vector image downloads, that part of the image will display on the browser screen while the rest of the movie downloads. Since over 98 percent of Internet users can view Flash content with the Flash player software already installed in their browsers, site visitors who prefer to view Flash-formatted content are able to do so. Therefore, Flash designs can benefit both Web designers and site visitors.

In terms of search engine visibility, however, Flash-based Web designs are not an ideal choice. Although a few of the major search engines are able to crawl the links embedded inside of Flash navigation schemes, the main problem with Flash sites is that they contain very little useful text for the search engines to index.

Splash Pages

Flash movies are typically used on splash pages. A splash page is a Web page that consists of either (a) a large graphic image and a link instructing visitors to "Enter" a Web site, or (b) a Flash animation, a link to skip the Flash animation (Skip Intro), and a redirect to a new page after the animation is completed. Many Web sites use splash pages as their home page.

Generally speaking, both site visitors and the search engines do not like splash pages because they contain little useful, high-quality content, even though the page design might be outstanding. Using a splash page as a home page is like trying to force all people who visit a supermarket to watch a 30-second commercial before entering a store. For example, Figure 3-6 shows a beautifully designed splash page with a Flash movie:

Figure 3-6
An example of a splash page. Note that there is no text for the search engines to index and no links for them to follow. Even the only text on the page ("skip intro") is a graphic image.

Viewing this page, you can immediately see multiple reasons why splash pages are not search engine friendly:

- **A splash page contains little or no text for the search engines to index.** Remember the most important text on a Web page is title-tag text and visible body text that can be copied and pasted into a text editor. This splash page contains no visible body text. Even the "Skip intro" text is formatted as a graphic image.

- **A splash page contains few or no links for the search engine spiders to follow.** Most splash pages link to a single page, which communicates to both search engines and site visitors that you consider only one page on your site to be important. If the link to an internal page is a JavaScript-generated link, many search engines will not follow that link.

■ **Most splash pages contain a redirect after the Flash animation is complete.** None of the search engines is interested in placing a redirect page in its index. Rather, they all prefer to crawl and index the final destination page. In fact, most search engines will not include splash pages in their indices because of the lack of content and the redirect.

One workaround is to simply add keyword-rich text and links to the splash page. If you wish to keep the flair and ambiance of the Flash movie, place the text and links below the fold so that your site visitors will have to scroll to view the text. In all likelihood, site visitors will click the "Enter site" or "Skip intro" button rather than scroll to the bottom of the Web page. But if your site visitors do scroll, the page will contain quality content and important links.

Figure 3-7
By adding keyword-rich text and important links to a splash page, the page becomes more search engine friendly without losing the impact of the Flash movie.

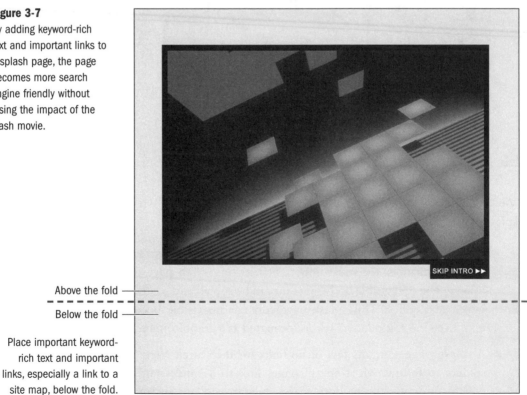

Above the fold

Below the fold

Place important keyword-rich text and important links, especially a link to a site map, below the fold.

SKIP INTRO ▶▶

One way to determine if a splash page is effective is to design two different home pages:

- A splash page as outlined in Figure 3-7, showing a large Flash movie and keyword-rich text below the fold.

- A home page that presents site visitors with keyword-rich text above the fold, without the Flash movie.

After analyzing your site's traffic logs for three to six months, determine which home page design your visitors prefer. If you find that your target audience prefers the splash page with the Flash movie, then keep the Flash movie and the quality content below the fold. If your site visitors prefer a less animated home page, then continue using the non-Flash page as your home page. Both page designs can attain search engine visibility, but one design will probably have a much higher conversion rate than the other.

Regardless of what your target audience prefers, a search engine friendly splash page must contain keyword-rich content.

Flash Sites

Some search engines have been able to follow the links inside of Flash sites since 2001, and they have become increasingly better at both extracting text and following links. Nonetheless, search data from multiple search engines found that extracting data from Flash files provided little value, and following Flash-generated links provided more value. Without the combination of keyword-focused text, easy access to text, and a strong information architecture and interface, Flash sites are generally not as search engine friendly as non-Flash sites.

Even so, Flash sites and Web sites containing Flash elements can and do receive qualified search engine traffic. The key to successful Flash optimization is to determine whether your target audience prefers to view your site's content through a Flash interface. And, if they do, are site visitors completing desired business transactions (Add to Cart, Sign Up for Newsletter, etc.) through this interface? Here are some Flash optimization techniques that are applicable to different types of Web sites.

> **Note**
>
> Always remove the redirect from splash pages. Most search engines will not include Web pages that contain redirects in their search engine indexes.

Flash site with a single page

On the surface, it might seem as if a Flash site consists of many different pages with unique content. This assumption is often incorrect. Many Flash sites consist of a single Web page with a single Flash movie.

If a site only has a few, noncompetitive keywords, optimizing the Flash site can work. In the absence of body text, search engines will look at the title-tag content, meta-tag content, and external, third party link development to determine relevancy.

Many site visitors prefer and use a Flash interface, particularly when the interface is creative, entertaining, and fun. In this situation, unusually high-quality link development is generally the main reason a single-page Flash site receives qualified search engine traffic.

However, a single-page Flash site communicates to the search engines that a Web site contains only one page, which is not the case with Flash sites. Even though the URL does not change in the browser, content changes when site visitors click a Flash link.

Thus, for increased search engine visibility, dividing Flash sites into multiple pages with unique URLs communicates to the search engines that a site contains more unique content. More URLs will be available for display in search engine results pages (SERPs).

Flash site with multiple pages

A Flash site with multiple pages often gets greater search engine visibility than a Flash site with a single page. As stated previously, more URLs with unique content means that more Web pages can be displayed in SERPs. If more Web pages are available for crawling and indexing, then there are greater opportunities for search engine visibility and sales conversions. More URLs also mean more opportunities for a variety of keyword phrase placement.

In addition, most HTML sites have multiple entry points. When searchers click a link from a SERP to Web site, they do not land on a home page. Instead, they tend to arrive on the page that contains the exact information they desire (a product, service, or article page) or a page that leads them to desired information (a category or customer service page). A single-page Flash site has only one entry point, and site visitors must always begin at the home page to find desired information. Therefore, multiple pages on a Flash site allow for multiple and direct points of entry for site visitors.

The same optimization strategies for HTML sites apply to Flash sites. Optimize each page with appropriate, unique titles and body content. In the absence of indexable content, make sure all pages have keyword-focused meta-tag content and the desired calls to action. Relevant cross-linking applies to Flash-site URLs as well as external, third party link development.

I highly recommend using focus groups or usability testing before launching a Flash site. All too often, designers and Web site owners want Flash, but the target audience may not. You might find your target audience prefers and uses Flash, but only in a specific area of a site. Flash can often be used on a section of a site and still convey the "wow" factor of a 100 percent Flash-formatted site.

Flash section of a site

An entire site does not necessarily need to be formatted in Flash to be effective. Sometimes, a site can be equally, if not more, effective if it is formatted as HTML overall and only one section of the site is formatted as Flash. The HTML version of the site can be optimized easily for search engine visibility and will probably deliver better ROI than the Flash-only site.

For this design strategy, use Flash movies whenever appropriate, and place the movies on HTML pages containing: (a) text for the search engines to crawl and index, and (b) a navigation scheme they can follow.

One example of a Flash section of a site might be the aforementioned site: one with a popular, interactive, and fun online game. Flash can be used to show people how to do something. The IKEA Web site uses Flash sections of the site effectively to show people how to construct various pieces of furniture, such as a bookshelf.

Another example might be a "Take A Tour" section of a real estate site. The virtual tour can be formatted in Flash. A page named "tour.html" can contain the Flash movie in a pop-up window. On the site, the "Take A Tour" link can be placed in the global navigation. Add some embedded text links or self-promotional banners as extra incentive to click that link. The page named tour.html can be optimized for search engine visibility as well.

Web site owners can implement link development to both a home page and Flash section of a site, especially since the Flash section's interactivity tends to be unique. With link development, though, remember to link directly to the URL containing the Flash section. For example, if a site uses Flash functionality to calculate the area of various shapes, such as a concrete calculator, do not suggest external links to the home page and force site visitors to navigate to the concrete calculator. Try to ensure the external link points directly to the Flash section with the concrete calculator. The description of the Web site (home page) and the description of the concrete calculator should be different as well.

Flash site vs. HTML site

When in doubt, create two versions of a Web site: Flash and HTML. On the home page, visitors can select their preference. Make sure the home page is not formatted as a splash page. It is important the home page contain keyword-rich text for the search engines to index, a link to a site map (at minimum) so the search engines can crawl all the pages on the HTML version of the site, and an option to view the Flash or HTML version of the site.

Web analytics software is imperative to keep track of visitor preferences. If the majority of visitors prefer the Flash site, keep it. If visitors prefer to view the HTML site far more often than the Flash, you know not to format an entire site in Flash. Only submit the HTML version of a site to the search engines.

Since Flash sites rarely contain keyword-rich content, allow your site visitors to communicate their preferences by creating both a Flash and HTML version of your Web site. On the home page, let your visitors select their preferred design, as SiteLab did on their former home page, shown in Figure 3-8:

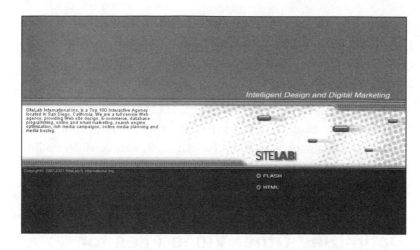

Figure 3-8
SiteLab's former home page contained keyword-rich text for the search engines to index and gives site visitors the choice to view the Flash version or HTML version of their Web site.

The main benefit of this type of layout is that the HTML version of the site will be able to attain maximum search engine visibility until all of the search engines are able to support Flash more effectively.

Questionable optimization techniques with Flash sites

If you have a Flash site, do not hire a search engine optimization firm that suggests any technique involving hidden text or hidden links.

Understandably, Web site owners who spent thousands of dollars on a beautiful Flash site do not want to hear that they must redesign their site in order to obtain search engine visibility in the natural search results. They do not want to hear that their site might not meet user expectations as well as search engine standards. Out of desperation, they are easy targets for unethical search engine optimization professionals who keep the Flash but place hidden keywords and hidden links within the Flash site.

Search engines are fully aware of the different techniques used to hide text and links. Sites that use these techniques rarely obtain search engine visibility. One of these techniques includes placing Flash sites inside invisible framesets, a technique called envelope pages. Invisible text is often placed between the <noframes> and </noframes> tags, and often between <noscript> and </noscript> tags even though the frameset page contains no JavaScript.

Another spam technique is to create invisible layers using Cascading Style Sheets (CSS) to present different content to the search engines than the content contained in a Flash movie. Part 5 of this book outlines a number of optimization practices that the search engines consider to be spam.

As search engines continue to evolve, they will find better ways of including Flash documents along with HTML documents in their search engine results pages. In the meantime, plan ahead. If you know your company is going to build a Flash site, consider its limitations in the search engines and budget for other means of marketing your Web site.

Optimizing Other Video Files for Search Engine Visibility

Even though the commercial Web search engines have been working with Flash and other video technologies for many years, video display in search results is still being tested and re-evaluated. In other words, video search engine optimization is still in its infancy. Therefore, as with image search optimization, apply to video files the same Web design, usability, and optimization principles that are applied to "regular" text-based Web pages. Text-based Web pages provide strong context for video files in the event that search engines have a difficult time accessing and determining a video file's true content.

Video files can be search engine friendly. As long as video creators and video editors keep usability principles and the building blocks of successful search engine optimization in mind, videos can deliver a great return on investment (ROI).

12 Steps to Successful Video Search Optimization

Below are guidelines for optimizing videos for search engine visibility:

1. **Research video-related keyword phrases before optimizing and categorizing video files.** When people search for video content, they often use the words "video" and "videos" as a keyword. Sometimes they use the keyword phrase "video clip" or "free

video" plus an important qualifier words. When you research keywords to use in your videos' metadata, file names, and other contextual information, make sure to include these keywords (and possibly file types such as Flash) in your research process.

You can use the keyword research tools offered at Yahoo, Google, and Microsoft's adCenter to get a clearer idea of the terminology your site visitors might use to find the videos your site offers.

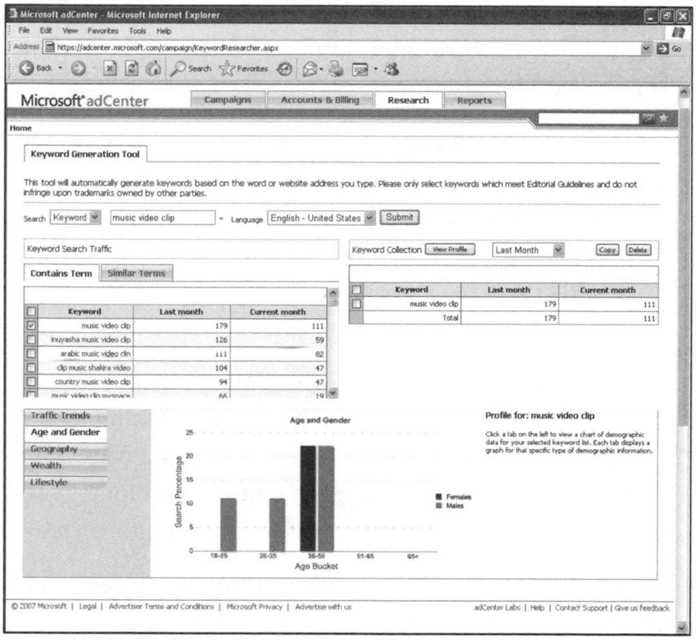

Figure 3-9
The keyword research tool at Microsoft adCenter shows some useful demographic information for people who search for music video clips.

2. **Always include user-friendly, keyword-focused metadata in all video files.** Meta-tag content is not as important for HTML files as it is for video files, because, in general, search engines are able to determine an HTML file's actual content more readily than a video file's actual content. Consequently, a video file's metadata has a far greater impact on ranking in the video search engines than an HTML file's meta-tag content in the main, organic search results.

The metadata fields currently used for ranking purposes include title, copyright string, author, keywords, and description.

Tip

Plan the metadata content formatting before you write the content to save considerable time and effort.

The same rules that apply for optimizing meta-tag content for HTML files apply to video files. Include words that your target audience is likely to type into search queries. Do not keyword stuff these metadata fields purely for search engine visibility. When this content appears in search results, it should be easy to read and it should encourage people to click the link to view your videos.

3. **Name the video with appropriate keywords, when applicable.** As I mentioned previously, since the search engines currently have a difficult time extracting text content from a video file, file naming is more important for video optimization than text-based optimization.

Site visitors should find video file names easy to type and easy to remember. Many image search engines display the file name in search results, and keywords are highlighted in the file name. As with image search, do not let software generate video file names. It is best for video creators and video editors to manually name videos based on keyword research and user testing.

For example, a file named honda-civic-crash-test.mpg or honda-civic-crash-test-video.mpg clearly communicates the video file's content, even with the numerous hyphens. Remember, though, that if a file name is too long, it will get truncated in the display on search engine results pages.

4. **Give video search engines easy access to your videos and video clips.** A video's file name appears on the URL (Web address) structure. URL structure provides search engine access to video content.

I like to set up the URL structure for videos as follows:

http://www.companyname.com/videos/flash/
http://www.companyname.com/videos/mpg/
http://www.companyname.com/videos/avi/

This type of URL structure is easy for search engines to access and communicates important information to both search engines and site visitors.

5. **Organize video content by file format.** The aforementioned URL format is an information architecture and interface strategy. Remember, a URL (Web address) structure is part of a Web page's interface. When the interface accurately reflects information architecture, Web pages and the files contained within those pages, including video files, appear more keyword focused to site visitors and search engines.

From a search usability perspective, I like to provide video files with as much context as possible to meet user expectations. If a site has a collection of videos, it is best to label (a) the types of video formats offered, (b) the platform and software support, and (c) the download times based on connection speed, as illustrated in Figure 3-10 below.

Figure 3-10

The Metalith Web site offers multiple formats for viewing their crash test videos. In the event that site visitors do not have the software needed to view the videos, there are links to download the software. Additionally, download times are given for both high- and low-speed Internet connections.

6. **Robots exclude redundant video content.** Even though the search engines are not currently proactive about filtering redundant video content, they will be in the future. Web site owners should be proactive about robots excluding redundant video content. Through Web analytics, Web site owners can determine the video format (swf, mpg, avi, etc.) that site visitors prefer and robots exclude.

I like to set up the URL structure for videos as follows:

http://www.companyname.com/videos/flash/
http://www.companyname.com/videos/avi/

In this example, if the Web analytics data show that site visitors clearly prefer viewing Flash videos, then robots exclude the subdirectory named "avi."

7. **Optimize the Web pages that contain videos.** A video will appear more keyword focused to search engines and site visitors if it is on a page where keywords are used in the surrounding HTML page's title tags, headings, locational breadcrumb links, other text-based body content, and calls to action. Using standard SEO practices is also applicable to video sharing sites. Make sure the video sharing pages are optimized as well as the actual corporate (or main site) pages containing the video files.

Search engines will analyze the text surrounding a video to determine its actual content. It is important to use keyword-rich captions or annotations next to embedded videos for a video's search engine visibility.

Another way to provide keyword-focused contextual information is to include the video transcript, an abbreviated "teaser" transcript, or even a short quotation (as a caption) on the page containing the video appears. The text surrounding the video should encourage visitors to watch the clip. The call to action "Click here" does not contain important keywords. The call to action "Click to view crash test video" is more specific and provides better context.

Tip

Put various video clips on a video sharing site and encourage your target audience to view the full video on the main Web site. Test a variety of video clips and corresponding captions to determine the ones that deliver the best ROI.

8. **Cross-link to other Web pages containing similar video content.** All too often, the only contextual information a video file has is the single Web page it's embedded in. A single Web page usually does not provide enough contextual information for accurate information retrieval, especially for multimedia files.

   Therefore, if other pages on a site contain similar video content, link to the other video pages. If you have cross-linked related content as outlined in Part 2 of this book, then some of the cross-linking might already be in place and only needs to be tweaked for visual display.

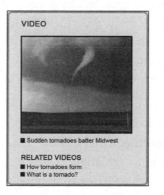

Figure 3-11
One way to cross-link related video content is to provide hyperlinks directly beneath the video caption.

9. **Create a video library or catalog.** A video library provides additional access and contextual information for the video search engines and site visitors. Video libraries are better to use than video site maps because libraries contain categorized information, not a long list of video URLs.

   The term "site map" is highly misunderstood in the search engine marketing, Web design, and usability industries. A site map is not a page full of links to every URL on a Web site. Likewise, a video site map is not a page full of links to every video offered on a site. A map or wayfinder to information should provide context and categorization.

   For example, the term "video index" is a label for Web pages containing links to video files, links that have been sorted alphabetically, since an index is an alphabetized list. A regularly updated video library and video index can be submitted to both video and content engines, and regularly updating these pages encourages search engines to crawl these pages more frequently.

A fully categorized and annotated video library provides far more useful information for both search engines and site visitors than a single page of hypertext links.

10. **Improve video quality.** One way to differentiate video conversions in search results pages is to have better video quality than competitor sites. How does a video look and sound on the intended Web page? Additionally, how does a video appear in search engine results pages and assorted video sharing Web pages? Does the video's color selection and color contrast naturally draw searchers' eyes to your specific video? Have your design team adjust video quality so that it displays well on both the Web site and video search results.

Ideally, all video creators and video editors should balance the best video quality with the smallest download time (for site visitors and searchers) and upload (for search engines). Video optimizers should regularly monitor required uploading specifications for each video search engine. Knowledge of video search engine specifications is especially important when working with large video files or a large number of videos because of potential wasted time and resources. No video editor wants to re-edit large amounts of video content.

11. **Watermark and/or brand your video content.** One way to make your video content stand out in video search results is to watermark and brand it. Not only will your videos appear unique, if your videos are shared across multiple sites, your brand will also be carried along.

12. **Submit and distribute your video files to video search engines and video-sharing Web sites.** Although it is better for search engines to access your site's text-based content through the natural crawling process, with multimedia files (including videos) it is better to manually submit video URLs and pertinent metadata via video search engine submission forms.

Below are the current URLs that contain links to video submission forms on Google, Yahoo, and AOL:

https://upload.video.google.com/
http://video.yahoo.com/
http://uncutvideo.aol.com/Main.do

As you can see, the techniques for optimizing videos for search engine visibility are not so different from optimizing graphic images.

Optimizing Podcasts and Audio Files for Search Engine Visibility

Audio search engines are similar to traditional search engines except that audio search engines crawl the Web constantly for rich media files. Like video search engines, audio search engines are fairly new compared to traditional text-based information retrieval systems.

A podcast is a collection of audio or video files that resides at a unique Web feed address. Each podcast is comprised of a series of individual episodes. Audio files are uploaded to a Web server where subscribers with iPods or other media players can download the content. With podcasts, subscribers automatically receive new episodes without having to go to a specific Web page to download each episode.

In the past, many audio and video search engines relied heavily on metadata content to determine relevancy. Though metadata content is still more important for audio-file optimization than text-file optimization, many audio search engines use speech recognition to determine the content of an audio file. With speech recognition, audio search engines are able to transcribe portions of an audio or video file. After transcription, content is analyzed for meaning, topics of conversation, and relevance to query terms (keywords).

Since audio files are generally prerecorded, with proper planning and implementation, they can be prepared and optimized for audio search engines as well as targeted listeners. Audio-file optimization is often more challenging than text-file optimization because speech occurs more quickly than writing. If Web content providers do not

Tip

Writing an interview script with keyword-focused questions ahead of time is an easy way to keep audio-file content focused on specific, targeted topics of interest.

naturally write using the words and phrases their target audience types into search queries, imagine how difficult it is to give a speech using the users' language.

As with all other Web files, keep usability principles and the fundamental building blocks of successful search engine optimization in mind when preparing audio files for search engine visibility.

8 Steps to Successful Audio Search Optimization

Below are guidelines for optimizing audio files for search engine visibility:

1. **Research and develop a comprehensive keyword list (including core and qualifier keywords) before creating a series of audio files.** When people search for audio content, they often use "podcast" or "mp3" as a keyword. When you research keywords to use in your audio files' metadata, podcast episode names, and other contextual information, include these types of keywords.

Figure 3-12
When MedicineNet optimized the audio newsletter section of their Web site, they included audio-related keywords in the title-tag content and body text. As a result, their podcast pages appear at the top of Google's main search results for audio-related terms.

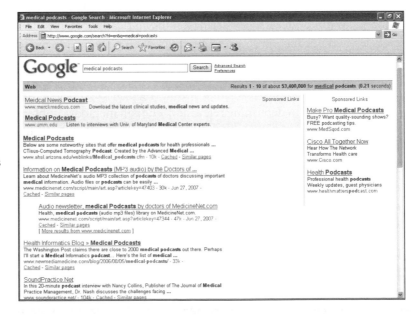

Keyword research is proactive. Before you come up with a name for your podcast show, see how people are searching for your type of product, service, and information. Funny podcast show names might seem cool and hip at first. They are not so cool when no one can find and listen to your podcast files. Incorporate important keywords into your podcast name, tag line, and episodes whenever possible.

2. **Always include user-friendly, keyword-focused metadata in audio files.** In the past, multimedia search engines relied heavily on metadata to determine relevancy. Currently, these engines are able to use speech recognition to determine the content of an audio file. However, like video optimization, an audio file's metadata has greater impact on ranking in the multimedia search engines than an HTML file's meta-tag content in the main, organic search results.

Each audio file or podcast episode should contain the following information: title (or the name of the episode), album (or the name of the podcast show), artist (or the company name and brand), year, genre (such as podcast or music type), track (or episode number), and comments/description.

The comments or description field can contain a URL, a summary or abstract, and relevant contact information.

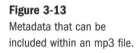

Figure 3-13
Metadata that can be included within an mp3 file.

Save time by building your audio file's metadata infrastructure in advance of creating the file so that you can rapidly build shows with multiple episodes.

3. **Name the audio file with appropriate keywords, when applicable.** Due to the limited allocation of screen real estate of podcast aggregators and directories, it is not always possible to use keyword-focused names for audio files. Other types of information are important, such as episode name and release date. If there is an opportunity for a useful keyword, put it in the file name.

   For example, a medical audio file about autism can be named autism051507.mp3 or autism03-051507.mp3. In the latter example, the file name communicates that episode 3 of the audio file contains information about autism, and the initial release date of this content was May 15, 2007. It also implies that the file is the third episode about autism following the files named autism01-(date).mp3 and autism02-(date).mp3.

4. **Create a fully optimized podcast library or catalog.** A podcast or audio library provides additional access and contextual information for the audio search engines and site visitors.

Figure 3-14

Example of a fully optimized podcast library at MedicineNet.com.

Sometimes, podcast show pages can be formatted and optimized in almost the same manner that ecommerce category pages are optimized. Each category page should contain keyword-focused titles, locational breadcrumb links, headings, and at least an abstract or introductory paragraph. Annotated links to each podcast episode provide further keyword focus.

Archive pages are useful in that they present a specific time and date of presentation, but searchers tend not to use archival or temporal keywords in search queries. Web site owners should provide more context than a single page full of hypertext links and/or audio file archive pages. Context is important for multimedia file optimization.

If podcast show pages are formatted as category pages, the headings, breadcrumb links, and other page text provide both a sense of place and a strong information scent, making the links to the audio files both user and search engine friendly.

5. **Create a useful, search friendly landing page for each audio file and/or podcast episode.** Landing pages are the perfect way to provide context to site visitors and search engines. Audio file landing pages can contain information such as a text-based (full) transcript or summary of the audio file's content, file type (mp3, wav, etc.), time duration of the audio file, subscription information, and relevant cross-links.

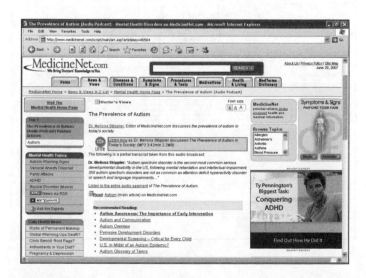

Figure 3-15

Example of a fully optimized podcast landing page at MedicineNet.com.

Whether to include a full transcript or a summary will depend on the audio file's time span. Test audio landing pages on the pay-per-click search engines. Determine whether searchers prefer to view the full transcript or only a well-written, keyword-focused summary. Usability tests will give Web site owners user feedback.

Often I have found that users prefer to view landing pages with a summary of an audio file's content with the choice to download the full PDF transcript or to click a link that leads to another Web page (or set of Web pages) containing the full transcript.

6. **Cross-link to other Web pages that contain similar audio content.** Audio/episode landing pages provide a fantastic opportunity for relevant cross-linking, not only from episode to episode but also from specific episodes to other content pages on a main Web site.

In Figure 3-15, notice that the landing pages contain links to Web pages with similar text content. In Figure 3-16, a main category (or channel) page links to the landing page containing the audio file in the event site visitors wish to listen to information about autism instead of reading it.

Figure 3-16

Example of a main category page that cross-links to an autism podcast landing page.

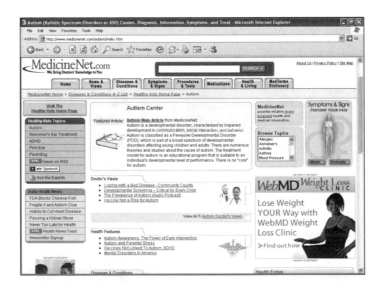

Not everyone wants to subscribe to a podcast. Therefore, providing additional cross-links with a strong information scent will encourage site visitors to continue browsing your site. If searchers find your site's content useful, they will usually bookmark specific pages and/or link to them.

7. **Preserve audio quality and validate feeds.** How do your audio files sound on the intended Web page or aggregator? How does an audio file listing appear in audio search engine results pages and assorted podcast directories? Have your audio team adjust sound quality without sacrificing download time.

8. **Submit and distribute your audio files to audio search engines and podcast Web sites.** Many podcast directories are categorized, which provides external, third party links to audio files that are more keyword focused. With audio files, it is better to manually enter their URLs and pertinent metadata via audio search engine submission forms or RSS feed programs. Search Engine Watch (www.searchenginewatch.com) and Search Engine Land (www.searchengineland.com) are Web sites that provide the best information about where to submit audio files for search engine visibility.

Finally, feed content should be properly formatted for all the major audio directories. Validate your feeds with feed-validator tools. Not all audio directories redistribute. So you might need to build multiple feeds in order to attain optimal audio search engine visibility.

Conclusion

The building blocks of search engine optimization apply to text-based files, graphic images, and multimedia files.

Whenever possible, graphic images and multimedia files need to contain the words and phrases that your target audience types in to search queries. In the event that search engines are unable to access the file's actual content, the text information that surrounds a graphic image or multimedia file should provide keyword-focused contextual information.

The way your Web pages are linked to each other also communicates contextual information about your site's graphic images and multimedia files. A keyword-focused information architecture, clear "you are here" cues, and a strong information scent not only help increase the search engine visibility of text files, but they also increase the search engine visibility of graphic images and multimedia files.

Web site owners should label, categorize, and describe Web files consistently, and in a way that meets user expectations. Web sites that satisfy user expectations experience higher conversion rates. An additional benefit of meeting user expectations is increased external, third party link development, which is the subject of this book's next section.

Part 4:

After Your Site Is Built

Once your new Web site is launched, you can submit it to Web directories and noncompetitive, industry-related Web sites. Once a Web site has some high-quality link development, the commercial search engines should easily discover your site through the natural crawling of the Web. However, submission is not the end of the optimization, design, and marketing processes. Individual Web page effectiveness must be monitored as well.

Understanding Link Development

Objective, third party link development is a key component to effective, long-term search engine optimization. Link development is one of the most overlooked components of a successful optimization campaign. Web site owners can write keyword-focused content and provide search engines with easy access to that content. But without well-planned and carefully implemented link development, search engine visibility is often short lived.

Link popularity vs. click-through popularity

To review, link popularity is the number and quality of objective, third party links pointing to a URL. The quality of a link carries far more weight than the quantity of links. Personally, I have seen many Web sites receive long-term, qualified search engine traffic with less than 50 links pointing to a site's home page. And I have seen sites with over 1000 low-quality links receive little or no qualified search engine traffic. Therefore, quality is certainly more important than quantity.

Click-through (or click-thru) popularity is the measurement of the number of clicks that a Web page receives from a search engine results page (SERP), and how long the searcher stayed on the Web site after clicking on the link from the SERP. If a searcher clicks on a SERP link and continues to browse the Web site, then it might be assumed that the searcher found the information he desired and did not need to return to the SERP to view other Web pages. However, if a searcher clicks on a SERP link and quickly returns to the SERP, then it might be assumed that the searcher did not find the information he desired on the Web page and/or site.

Unfortunately, some Web developers and programmers have created clickbots to deceive the search engines into calculating more clicks to a Web site, making it seem as if a Web page receives more qualified clicks from human beings. In other words, the clicks do not come from actual searchers; they come from cleverly designed software. Due to the rise in click fraud in both organic search results and search engine advertising, click-through popularity is a less important or a nonexistent factor in determining a Web page's relevancy. Search engines do measure click-through popularity; however, it has little or no value for determining positions in the main search results.

Thus, when search engine optimizers refer to link popularity, they are referring to the number and quality of links pointing to a URL, not click-through popularity.

Link development, or the popularity component, is off-the-page criteria because Web site owners do not ultimately control how other people link to their sites' content. Web site owners can influence how other people link to their sites' content by using keyword-focused titles, headings, meta-tag descriptions, and page abstracts. In the end, though, other people will determine how they prefer to link to a site's content.

True long-term link development is difficult to imitate. Copywriting, information architecture, and site design can be easily imitated. All too often, the imitation constitutes a violation of copyright. Even so, it has not stopped a large number of search engine optimizers from stealing another site's content and site design. Cloaking, a form of search engine spam, often hides copyright infringement. Unique link development is equally important as keyword-focused text and an intuitive information architecture for obtaining long-term search engine visibility.

What I like about the entire link development concept is that Web sites will not be able to maintain search engine visibility unless they contain unique content and are easy to use. If two sites contain similar unique content, the one that is easier to use is more likely to receive more objective, third party links.

Link Development Strategies

High-quality link development is rarely an instantaneous occurrence. It takes time and patience. With careful planning and implementation, quality link development can help a site receive and maintain targeted search engine traffic.

Web Directory Submission

One of the quickest ways for a site to receive legitimate, objective, high-quality, third party links is to submit the site for inclusion in the major Web directories.

When submitting to Web directories, there is no "magic" formula. All Web directories are unique, generally having different categories and different rules for submission. Directory submission can be quite time consuming because each submission must be tailored for a specific directory. Some Web directories allow 15-word descriptions. Some allow 30 words. Some allow up to 200 words. Therefore, when submitting your site to the most popular Web directories, always keep their unique characteristics in mind.

Planning an effective Web directory submission campaign is crucial to your site's search engine visibility. And, in some ways, directory submission is even more important than search engine submission because, with Web directories, you basically have one chance to submit your site correctly. As long as a Web site's directory listing is factually accurate, directory editors have no reason to modify the listing. Directory editors' main concern is not how Web site owners market their Web sites. Directory editors care that the information in their directory is unique, timely, and accurate.

Some Web directory results come from human editors who find sites through their own research and surfing. Although this is not a common occurrence, most Web site owners prefer the opportunity to write their own titles and descriptions. So rather than risk a directory editor finding your site and writing a title and description you don't like or isn't effective for search visibility, plan and implement your unique Web directory submission campaign.

Planning a Web directory submission campaign

Before submitting your site to the Web directories, create a log file to keep track of your submissions. Web directory editors keep records of all submissions and can verify this information quickly. In the event your submission is rejected or the current listing must be modified due to factual errors, careful record keeping will help your directory submission campaign run more smoothly. Directory editors will appreciate your careful record keeping as well.

In this log file, keep records of the following information:

- Name of the Web directory

- Name of the person submitting the Web site

- Email address of the person submitting the Web site

- URL submitted

- Date(s) of submission

- Categories selected

- Web site title

- Web site description

- Any additional information entered in a "Comments" field

- Relevant contact information of the company and organization including physical address, telephone number, and fax number

- If using paid submission, a copy of the receipt and the tracking or order number

Tip

I prefer to make the email address of the person submitting the Web site a generic and unique email, such as development@company-name.com. In the event that the person in charge of a site's link development leaves the company, then the submission email will not have to be modified.

An effective Web directory campaign involves careful keyword research and copywriting. Remember that search engines look at anchor text, and text that is near anchor text, when calculating a URL's (and a site's) link development.

How many of you truly, honestly spend hours researching the most appropriate directory categories and writing the best descriptions so that both the Web directories and your site can benefit? Does your site really have unique content or does it contain the same content that other sites contain? Web site owners, or a company's marketing department, tend to write the descriptions that benefit the business or organization more than the Web directory and actual searchers.

If you plan on using the Web directories as part of your online marketing plan, try not to think solely about your own Web site. Try to imagine how the Web directory and Web directory users might benefit from your information. That is what directory editors are thinking about when they evaluate your submission: what sites add value to their directories. Web directories do not benefit from keyword-stuffed titles and descriptions. Categories with keyword-stuffed titles and descriptions denigrate the search experience. Web directories directly benefit from sites with unique, quality content that is placed in the most appropriate category (or categories) and is described accurately with the searchers' language.

So help directory editors reach their goals. Build a good Web site and do your research before you submit.

Selecting the best category

One of the biggest mistakes Web site owners make during Web directory submission is not doing the necessary research on each directory.

To select the most appropriate category (or categories) for your Web site, type in your selected keywords in each Web directory, and study the results. Remember the 20- to 30-word keyword list you came up with in Part 2? These are the words that you will be entering in the Web directory search boxes.

Let's look at our fictional TranquiliTeas site. From our keyword list, we know that we must perform a search in each directory using the following keywords:

organic teas	organic tea	oolong tea
green tea	organic oolong tea	organic green tea
herbal green tea	organic tea recipes	herbal teas
tea recipes	herbal tea recipes	black tea
decaffeinated tea	decaffeinated teas	loose leaf teas
whole leaf teas	tea accessories	Chinese teas
English teas	Indian black tea	tea sets
porcelain tea sets	gourmet teas	

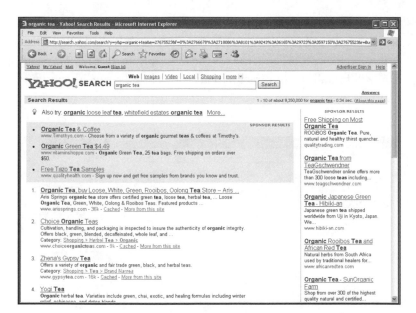

Figure 4-1
Make sure you are search-
ing in the Yahoo directory
results, not the Yahoo
spidered results, when
researching the most
appropriate category for the
Yahoo directory. The Yahoo
directory results will show
categories listings with categories listed above the URL.

You might want to begin with the most generic search term, such as
the word *tea*. When you begin with a generic search term, categories might appear at the top of the search results. In all likelihood, your site will belong in one of the categories that appear at
the top of the search results.

Sometimes, you can search for your top keyword phrases and discover that no categories appear in the search results, only Web sites. If this happens, look underneath the descriptions of each Web site. You will find different directory categories listed there, as shown in Figure 4-2:

Figure 4-2

When you perform a search on the Yahoo Web directory for the keyword phrase "organic tea," a number of categories appear in the directory search results, including local or geographically specific listings. If you scroll down to the bottom of the screen, you can see the different categories available for an organic tea site.

Do not automatically select the category that appears at the very top of the Web directory search results. Your Web site must truly be suited to a category in order to be accepted. Are your competitors listed in that same category? Is the type of information you are offering on your Web site similar to the information offered by other Web sites in that category? You might find that your site can easily fit in multiple categories. If this is the case, then it is safe to select the category that appears at the top of the list.

For the TranquiliTeas Web site, the most appropriate category in Yahoo is the following:

> Business and Economy > Shopping and Services > Food and Drinks > Drinks > Tea > Organic

The Open Directory displayed multiple categories that might be appropriate for the TranquiliTeas site:

> Shopping > Food > Beverages > Coffee and Tea > Tea
>
> Business > Food and Related Products > Beverages > Tea
>
> Recreation > Food > Drink > Tea
>
> Home > Cooking > Beverages > Tea
>
> Shopping > Health > Alternative > Herbs > Teas and Tonics

The first Open Directory two categories contain a large number of tea sites, and the TranquiliTeas site will probably be buried in the search results. It might be better to find less populated categories. However, based on the types of sites listed in these categories, a submission to either category would be appropriate.

The fourth category is not the best category for home page submission because upon careful inspection, most of the listings specifically mentioned recipes. Even though the TranquiliTeas site contains recipes, the majority of its content is geared toward selling tea.

If a company or organization has a physical location, then the site often can have an additional Web directory listing under geo-specific, or local, categories.

Suggesting a new category

Sometimes, after performing several searches, you might not find a Web directory category that accurately reflects the content of your Web site. In this situation, you can suggest an additional category to the directory editors.

To be safe, suggest a category that is similar to other categories in the Web directory.

For example, a particular state (in the United States) might display a specific category, but a different state might not. This situation arose when I submitted a Web site from a domestic violence shelter located in Waukegan, Illinois. A domestic violence shelter listing belongs in a directory's regional section. In all likelihood, a person who is seeking domestic violence help in Connecticut is not going to travel to Illinois to seek an emergency shelter.

When I performed a search on Yahoo, I found that there was a category in Woodstock, Illinois for domestic violence shelters (see Figure 4-3).

Figure 4-3
Regional domestic violence shelter category in Yahoo.

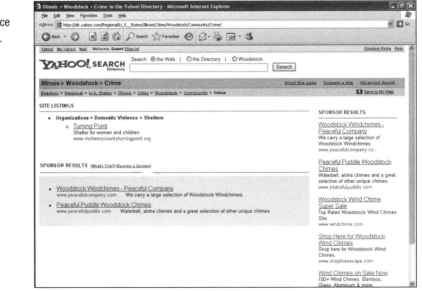

However, there was no domestic violence shelter category in Waukegan, Illinois. In this situation, it was safe for me to suggest an additional category to Yahoo because there were similar categories in other regions. To be sure that my additional category would be accepted, I also checked other states. I found the same categories existed in Texas, California, Minnesota, and North Dakota regional listings. I even found domestic violence shelter listings in other countries.

Types of Web sites that belong in regional categories are physician sites, hospitals, landscaping firms, real estate offices, restaurants, local government offices, Chambers of Commerce, and any other organization that does business in specific areas. If you do not see the appropriate category for your type of business and organization, check out categories in other states.

Yahoo's submission form does allow you to suggest an additional category in a field called "Additional Information." Other directories might not have this field. If you find yourself in that situation, feel free to suggest an additional category in the "Comments" field in the submission form, if it is provided (see Figure 4-4).

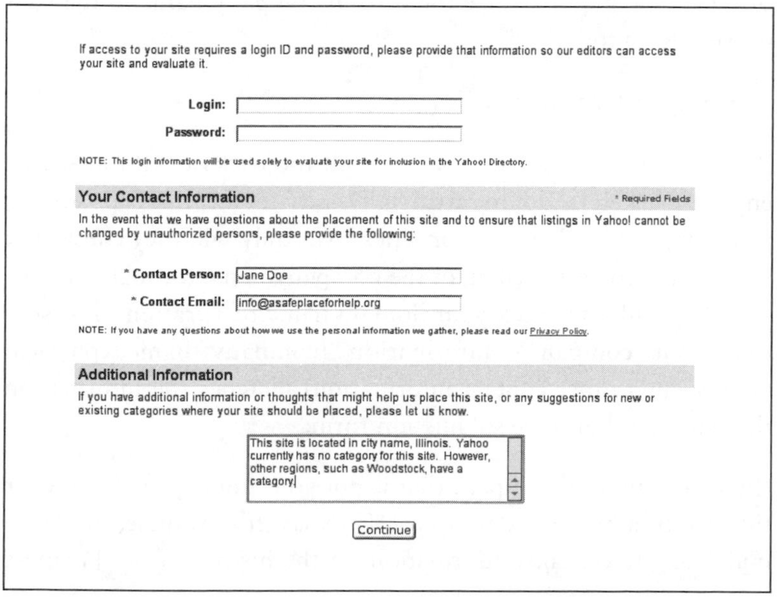

Figure 4-4
Yahoo's Additional Information field in the submission form.

Writing an effective Web site title

Most of the time, a Web site's title will be the official company name, and, as previously mentioned in Part 1, Web directory editors are looking for the official company name in one of four places:

- A header or footer
- The About Us page
- The Contact Us page
- A Locations page

The About Us page should always contain the correct spelling of your company name. So even if you use your official company name in other places throughout your Web site, it is still a good idea to always place that information in your About Us section.

Do not try and trick directory editors into using a company name that contains keywords if the official spelling of your company name does not contain keywords. For example, an unethical search engine marketer might not like that the official company name of TranquiliTeas Organic Tea, Inc. does not contain the plural version of "tea." He might change the official company name in the submission form to:

Tranquili Teas Organic Tea, Inc.

Web directory editors are aware of all the tricks unethical search engine marketers do to artificially inflate directory positions, including stuffing keywords in titles. Not only will they check that you use the correct spelling of the company name throughout your site, they will also check your domain name registration to be sure that your company's information (company name, physical address, and other contact information) matches the information that you typed into the submission form.

If you are submitting a page that is not your home page, then your title can be a bit more descriptive. Let's say, for example, the TranquiliTeas site contains information on the history of the Japanese tea ceremony. If site owners were to submit this particular page (or set of pages to Yahoo), the title might be:

History of the Japanese tea ceremony

Notice that the titles in both of these examples are factual and contain no sales and marketing hype. The keywords "organic" and "tea" are in the home page title submission. The keywords "Japanese" and "tea" are in the individual Web page submission. Even if your keyword research showed that your target audience typed in "teas" more often, the acceptable titles do not use that form of the word.

Writing an effective Web site description

At first, it might seem that Web directory editors and Web site owners have conflicting interests. Directory editors want to preserve the quality of their directory results. They want descriptions to accurately describe the contents of a Web site without any sales and marketing hype. Web site owners do not necessarily want their description to be objective. If a slogan or a set of keywords has worked for their businesses over the years, they want to preserve that branding and marketing strategy. With these seemingly conflicting goals, how can Web site owners have their Web sites displayed in directories the best way possible?

In reality, Web directory editors and Web site owners actually have the same goals. As a Web site owner, you have complete control over how your pages are displayed and the content that you place on your pages. You would not like it if complete strangers ordered you to change the content on your site because they did not agree with what you had to say or the manner in which you stated information. No stranger should control the contents of your Web site.

Likewise, Web directory editors must deal with thousands of strangers telling them, every day, how they should display the contents of their Web sites. Directory editors have a tough job. Viewing hundreds of submissions a day for hundreds or thousands of different categories while preserving the quality of the directories must be a daunting task.

Approach Web directory submission knowing that the editors must deal with thousands of submissions every week. Directory editors are trying to preserve the quality of the information they deliver. So by making their job easier and following their guidelines and examples, your submission is less likely to be modified or rejected.

To best accomplish this approach, after you have determined the most appropriate category for your Web site, review all of the descriptions listed in that category. How many words, on average, does the directory editor appear to allow on the page? If you notice that most of the descriptions contain 12 to 15 words, then you know that the directory editor might prefer a 15-word description instead of a 25-word description, even though the guidelines might state you can submit a description of up to 25 words.

What appears to be the writing style of the descriptions that are listed? Even though your description should resemble the description style of other sites listed in your targeted category, your description should be unique. So if your company specializes in three types of services, mention those three services in your description. If your company targets a specific audience, mention the audience as well.

Do not write a description that is identical to other descriptions in your targeted category. Web directory editors understand that their end users do not want the same information delivered to them over and over again in search results. Editors want to know that each Web site they accept offers unique and valuable information. So make sure one of your unique selling propositions (USP) is somehow shown in your description.

Also, do not stuff too many keywords into the description. Directory editors and people who view search results do not want to read a list of keywords.

I tend to follow a basic description format and tailor the description based on directory research. This description format appears to satisfy the needs of both directory editors and Web site owners:

> (Keyword phrase 1) firm specializing in (keyword phrase 2), (keyword phrase 3), and (keyword phrase 4).

Using this format, a possible description for TranquiliTeas look might be:

> Wholesale organic tea distributor specializing in oolong, green, herbal, decaffeinated, and black teas. (13 words)

This description (a) objectively and accurately describes the contents of the Web site, making the directory editors happy, and (b) contains the keywords that the Web site owner is targeting.

This 13-word description contains the following keyword phrases:

Tea	Green tea	Organic green tea
Teas	Green teas	Organic green teas
Organic tea	Herbal tea	Organic herbal tea
Organic teas	Herbal teas	Organic herbal teas
Wholesale tea	Decaffeinated tea	Organic decaffeinated tea
Wholesale teas	Decaffeinated teas	Organic decaffeinated teas
Wholesale organic tea	Black tea	Organic black tea
Wholesale organic teas	Black teas	Organic black teas
Oolong tea	Organic oolong tea	
Oolong teas	Organic oolong teas	

If Web site owners have a specific target audience, then it might be a good idea to include that information at the end of the description.

> Wholesale organic tea distributor specializing in oolong, green, herbal, decaffeinated, and black teas for stores and restaurants. (17 words)

Sometimes, Web site owners have more keywords they would like to target. For example, the Tranquiliteas site might offer teas as loose tea or in tea bags. This information is important to the target audience: store and restaurant owners. So another possible description might be:

> Wholesale organic tea distributor specializing in oolong, green, herbal, decaffeinated, and black teas. Choose from loose tea or tea bags. (20 words)

This 20-word description contains an even longer list of keyword phrases:

Tea	Green loose tea	Organic oolong tea bags
Teas	Green loose teas	Organic green tea
Loose tea	Green tea bags	Organic green teas
Loose teas	Herbal tea	Loose organic green tea
Organic tea	Herbal teas	Loose organic green teas
Organic teas	Herbal loose tea	Organic green tea bags
Loose organic tea	Herbal loose teas	Organic herbal tea
Loose organic teas	Herbal tea bags	Organic herbal teas
Wholesale tea	Decaffeinated tea	Loose herbal green tea
Wholesale teas	Decaffeinated teas	Loose herbal green teas
Wholesale organic tea	Decaffeinated loose tea	Organic herbal tea bags
Wholesale organic teas	Decaffeinated loose teas	Organic decaffeinated tea
Wholesale loose tea	Decaffeinated tea bags	Organic decaffeinated teas
Wholesale loose teas	Black tea	Loose decaffeinated green tea
Wholesale tea bags	Black teas	Loose decaffeinated green teas
Oolong tea	Black loose tea	Organic decaffeinated tea bags
Oolong teas	Black loose teas	Organic black tea bags
Oolong loose tea	Black tea bags	Organic black tea
Oolong loose teas	Organic oolong tea	Organic black teas
Oolong tea bags	Organic oolong teas	Loose black green tea
Green tea	Loose organic oolong tea	Loose black green teas
Green teas	Loose organic oolong teas	Organic black tea bags

Notice that the target audience was eliminated from the 20-word description. If the words used to describe the target audience (stores and restaurants) are targeted keywords, why should they be eliminated from the description? Many directories allow 25-word descriptions. A longer description would still follow directory guidelines.

When submitting your site to a directory, remember to *always* follow the lead of the editor. If you noticed that the current listings in the directory have a shorter description, then a longer description stands a higher chance of being modified. You might not like the way the editor modifies your longer description, especially if the editor eliminates one of your most important keywords. Since I recognized that "stores and restaurants" was not one of the keyword phrases on the keyword list I came up with in Part 2 of this book, I eliminated that phrase to make the description as concise as possible.

Since all Web directories are different and vary in the number of words they will accept in their submission forms, write descriptions of varying lengths. Write 7-, 10-, 15-, 20-, 25-, 30- and 50-word descriptions and save them in a text file. When you begin the directory submission process, you will be able to easily cut-and-paste the appropriate description into the submission form.

Paid submission

If your budget allows, use the paid/expedited submission programs whenever possible. Since most of the major search engines measure link development as a part of their ranking algorithms, the faster your site can be listed in the Web directories, the faster your site can receive the external link development boost.

Paid submission does not guarantee that your site will be accepted into the Web directory. Rather, the fee guarantees that your site will be reviewed within a specified time, generally 48 hours to one week. The fee pays for the time it takes for a directory editor to evaluate your title, description, and Web site plus the time it takes to add your site to its database, if your site is accepted.

Multiple listings from a single Web site

Getting multiple listings from a single Web site in a Web directory is the exception rather than the rule. Again, Web site owners and directory editors appear to have conflicting interests. Web site owners desire multiple listings to increase their site's popularity and overall search engine visibility. Directory editors want to list URLs with unique, quality content. Web site owners' ultimate goal is to sell their products and services. Directory editors' ultimate goal is to find sites that provide information and that add value to the Web directory.

Important

When writing your descriptions for Web directory submission, remember editors are most likely to view your home page first. Therefore, on your home page directory editors should be able to see the products or services you highlighted in your description. If editors and site visitors are unable to determine that your site specializes in the very services that you claim to offer in your description, editors are likely to modify your description.

One way to determine whether a site can be successfully submitted for an additional listing is to ask, "Can people benefit from visiting your site without having to spend money?" If your site provides information such as free tips, a how-to section, recipes, a dictionary or a glossary, your site provides information for the clear benefit of your target audience. Both Web directory editors and end users like to see this type of information.

If your Web site has been approved for admission into a directory, then your specialized-topic Web page stands a better chance of being selected for a different category. Once your main site is accepted, you know that your site has met the Web directory's rules and guidelines. The editors found your site's content easy to read and informative.

You will have to go through the same submission process as outlined for your main site. You will have to suggest an additional category and write a unique title and description for each additional URL you submit.

A general guideline is to not submit multiple pages from the same site in the same branch of a directory. For example, in the Open Directory, the category selected for the TranquiliTeas main site was:

Business > Food and Related Products > Beverages > Tea

Suppose TranquiliTeas site owners had a collection of unique organic tea recipes and wanted to submit their main Recipes page to additional categories.

First, they would have to find the most appropriate category. After performing multiple keyword searches in the Open Directory, the most appropriate categories might be:

Home > Cooking > Beverages > Tea

or

Recreation > Food > Drink > Tea

Notice that both of these categories are not in the Business branch of the Open Directory.

Since the sites in the first category contain tea recipes in their descriptions, the first category is probably the better selection.

Before submitting the Recipes page, the TranquiliTeas site owners should check to see that: (a) the site's recipes are unique, and (b) the content is substantial. Some of the sites listed in this category have a single tea recipe that is unique. Other sites have collections of tea recipes. Therefore, if the TranquiliTeas site has a collection of unique organic tea recipes, the Recipes URL is likely to be accepted into this category.

Assuming that the TranquiliTeas site does have a collection of unique organic tea recipes, the site owners can now write a unique title and description for this submission. Many of the sites listed in this category mention the company name. So it might be appropriate to submit a title such as:

Organic tea recipes from TranquiliTeas Organic Tea

A directory editor might not like that title due to the repetition of the keyword phrase "organic tea." So another appropriate title might be:

Organic tea recipes from TranquiliTeas

This title is more concise and still accurately conveys the necessary information. If site owners wish to keep the full company name intact without giving the appearance of keyword stacking, another appropriate title might be:

TranquiliTeas Organic Tea recipes

Additionally, no Web sites in this category specifically highlight organic teas. So another appropriate title might simply be:

Organic tea recipes

Since the sites (in the targeted category) that contain a collection of tea recipes mention the company name in the title, follow the directory editor's lead. Submit a title containing the company name.

Now that both the title and category are selected, it is time to write an appropriate description. Note that in the initial TranquiliTeas site submission the word "recipes" was not mentioned:

> Wholesale organic tea distributor specializing in oolong, green, herbal, decaffeinated, and black teas. Choose from loose tea or tea bags.

Search engine and Web directory users do not want the same sites appearing over and over in the search results. In general, end users and directory editors do not want to see the both the TranquiliTeas main site and the individual Recipes section appearing together in search results.

Keeping the words "recipe" or "recipes" out of the initial description was a strategic move. If a search engine marketer kept the word "recipes" in this description, the main site might show up in search results for the search query "organic tea recipes." And the additional listing might be rejected.

Note

In some cases, multiple listings are difficult to obtain. Even if your site offers a variety of products and services, do not submit each service to a different category, even if the category is in a different branch. Most of the time, a single submission with a well-written description will satisfy Web directory editors. Content must be truly unique to warrant multiple listings.

When people perform searches, they do not necessarily want to go to the home page. Searchers prefer to go straight to the page that contains the information they desire without having to surf. By keeping the word "recipes" out of the main site submission and using that word in the additional submission, the TranquiliTeas site owners are thinking about their target audience by delivering them directly to the Recipe section.

Additionally, the site owners are helping to preserve the quality of the Web directory category. If the TranquiliTeas site offers a unique collection of organic tea recipes, the site provides free information for visitors without forcing them to go to the home page first. Therefore, the additional listing benefits everyone. End users are delivered directly the appropriate page. The directory has unique and accurate information. And site owners have an additional listing.

To avoid possible rejections, before you submit your site to a major directory, review your entire site using the following checklist.

Web directory submission checklist

To save time and costs involved in Web directory submissions, use the following checklist to ensure that your site is ready for directory editors to review:

❏ Yes ❏ No   Did you read the Terms and Conditions on each individual Web directory *before* submitting your site to ensure you are following the guidelines?

❏ Yes ❏ No   Does your site contain unique content? Have you researched your targeted categories to ensure that your site contains unique content?

❏ Yes ❏ No   Is all the text on your Web site legible, both the HTML text and the text within graphic images?

❏ Yes ❏ No   Does your site have any broken links? Any type of broken link, be it an Error 404 page or a graphic image that does not load, is reason for a site to be rejected.

❏ Yes ❏ No   Is the site legible on current versions of two major browsers, Firefox and Internet Explorer?

❏ Yes ❏ No   Is all of your contact information (physical address, telephone number, fax number, email address) easily found on your site?

❏ Yes ❏ No   Is the correct spelling of your official company or organization name on an About Us, Contact Us, or Locations page, even if this information is available in a header or footer on your Web site?

❏ Yes ❏ No   If you have a business site, do you have a virtual domain name (i.e., www.companyname.com)?

❏ Yes ❏ No   Do all of your links work, both internal links (to pages within your site) and external links (to other Web sites)?

❏ Yes ❏ No   Does your site have secure credit card processing (for sites that accept credit cards)?

❏ Yes ❏ No   If your site sells products, does your site have a return policy and a money-back guarantee?

❏ Yes ❏ No   If your site collects confidential information, does your site have an official privacy policy?

❏ Yes ❏ No   Does your site have a copyright notice? If so, is the most current year published?

❏ Yes ❏ No   Do visitors have to download a plug-in in order to view the site? Requiring a plug-in might cause a site to be rejected.

continues

(continued)

❑ Yes	❑ No	Does your site have at least six to eight pages of substantial content? Sites with too few pages generally get rejected.
❑ Yes	❑ No	Are both your Web pages and your graphic images quick to download?
❑ Yes	❑ No	Is your site fully functional 24 hours a day, seven days a week? Make sure your shopping carts, forms, search engines, and any other dynamically generated functions work properly.
❑ Yes	❑ No	Have you tested all of your forms to be sure they are working properly? Do forms have an appropriate "Thank You" page after your visitors hit the Submit button?
❑ Yes	❑ No	Have you spell checked all of your content?
❑ Yes	❑ No	Do you have redirects (other than 301 redirects) on any of your pages? Most redirects are considered search engine spam. Additionally, Web directory editors are not likely to list the submitted URL but rather the destination URL.
❑ Yes	❑ No	Does your site require a user name and password in order to view its contents? If so, have you provided Web directory editors with this information so they can verify your site's content? Many sites are rejected if there is no substantial content outside of a password-protected area or if you require your visitors to give you confidential information before viewing a site's content.
❑ Yes	❑ No	Did you perform extensive category research to choose the most appropriate categories for your site?
❑ Yes	❑ No	Did you select the most language-appropriate categories?
❑ Yes	❑ No	Is the title of your main site your official company or organization name?
❑ Yes	❑ No	Have you removed unnecessary punctuation, sales hype, and buzz words from your title and description?
❑ Yes	❑ No	Is your title written with all capital letters? Remove all unnecessary capitalization.
❑ Yes	❑ No	Did you repeat the site's title or the category in the description? Editors do not like this.
❑ Yes	❑ No	Did you use abbreviations or acronyms that are commonly understood in your description? When in doubt, spell out the acronym.
❑ Yes	❑ No	Did you capitalize the first letter of the description?
❑ Yes	❑ No	Did you carefully review the current descriptions in your targeted categories for a standard word count?

❏ Yes   ❏ No   Does your description contain only a list of keywords? If so, review again the current descriptions in your target categories and rewrite following the editors' lead.

❏ Yes   ❏ No   Did you highlight your most important products and services, using keywords, in your description?

❏ Yes   ❏ No   Did you highlight your unique selling propositions in your descriptions?

❏ Yes   ❏ No   Can directory editors easily find your most important products and services just by viewing your home page?

❏ Yes   ❏ No   If you submit additional pages within your site, is the information on those pages substantial and unique?

❏ Yes   ❏ No   Are additional pages submitted to categories in a different category branch than the main site?

❏ Yes   ❏ No   Do your additional page title and description contain keywords that clearly, concisely, and accurately describe the contents of the page?

❏ Yes   ❏ No   If it is within your budget, did you use the paid, expedited submission form?

❏ Yes   ❏ No   Did you check to see if your site is already listed in the directory? If so, you will have to fill out a Change Request form.

❏ Yes   ❏ No   Did you create a log of all directory submissions information, including dates, names, titles, descriptions, and contact information?

❏ Yes   ❏ No   If your site has not appeared in the directory, did you wait at least three weeks before resubmitting?

❏ Yes   ❏ No   If you are suggesting an additional category, did you model that category after other categories that already exist in each individual Web directory?

❏ Yes   ❏ No   If your submission was rejected, did you appeal within 30 days? Was your appeal written in a polite and professional manner?

❏ Yes   ❏ No   Are all submissions tailored for each Web directory?

❏ Yes   ❏ No   Did you double-check each Web directory's Terms and Conditions to ensure that your submission follows all the rules and guidelines?

Most of the time, site owners have only one chance to "do it right" with Web directories. Modifying a directory listing can be very difficult, if not impossible. Nonetheless, with proper planning and execution, Web site owners can reap the rewards of directory listings years after submission.

Third Party Web Site Submission

New Web sites often achieve initial search engine visibility from fresh Web directory listings. To maintain this visibility over time, however, a site should receive links from noncompetitive, industry-related Web sites. The quality of third party links always carries more weight than the quantity of links.

Thus, the focus of all link development is to think as your target audience thinks and to understand their search behavior. What types of Web sites does your target audience tend to visit, bookmark, and revisit periodically? These types of Web sites are good places to research and analyze for high-quality link development opportunities.

Usability testing for search behaviors

In an ideal situation, usability testing should be the first step in a competitive link analysis. Why should usability testing be the first step? The reason is simple: Web site owners need to determine the most common search behaviors, particularly the querying behavior, of their main target audience.

Many Web site usability professionals create profiles or personas to assist them in the Web development process. A persona is a user archetype that drives the design and interface of a Web site. A profile is somewhat similar to a persona, but it is not as specific. People who fit the descriptions of a persona or profile are the best ones to observe for search behaviors.

For example, if you know that your target audience primarily consists of information technology professionals, you can give your persona an appropriate name and job title to make the persona seem like a real person. Without a name or a visual image, a persona will not become a concrete individual in the minds of the business team (content providers, developers, marketers, search engine optimizers, etc.). My favorite persona name for an American male is Bob, just because the name often conjures images of a likable person. If the business team likes the persona, then the team tends to work harder to make a Web site easy to use for Bob.

Until a persona is clearly defined, the persona is too elastic. This elasticity commonly results in the persona sharing the same characteristics as business team members. When you optimize a Web site, you must use the words and phrases that your target audience types into search queries, not necessarily the words that the site's business team wants to use. Usability professionals often chant the mantra, "Use the users' language." They do not chant, "Use marketing hype."

Of course, I am not saying that a Web site should contain no sales or marketing language. A successful Web site generally strikes a balance between user expectations and business goals. Sales and marketing language encourages site visitors to take desired calls to action and is necessary for a site to achieve business goals. Nonetheless, very few people link to a site that merely acts as a giant ad for a company or organization. Finding and maintaining the balance is crucial for long-term search engine visibility.

Once Web site owners have six to ten participants for usability testing, they should observe how these participants use the commercial Web search engines for the products, services, or information offered on their Web sites. The idea is not to monitor for search engine positioning but rather for how participants formulate queries and which types of Web sites they gravitate toward.

Figure 4-5

A query for the keyword phrase "green tea benefits" (without the quotation marks) on Google yields some potential link development opportunities, including an About.com guide and some news sites.

Which Web pages do participants read, and which pages do they skip? Are participants likely to bookmark a Web page because its content was helpful in some way? The results of these usability tests will reveal some of the sites to target for future link development opportunities and further research.

Observing querying and other search behavior

Many information retrieval and usability professionals have identified a number of different search behaviors, including but not limited to:

- Querying
  - Refining
  - Expanding
- Browsing or surfing
- Foraging
- Scanning
- Reading
- Pogosticking

One landmark search behavior that was identified long before Google came into existence is berrypicking. Many of the aforementioned search behaviors are actually components of berrypicking behavior. What is so phenomenal about berrypicking research was the conclusion that search is not a linear process.

Though Marcia Bates did not specifically mention the Web in her research (http://www.gseis.ucla.edu/faculty/bates/berrypicking.html), her observations are applicable to the Web and the commercial Web search engines. Many people consider the word *search* to only mean only querying behavior, when, in fact, "search" encompasses a wide variety of behaviors.

For example, a single Google query involves many types of search behavior. After a searcher types in a series of keywords in Google's search box and clicks the search button, the searcher will either read or scan search results to see which listings best match the query. If the search results are unsatisfactory, the searcher might add more keywords in the search box. Then the searcher might read or scan more search results.

If the searcher visits a site after clicking a link from a commercial Web search engine, the searcher will read or scan the page to determine if the page content matches the query. Browsing a site for further information is also a common occurrence. Searchers often pogostick between search engine results pages and commercial Web sites to find the best answer to their questions.

Look at all of the search behaviors I just mentioned: querying, scanning, reading, refining, and pogosticking. In reality, pogosticking is a negative search behavior because it indicates that the searcher is unsure of the information presented and is less likely to take a desired call to action.

What does search behavior have to do with link development from objective, third party Web sites? By observing the search and querying behaviors of actual users who fit a desired profile or persona, Web site owners can determine the types of sites they like and actually use, and the types of sites they dislike and abandon. The sites that usability participants like and use are targets future link development and link development research.

Link development procedure

As I mentioned previously, in an ideal situation, usability testing should be the first part of link development research. Gathering a list of Web sites and their corresponding URLs from target audience members is an important part of the competitive analysis process.

In the event that your company or organization does not have the time, budget, or other resources to incorporate usability testing, then optimizers can research competitor Web sites on their own. Keep in mind, however, that there is no substitute for user observation and analysis. Even seasoned search engine optimizers are making educated guesses (and often false assumptions) without usability testing.

The following list is the process that I use for determining link development opportunities and link requests:

Important

Like link development, usability testing, analysis, and results implementation should be an ongoing process. The idea behind search usability™ is to accommodate a wide variety of search behaviors, not only querying behavior. By making the information on your Web site easy to find externally (via the commercial Web search engines) and internally (after people arrive on your site), a site can meet both business goals and user expectations.

1. **After Web directory research, search for useful content on all major search engines.** This process is probably the most time-consuming part of link development. Google ranks content different from Yahoo. And MSN's Live ranks content differently from Ask. What you are looking for are sites that appear on all of the search engines results pages consistently over time.

   A one-time search for keyword phrases might yield poor quality sites (that achieved search engine positions through unethical means). To get the best return on investment, you want to find sites with high quality content and long-term search engine visibility. These sites are usually the ones with the most credible information.

2. **Read the site's content and see if the site has a section for external linking.** What you are looking for is a content "hole." You might have content available on your site that is not available on the other site. If the site allows external linking, then there is an opportunity for link development.

3. **Make sure the site is not your competitor's site.** Only in rare instances should your site link to a competitor. You also do not want to link to a site that is considered search engine spam.

   Search engines will not penalize a Web site for incoming links because Web site owners do not have any control over whose sites link to their sites. However, they will penalize sites that link to poor quality sites. The reason for this is that Web site owners have complete control over the sites they choose to link to. So be selective about the sites you link to. Yahoo's Site Explorer tool can help you determine whether or not a site is part of a poor-quality link farm.

4. **Send a personalized message to the Web site owner, editor, or guide via a form or email.** If the link request is in an email, it should originate from your company's or organization's email address, not the address of a search engine optimizer.

   Once you have determined some link development opportunities, find the form or email for requesting the link. I like to keep a database (or an Excel spreadsheet) of URLs, email addresses and/or form URLs, and submission dates. If the email has a person's name in it, always address the person by name.

5. **Always be polite and sincere.** Show the Web site owner that you have content that will benefit his target audience. Additionally, prove to him that you have read the content on his Web site. If you found the site's content to be particularly helpful, let him know how and why it was helpful. Mention the specific URL or headline of the content that you found helpful. Don't lie or stroke an ego just for the link. People can usually detect insincere flattery. Then, let the Web site owner know about your supplemental content and how it might help his site's visitors.

6. **Give the site owner all information for linking back to your site,** making it as easy as possible for him to provide the link. Present a suggested title, description, and URL. The title and description do not have to be a Web page's HTML title-tag content or meta-tag description. Personally, I recommend following the writing style of the Web site owner so that your suggested link will blend in seamlessly with the Web site's owner's content.

7. **Follow up.** If a Web site owner links to your site, thank him. If the Web site owner does not link to your site right away, follow up with a second or third link request. If sending multiple submissions, make sure the email's content changes a little.

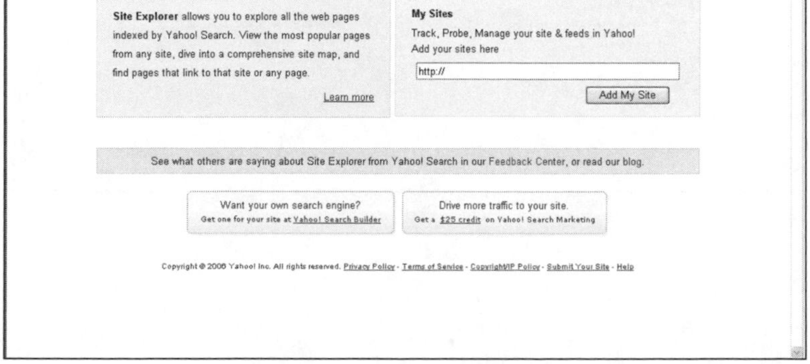

Figure 4-6

Yahoo's Site Explorer is a great way to get a snapshot of a site's link development.

Figure 4-7

Type the URL of a competitor site or a link development target into the search box and click the Search button.

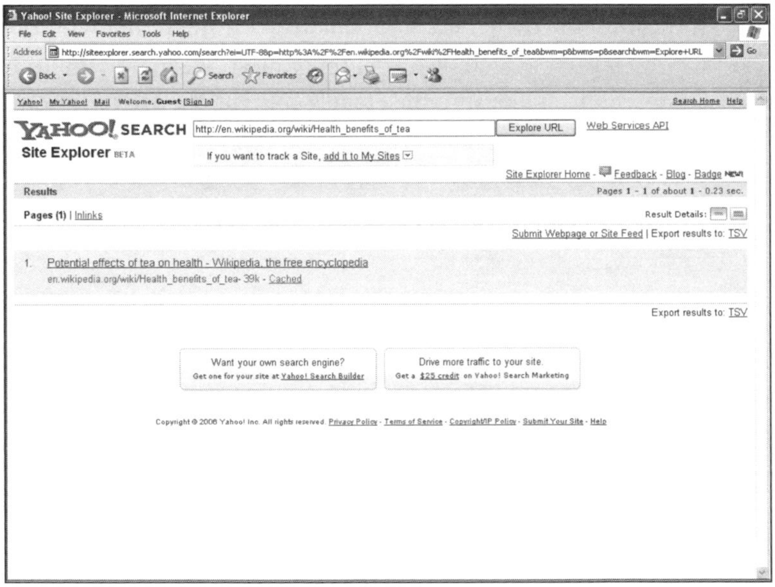

Figure 4-8

The search results page will display the URL (or a collection of URLs, if you entered a home page URL in the query). What you are interested in determining are the external, third party links pointing to the target URL. Click on the hypertext link named Inlinks.

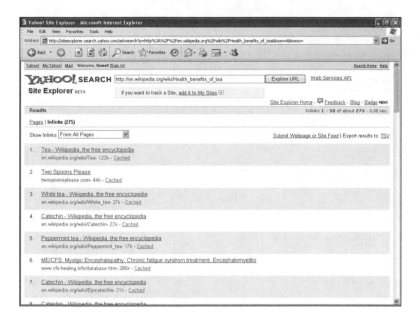

Figure 4-9
The search results will display internal links (from site navigation and cross-linking) and external, third party links. For link development research, you only want the external, third party links.

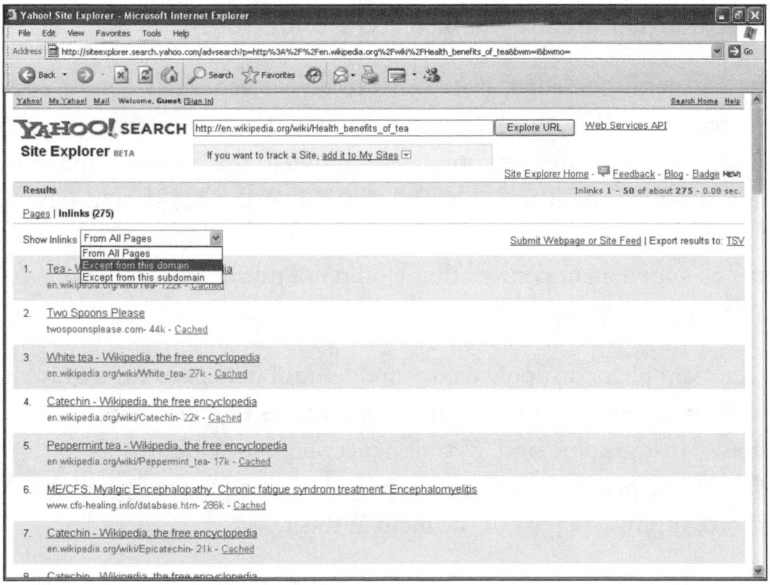

Figure 4-10
From the Show Inlinks drop-down menu, select "Except from this domain."

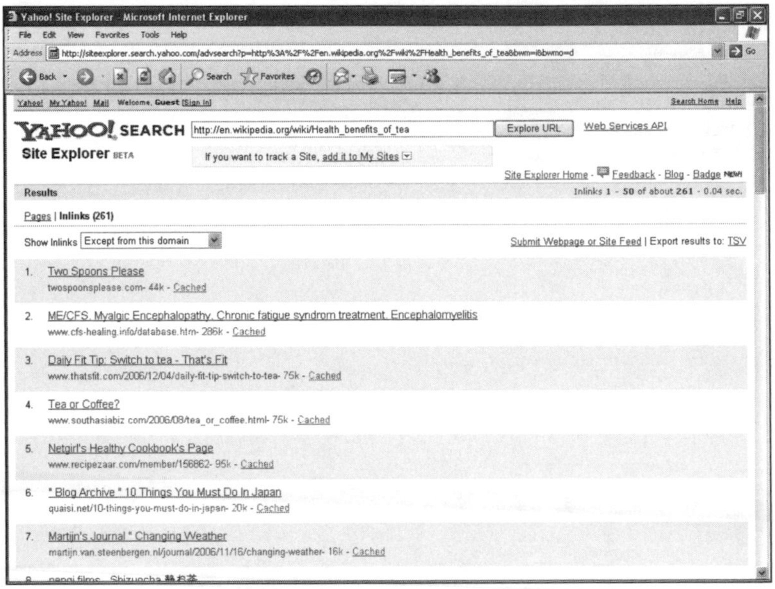

Figure 4-11
The search results will display a list of external, third party links.

Do not be a pest. If a site owner is genuinely interested in linking to your site, they usually will link after a third request.

As a general guideline, if a Web site owner genuinely found your content to be helpful, reciprocation should not be a requirement, especially if you are not completely confident that the link opportunity is 100% spam free. Nevertheless, all Web sites should have a Links and/or a Resources section for link development purposes and to supplement content that would not normally be available on a particular type of Web site.

One example of a supplemental and useful Links page for a graphic or Web design site is one that provides links to stock photography sites. Most graphic and Web designers use stock photos as part of the design process, but these types of Web sites rarely sell stock photography as a part of the main Web site.

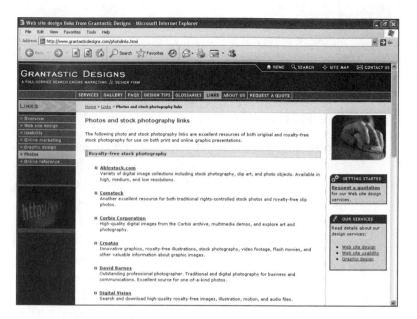

Figure 4-12
A specific stock photography links and resources Web page.

Legitimate vs. search engine spam link requests

Because link development is part of the fundamental core of effective search engine optimization, many unethical search engine marketers have created entire networks of low quality Web sites purely for link popularity purposes. Here are some ways to tell whether you are receiving a legitimate link request vs. a spam link request:

- **The site requesting a link is off topic.** Do you ever receive link requests from a site whose content has absolutely nothing to do with the content on your site? For example, this book has a companion Web site at http://www.searchenginesbook.com/. From my book site's contact form, I get many requests to ecommerce sites, software sites, etc. In other words, I receive thousands of link requests from sites that have nothing to do with search-engine friendly Web site design. Many search engine marketers send out a link request template email once they see a high PageRank score (a number between 1 and 10) on the Google Toolbar. Do not reply to template emails, and do not grant links to sites that fail to provide useful, unique content to your target audience. Link development should always benefit your site visitors.

- **Reciprocation is required.** I feel that the whole reciprocal linking and Web ring strategy was fundamentally flawed. If I find another Web site's content to be useful, I will link to that Web site. No reciprocation is required. However, if a Web site owner will not link to my content without reciprocation, that person must not have found my content to be *that* useful, did he?

- **Link request is from a competitor.** Sometimes, common sense does not appear to be a part of the link development process among search engine marketers. Why would anyone link to competitor Web sites and provide them with high quality link development? However, if some colleague sites have very informative newsletters that do not compete with the products and services your site offers, you might want to link to that section of their sites because their newsletters contain credible, unique information about a specific topic. But do not link to any colleague who spams the search engines. Ultimately, it will hurt your site's overall link development.

- **Email request demonstrates that a person has not read your site's content.** Many link requests to my book Web site originates from Web positioning software companies. Interestingly, I state very clearly in this book and in my companion Web site I do not use nor endorse position-checking software. Clearly, the person who sends me these types of link request has not read my site. When requesting a link, you should prove to the site owner that you have read his/her site.

- **Email request mentions PageRank.** I understand that receiving a link from a site with a high PageRank might be a tempting offer. Who doesn't want high-quality links? But PageRank is not flawless. Sometimes a high PageRank is the result of a large free-for-all spam link farm, which is spam.

  Look at the Web site with the high PageRank. Do some digging. If the site is poorly designed and has a wide variety of unrelated topics and links, that high PageRank site is probably due to a link farm. Additionally, many Web sites with a low PageRank generate thousands and millions of dollars in sales.

And many Web sites with a high PageRank generate little or no income. A number between 1 and 10 yields little useful information as to the success or failure of a Web business.

These rules are certainly not applicable 100% of the time. However, these guidelines have helped me save hours of time filtering out low quality link requests.

Search Engine Submission

The guidelines for submitting to search engines are different than the guidelines for submitting to Web directories and third party, industry-related Web sites. With directories, a human editor evaluates your Web site and ensures that it is placed in the most appropriate category. With search engines, no editors or categories are involved. In fact, over time, most search engines will find a naturally spider-friendly site without direct human submission.

Search engines begin finding Web pages through lists of heavily used servers from major Internet Service Providers and the most frequently visited Web directories, such as Yahoo. Because the major Web directories are a starting point for many search engine spiders, submitting your site to directories is the first step in effective search engine submission. The popularity boost can greatly affect search engine visibility.

Planning a search engine submission campaign

Many Web site owners feel that they will get maximum search engine visibility by having every single page on their site listed well in the search engines. This belief is a common misconception. Every page on a Web site does not have to be optimized in order to obtain effective search engine visibility. In fact, many successful small business sites only need 20 to 25 optimized pages, and larger sites usually do not need more than 200 optimized pages.

Ideally, Web site owners should never need to submit their site's URLs to the commercial Web search engines. Search engine spiders should be able to discover new and updated content with little human intervention.

Generally speaking, if a Web site has: (1) a URL structure, (2) at least one navigation scheme, and (3) relevant horizontal and vertical cross-linking that search engines can follow, and if the site has some high-quality, objective, third-quality link development, then search engine submission is an unnecessary process.

If Web site owners are finding it difficult to encourage search engine spidering, or if they find that search engines will not crawl their sites without site map submission or participating in a paid inclusion program, then the Web site probably has a substandard site architecture and interface. Or a site's external, third party link development might not be substantial enough to encourage deep crawling.

Either way, end users (be they qualified prospects or Web directory editors) are not finding the site to be intuitive and easy to use. Perhaps desired information and clear calls to action are difficult to find. Perhaps the navigational elements are confusing. Maybe clickable elements do not look clickable, and unclickable elements look clickable. In other words, the site might not clearly communicate desired information to both humans and search engine spiders.

Coming to the aforementioned realization after a site is built is a more common occurrence than one might expect. If a Web site receives thousands or millions of visitors per day without search engine visibility, then one logical conclusion is that there must be something wrong with the commercial Web search engines. And the search engines should change or make exceptions to accommodate a clearly user-friendly site.

I am always fascinated with this conclusion. Reason? I would never have the audacity to demand that the *Wall Street Journal* newspaper publish one of my articles on its front page, every day, and provide a link to my Web site. I doubt that any major company or well-known organization would, either. Yet people who work for these same groups have no problems making the same demand of the commercial Web search engines.

If your boss, clients, or other powers-that-be insist on search engine submission as a job responsibility or a required client service, the pages you should submit to the search engines are the home page, site map, and/or site index, and pages that are properly optimized. Some search engines only need your home page URL, and search engines should be able to crawl the rest of your Web site from the links on your home page and subsequent navigation schemes and cross-linking on other Web pages. Nonetheless, always be sure that your home page is properly optimized.

To get optimal visibility in search engine results, keywords and keyword phrases must be placed strategically throughout your Web pages. To summarize, keywords need to be placed in:

- Title tags
- Visible body text
- Within or near hypertext links
- Meta tags
- Alternative text
- URL (subdomain, subdirectory, and/or file names)

Your title tags, visible body text, and anchor text are considered primary text because all of the major search engines place a great deal of emphasis on this text. Meta-tag content, alternative text, and URL structure text are considered secondary text because not all search engines use this text to determine rankings.

To ensure that the search engines are able to find your optimized pages, your site designer should provide multiple means for the search engine spiders to access those pages. Effective cross-linking within your site is beneficial for both your site's visitors and the search engine spiders. If cross-linking is too difficult or time consuming to implement, creating and submitting a site map will give spiders access to many URLs within your site. However, a site map is often used as a Band-Aid for poor or substandard information architecture. Be prepared to re-evaluate your site's information architecture and interface if you find that the only way search engines access most of your site's content is via a site map.

With free submission, it can take anywhere from a few weeks to a few months for your pages to appear in the search results. If your search engine marketing campaign has specific deadlines, using paid inclusion programs and pay-per-click search engines are your best options because of the quick turnaround time.

To succeed with both paid inclusion programs and pay-per-click search engine advertising, remember their unique characteristics. Pages submitted to paid inclusion programs must be properly optimized to rank well. Select only your best optimized, most targeted pages for paid inclusion programs.

Effective pay-per-click search engine advertising involves careful keyword research and selection as well as writing a series of ads. Designing and/or selecting appropriate landing pages for your pay-per-click advertising are also essential. Design landing pages and write a series of possible ads *before* you sign up for any pay-per-click program.

Search engine submission checklist

To avoid potential spidering and indexing difficulties, duplicate/redundant content delivery, spam penalties, and wasted time and effort, review your site using the following checklist to be sure your site is ready for submission.

☐ Yes	☐ No	Are you creating Web pages with content your target audience is interested in reading?
☐ Yes	☐ No	Does your content contain highly focused keyword phrases rather than phrases that are too general and competitive?

❏ Yes   ❏ No   Are you optimizing your Web pages for at least three to five keywords at a time?

❏ Yes   ❏ No   Are you using regionally specific keywords, when applicable?

❏ Yes   ❏ No   Are you using the most commonly used variations of your keywords, based on your keyword research?

❏ Yes   ❏ No   Does each optimized page contain unique HTML title-tag content?

❏ Yes   ❏ No   Are you using multiple keywords in your title tags, using the power combo strategy, when appropriate?

❏ Yes   ❏ No   Are your most important keywords (a) appearing above-the-fold, and (b) throughout each optimized page?

❏ Yes   ❏ No   Are you including keywords in hypertext links whenever possible?

❏ Yes   ❏ No   Does each optimized page have at least one appropriate primary and secondary call to action?

❏ Yes   ❏ No   Does each optimized page contain a unique meta-tag description?

❏ Yes   ❏ No   Do your meta-tag descriptions contain both targeted keyword phrases and a call to action?

❏ Yes   ❏ No   Does each optimized page contain a unique meta-tag keyword list?

❏ Yes   ❏ No   Does each set of meta-tag keywords contain words and phrases that you actually use within the visible body text?

❏ Yes   ❏ No   Do you place common misspellings of your keywords within your meta-tag keywords?

❏ Yes   ❏ No   Do your graphic images contain descriptive keywords within the alternative text attribute when appropriate?

❏ Yes   ❏ No   Do you provide at least two means of navigating your site: one for your site visitors and one for the search engines?

❏ Yes   ❏ No   Does your site have a site map and/or a site index to assist both your visitors and the search engine spiders?

❏ Yes   ❏ No   If your site uses frames, is your site navigational with and without the frameset?

❏ Yes   ❏ No   If you are using JavaScript on your site, did you place the JavaScript in an external .js file?

❏ Yes   ❏ No   If you are using Cascading Style Sheets on your site, did you place the style sheets in an external .css file?

continues

(continued)

❏ Yes ❏ No   Do you have any redirects on your site? If so, have you placed the Robots Exclusion Protocol or appropriate 301 redirects on pages that use redirects? Search engines will list the destination URL.

❏ Yes ❏ No   Are your most important optimized pages placed in the root directory (along with your home page) on your Web server? Or if your site's URLs are dynamically generated, are the most important URLs as short and easy to read as possible?

❏ Yes ❏ No   Is your robots.txt file placed in the root directory on your Web server? Did you remember to transfer your robots.txt file before you transfer any other Web pages to your server?

❏ Yes ❏ No   Are you using subdomains or subdirectories, and is the content for each subdomain or subdirectory unique and substantial?

❏ Yes ❏ No   If you are submitting pages to non-U.S. search engines, are you writing your pages in the appropriate language?

❏ Yes ❏ No   If it is within your budget, do you submit your optimized pages to paid inclusion programs?

❏ Yes ❏ No   If you use pay-for-placement search engine advertising, are your keyword purchases based on detailed keyword research and selection?

❏ Yes ❏ No   If you use pay-for-placement search engine advertising, do you carefully monitor your bids to get the best search engine visibility at the most reasonable cost?

❏ Yes ❏ No   Did you name your Web pages something that your target audience will remember easily, using keywords whenever possible and appropriate?

❏ Yes ❏ No   Did you design or select a series of landing pages for your pay-for-placement advertising? If the landing pages do not contain substantially unique content, did you place the Robots Exclusion Protocol on those pages?

❏ Yes ❏ No   Do the search engines and your site visitors view the same content? (The only exception to this rule is sites that participate in XML-feed programs.)

The time between page submission and addition of the page to the index is called the search engine lead time. You will not see results in your site statistics software until the lead time has passed.

Position checking software

Many search engine marketers like to check positions using automated query software to see if a Web page listing has been added to the search engine index and to see how the page ranks.

Unfortunately, all of the major search engines frown on this practice. The goal of this practice is primarily to tweak a site for positioning purposes, not to create content that truly benefits site visitors. Furthermore, the use of automated position checking software places a considerable load on the search engines' servers. For these reasons, many search engines have tried to limit or ban this software usage.

Too many search engine marketers focus only on positioning without reviewing the Web site's entire online marketing processes and how they interact with each other. Top positions are useless if your target audience is not clicking on the links to your site and converting into customers. In addition, search engine positions alone do not communicate desired user behavior, or the roadblocks that inhibit desired user behavior. Instead of overzealously focusing on maintaining top positioning, online marketers should spend more time and money measuring and analyzing visitor behavior.

Therefore, when checking the effectiveness of your search engine marketing campaign, do not rely on position checking software. Rather, monitor your site statistics software to see how your target audience is finding and using your site.

How To Resubmit a Listing

If your site is listed in one or more of the major Web directories, search engines usually will find your new and updated pages without resubmission. Therefore, resubmission is not a necessity. However, resubmission alerts the search engine spiders and directory editors that you have made changes to pages on your site.

The search engine spiders will usually find your site's new information each time they visit your site, generally every two to eight weeks. Web directories are different. Remember, editors are sorting through hundreds of submissions per day. They might not notice the subtle changes on your site. Therefore, if your business has significantly changed, your URL or company name has changed, or your site clearly belongs in a different category, resubmission to Web directories is essential to preserve the factual representation of your Web site in the directories.

Modifying a Web directory listing

Once your site has been added to a Web directory, you should not have to request a modification unless your business or organization name, company location, domain name or URL has changed. Another good reason to request a listing modification is if your company no longer offers a product or service that is shown in your site description.

For example, suppose your business no longer offers a service that is shown in your site description. Directory editors will be more than happy to modify that description because the description no longer illustrates, accurately, the contents of your Web site. If your business no longer offers a specific product and that product is reflected in the directory category, then directory editors will allow you to change your category. Editors want the information in their directories to be accurate.

One of the simplest changes to request is a regional listing. If your site has a regional listing and your main office is no longer in that region, directory editors want you to modify the listing to the more appropriate region. Quite often, if you modify the physical address on your Web site, a directory editor might notice and move your site to the more appropriate regional category without the site owner taking any action. However, it is always best to point out this modification to the editors right away rather than wait for an editor to discover it.

Careful record keeping can make the change process move more smoothly. If you have a tracking or order number, the initial date(s) of submission, and the other relevant information, directory editors will be able to locate your site more quickly and make any suggested modifications.

If a Web directory has a Change Request Form, fill it out exactly as requested. If a directory allows paid, expedited submission with its Change Request Form and your budget will allow it, the change request will be processed more quickly.

Most Web directories do not allow for expedited submission, however, and the change requests might take some time to process. Again, careful record keeping is essential in order to get the best results.

With a Web directory, your site must be reviewed first, accepted into the directory, and then added to the database. This lead time for free Web directory submission is generally between three to four weeks, but could take as long as four months.

If your change request has not been added to a Web directory within a specified lead time, then resubmit the Change Request Form. Wait another three to four weeks to allow directory editors time to evaluate and process your suggested modifications.

In the event that your change request is not processed after three submissions, then contact a Web directory representative via email. Immediately following your third change request, send an email to the appropriate editor. Figure 4-13 shows a sample email to Yahoo requesting a category and a description change for the fictional TranquiliTeas Web site:

Figure 4-13

Sample email requesting a change to a Yahoo listing.

To: url-support@yahoo-inc.com

Dear Yahoo,

I am writing you regarding the following URL:

http://www.tranquiliteasorganic.com/

In your directory, the title of the site is "TranquiliTeas Organic Tea" and the Express order number for the initial submission is #XXXXXXX. The current description is as follows:

"Whol-esale organic tea distributor specializing in oolong, green, herbal, decaffeinated, and black teas. Choose from loose tea or tea bags."

The site is currently listed under the category:

Regional > U.S. States > Washington > Cities > Seattle > Business and Shopping > Business to Business > Food and Beverage > Beverages > Coffee and Tea

I have filled out the Change Request Form, exactly as instructed on your Web site, on the following dates:

MM/DD/YY – first submission

MM/DD/YY – second submission

MM/DD/YY – third submission

Since I understand that Yahoo likes to have the most accurate, up-to-date information in the directory, I would like to be sure that our listing reflects your standards.

The current regional category is no longer accurate since we moved our offices to Chicago. We have reflected this change on our Web site on the About Us page and the Locations page. We request that our current listing be moved to the following category:

Regional > U.S. States > Illinois Cities > Chicago > Business and Shopping > Business to Business > Business and Shopping > Shopping and Services > Food and Drink > Drinks > Coffee and Tea

Also, our company no longer offers herbal teas; therefore, the current description does not accurately reflect the contents of our site. We request that our current description be modified to state:

"Wholesale organic tea distributor specializing in oolong, green, decaffeinated, and black teas. Choose from loose tea or tea bags."

We have also reflected this change in the Products section and throughout the entire Web site.

Thank you for your time and consideration.

Sincerely,

John Doe, Marketing Director
TranquiliTeas Organic Tea, Inc.

info@tranquiliteasorganic.com

The person who made the initial submission to a Web directory should be the person sending the change request email. If a different person is sending this email, be sure to mention the initial submitter's name and email address in a short paragraph at the beginning of the letter. Let the editors know that you are the new person responsible for your Web site.

Free submission

Check your site statistics software regularly to see when the site has been modified in a Web directory, or just search for your listing within the directory. If your site has not been added to a directory within three to four weeks, then resubmit. Keep track of your dates of submission, categories, descriptions, and titles.

In the event that your change request is not accepted into a Web directory after three submissions, then contact a directory representative via email.

Paid submission

If paid submission is within your budget, use this method for directory resubmission. The turnaround time is much faster.

If your submission is rejected

Submissions are rejected for a variety of reasons. The site might be submitted to the wrong category. The site might not offer truly unique content. The Web server might not have been functioning properly when a directory editor was evaluating a submission. The designer left some "Under Construction" pages on the site. The description might not accurately reflect the contents of the site being submitted.

If your submission is rejected, try to find out why. If you can find out the specific reason, it will be easier to appeal the decision. For example, if your site was rejected because it contained " Under Construction" pages, those pages can be easily removed.

Other rejections are not so easily appealed. In one situation, a Web site owner created a unique glossary of over 1,000 terms on her site. The content was truly unique because it encompassed a specific industry, and most of the definitions were not available in other glossaries currently listed in the Web directory. After the main site was accepted, the Web site owner submitted this glossary to an additional category. Figure 4-14 is an email excerpt from Yahoo explaining the initial reason the additional listing was rejected:

Figure 4-14

Excerpt from a Yahoo! rejection email.

> We're sorry to report that we've decided not to include your site in the Yahoo! directory. The URL appears to be part of a larger site that is already listed in Yahoo!. After reviewing both your URL and the existing URL that encompasses it, we've determined that the existing listing is adequate for users to find your site.
>
> The Yahoo! Express Terms of Service state that in order to be listed in the Yahoo! directory, a site must meet the following minimum criteria:
>
> "The site must contain substantively unique content that is not already accessible in the Yahoo! directory." In general, rather than separately listing every sub-page of a large site, we try to find the core or hub page of the site and point users to that. Our users appreciate this because it means they do not have to sift through multiple listings from the same site, and it gives your site more prominence as it won't get lost among many separate listings of other sites.
>
> If you have questions, or would like to request a reconsideration of this decision, please email us within 30 days by replying to this message.

If a submission is rejected, in general, you have 30 days to appeal the decision. When appealing via email, above all, be polite. Directory editors are human beings. They are looking out for the best interests of their end users. If they rejected your submission, they have reasons to do so, though you might not agree with them.

Figure 4-15 shows a sample email we helped our client write to Yahoo to appeal a rejection email. After reviewing the contents of this email, the additional listing was accepted.

Remember, editors are looking out for the best interest of their directories and their end users. They are not looking out for the best interest of your individual Web site. If they feel that your resubmissions meet their guidelines, then your site will be accepted and/or modified.

Search engine resubmission

As stated previously, crawler-based search engines will find your new and updated pages without resubmission. Therefore, resubmission is not always necessary.

Sometimes, due to technical reasons, a page might be dropped from a search engine index. For example, your Web host might have upgraded or rebooted your server when a search engine spider visited your site, making it impossible or difficult for the spider to

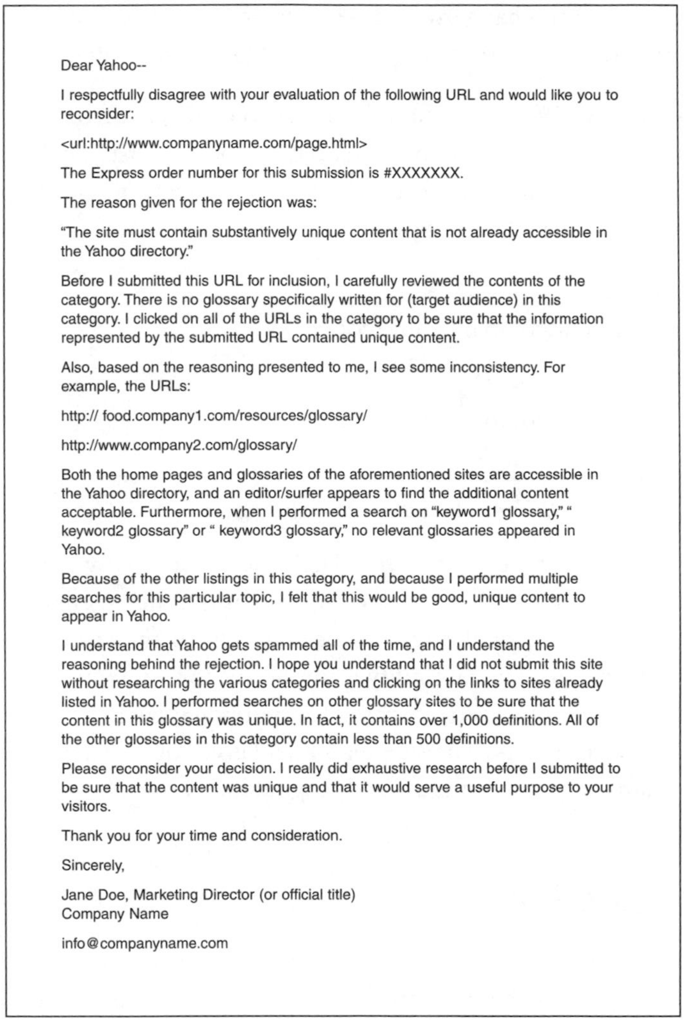

Dear Yahoo--

I respectfully disagree with your evaluation of the following URL and would like you to reconsider:

<url:http://www.companyname.com/page.html>

The Express order number for this submission is #XXXXXXX.

The reason given for the rejection was:

"The site must contain substantively unique content that is not already accessible in the Yahoo directory."

Before I submitted this URL for inclusion, I carefully reviewed the contents of the category. There is no glossary specifically written for (target audience) in this category. I clicked on all of the URLs in the category to be sure that the information represented by the submitted URL contained unique content.

Also, based on the reasoning presented to me, I see some inconsistency. For example, the URLs:

http:// food.company1.com/resources/glossary/

http://www.company2.com/glossary/

Both the home pages and glossaries of the aforementioned sites are accessible in the Yahoo directory, and an editor/surfer appears to find the additional content acceptable. Furthermore, when I performed a search on "keyword1 glossary," " keyword2 glossary" or " keyword3 glossary," no relevant glossaries appeared in Yahoo.

Because of the other listings in this category, and because I performed multiple searches for this particular topic, I felt that this would be good, unique content to appear in Yahoo.

I understand that Yahoo gets spammed all of the time, and I understand the reasoning behind the rejection. I hope you understand that I did not submit this site without researching the various categories and clicking on the links to sites already listed in Yahoo. I performed searches on other glossary sites to be sure that the content in this glossary was unique. In fact, it contains over 1,000 definitions. All of the other glossaries in this category contain less than 500 definitions.

Please reconsider your decision. I really did exhaustive research before I submitted to be sure that the content was unique and that it would serve a useful purpose to your visitors.

Thank you for your time and consideration.

Sincerely,

Jane Doe, Marketing Director (or official title)
Company Name

info@companyname.com

Figure 4-15
Sample appeal letter sent to Yahoo.

access your pages for a short, temporary period. Pages that have been dropped can be safely resubmitted, as long as they are not spam pages.

If a page is already in a search engine index, do not resubmit the page unless you have updated with new and significant information. If the information is significant, then visitors should be able to view that information change in a standard Web browser. Changes in your visible body text, and the addition or modification of a product photo, constitute a significant change.

An insignificant change would be rewriting a meta-tag description or a title tag purely to increase search engine positioning.

To see if your Web pages have been added or deleted from a search engine, go to each of the major search engine sites listed below and type in the string listed below the search engine name. Replace "companyname.com" with your domain.

- Google
  site:www.companyname.com

- Live (Microsoft)
  site:www.companyname.com

- Yahoo (Site Explorer)
  Use http://siteexplorer.search.yahoo.com/

You can also type in the full URL (www.companyname.com/pagename.html) or info:www.companyname.com/pagename.html to see if an individual page has been added to the search engine index. If search engine visibility is important for individual targeted pages within a site, then searching for individual URLs versus a site can be an easier task. The site: search will give you a general idea of how many pages are in the search engine index overall.

Conclusion

Effective link development campaigns are crucial to your site's search engine visibility. Web directories generally allow Web site owners one chance to submit correctly, with few exceptions. Objective, third party link development is an ongoing process. With the crawler-based search engines, spiders should be able to find your pages without direct submission as long as the URLs exist on your Web server.

A Web site is always a work in progress. Technology and visitor preferences constantly evolve. With successful search engine optimization and careful traffic analysis, Web site owners can continually modify their sites for their visitors and maximum search engine visibility.

Part 5:

Best Practices: Dos and Don'ts of Search Engine Optimization

Parts 1 through 4 of this book presented strategies for creating a search engine friendly Web site. These strategies not only help increase your site's overall search engine visibility, but they also increase Web site usability, leading to increased visitor satisfaction, qualified leads, and closed sales. This section shows you what methodologies to avoid and addresses common misconceptions about search engine marketing.

To keep search results relevant and accurate, search engines actively work to thwart excessive and unethical optimization tactics. *Spamdexing*, commonly referred to as spam, is taking extreme or excessive measures to achieve top search engine positions. Spam is also using any words, HTML/XHTML code, scripting, or programming on a Web page that is not meant to benefit the user experience.

Many search engine optimization and marketing firms spend a great deal of time utilizing spam techniques to gain top search engine positions for their clients, particularly if clients are unwilling to modify their sites to be more search engine friendly and user friendly. The reason for this is twofold: First, many Web site owners do not want to accept that anything is wrong with their sites. Providing a consistent "sense of place" and "scent of information" is paramount to achieving both search engine visibility and a positive user experience. If a site is profitable without providing these two items, the owner often views the profitability as proof that the site does not need any modifications, making the Web site owner easy prey for search engine spammers.

Second, very few Web developers and search engine optimizers have education, training, or experience in user-centered design. Likewise, very few usability professionals have a background in search optimization. As a result, both groups feel that search engine optimization and Web site usability are at odds. They often conclude that search engine optimization techniques are done at the expense of site usability, and that optimization negatively impacts the user experience. In fact, making products, services, and information easy to find benefits the user experience and increases search engine visibility as well. I believe that this willful ignorance in both groups makes it easy for unethical search engine marketers to thrive in the information retrieval industry.

Although Web pages that achieve top positions through spam techniques often manage to slip through the search engines' spam filters, top positions achieved through spamming are generally sporadic and short-lived.

Another reason to avoid spamming the search engines is that search engines can penalize or permanently ban Web pages (and sites) from their indices if they detect excessive use of spam techniques. Your competitors or human "spam police" can also spot the use of spam techniques on Web pages. Never discount your competitors. They compete for the same positioning you desire, and if they can eliminate your site from top positions because of spam, they will not hesitate to report your site to the search engine spam police.

If a site is banned, it is placed on a search engine blacklist. The only way to have your site removed from the blacklist is to contact the group of search engine staff members who actually banned or penalized your site. Then you must convince someone in that group that you no longer practice the spam technique(s) that got your site banned. The odds of contacting the exact group or person who banned your site are not high. If your site is re-admitted to the search engine indices, future Web pages from your site are likely to be subject to higher scrutiny.

In my opinion, spamming the search engines is not an effective use of time or budget. The amount of effort required to trick and exploit the search engines would be better spent on developing a more effective Web site, one that pleases both your target audience and the search engines. Very few Web site owners, developers, and even usability professionals focus on building a strong search friendly foundation. Regrettably, many professional search engine marketing firms focus more on tricks and gimmicks than building a strong foundation.

What Is Search Engine Spam?

As much as we all would like the search engines to give us clear guidelines as to what does and does not constitute search engine spam, that is an unrealistic expectation. Once the search engines present a clear-cut spam guideline, unethical search engine marketers will try to implement exceptions to it. Then the search engines must update the guideline to include the new exceptions, and so on and so on. It will be a never-ending process. Therefore, the search engines present general rather than specific guidelines as to what constitutes spam.

Search engine spam is more about how and to what extent a marketing technique is used rather than *whether* a technique is used. In other words, the search quality team at the search engines will not automatically using a design technique if the technique is used in an appropriate manner. For example, a site that uses invisible DHTML layers for drop-down menus, such as the XYZ site (Figures 5-1 through 5-3) will not be penalized because the invisible navigation layers serve a specific purpose: to help site visitors navigate the Web site. However, if a design or writing technique is used to deliberately trick a search engine into offering inappropriate, irrelevant, redundant, or poor-quality search results, then the site will likely be penalized (or banned) for spamming.

Figure 5-1

An earlier version of the Position Technologies Web site uses DHTML layers as part of the navigation scheme. The menus are not visible to site visitors at first.

Figure 5-2

But when a visitor places his cursor over the top navigation, the menus appear. Since the menus are clearly meant to be seen by site visitors, even though they are not initially visible, the hidden DHTML layer is not considered search engine spam.

To determine whether a search engine marketing strategy is spam, ask yourself the following questions:

1. Does your site's content genuinely benefit your target audience and site visitors? (Hint: Do not ask anyone in your marketing or IT department. They are not the most objective people for determining the usefulness of your site's content. It is preferable to ask objective third parties such as new or current site visitors.)

2. Would you utilize a search engine marketing strategy if the commercial Web search engines did not exist?

3. Are you building pages primarily for Web search engine positioning?

If you answer yes to questions 1 and 2, and no to question 3, then in all likelihood the search quality team will not consider the use of your design or writing strategies as spam.

Types of Search Engine Spam

The Web search engines are commercial enterprises. They have a right to control how information is displayed in their search results. If a Web site does not follow a search engine's guidelines for inclusion, then the content of that site should not be made available in search results.

If the search quality team discovers that a Web site owner or search engine marketer is deliberately trying to trick the search engines into giving a Web page higher relevance than it deserves, the individual page, or the entire site, can be penalized. Most of the time, the search quality team will modify a search engine algorithm so that the spam pages will no longer appear at the top of search results. In more extreme cases, the page itself, or the whole site, will be removed from the search engine index. Therefore, avoid the following types of search engine spam:

Promoting Keywords Not Related to Your Web Site

To gain top search engine visibility, many spammers will place words on Web pages that are not related to the pages' actual content. For example, many people take the most popular search phrases (such as *sex* or a celebrity name) and place those words inside a meta tag only because the word is popular, not because the word relates to the content of a Web page.

As a general guideline, if you are not using a keyword or keyword phrase on the visible content of your Web pages, then do not place it in your meta tags, title tags, alternative text, or CSS layers.

Keyword Stacking

Keyword stacking is the repeated use of a keyword or keyword phrase to artificially boost a Web page's relevancy in the search engines. Keyword stacking, at its simplest level, looks like the following:

> organic tea organic tea organic tea organic tea organic tea
> organic tea organic tea organic tea tea tea tea tea tea tea
> tea tea tea tea tea tea tea tea tea tea tea tea tea tea tea
> tea tea tea tea tea tea tea tea

No matter where this type of text is placed, it is still considered search engine spam because the wording is gibberish and is clearly there to boost relevancy, not to benefit site visitors.

Keyword Stuffing

Keyword stacking and keyword stuffing often have the same meaning. Some search engine marketers differentiate the two forms of spam. Keyword stacking often refers to the writing of gibberish "sentences." Keyword stuffing usually refers to placing gibberish "sentences" inside graphic images or Cascading Style Sheet layers.

For example, many unethical search engine marketers will create a small, transparent image called blank.gif, clear.gif, spacer.gif, or shim.gif, ranging from 1 x 1 pixel to 25 x 25 pixels. Then they will place a series of keywords in the alternative text of the graphic image. The HTML code for keyword stuffing generally looks like the following:

```
<img src="images/blank.gif" alt="organic tea organic teas
Organic Tea Organic Teas ORGANIC TEA ORGANIC TEAS" />
```

If you place text inside a graphic image that: (a) does not describe the graphic image, or (b) describes the graphic image and the page/section of the Web site where it appears, then the search engines will consider the text to be spam. Below is an example of acceptable alternative text:

```
<img src="images/green-tea.gif" width="75" height="125"
alt="Organic loose leaf green tea – product photo" />
```

Hidden Text

As stated previously, in order for Web pages to appear at the top of search results, the words that your target audience types into a search query should be used on your Web pages. One way to place keywords on your Web pages without changing the look and-feel of your site design is to hide the text, or make it invisible.

Hidden keywords and keyword phrases are supposed to be visible to search engine spiders but not to site visitors.

Unethical search engine marketers can make text invisible via multiple means:

- Using colored text on a same-colored background. Common ways of doing this include using <font> tags, tricky graphic images, and Cascading Style Sheet attributes and layers.

- Using hidden text in the HTML forms tag <input type= "hidden" /> even though a Web page does not contain a form.

- Placing keywords between the <noframes> and </noframes> tags even though the page layout is not a frameset.

- Placing keywords between the <script> and <noscript> tags when no scripts are used on a Web page. The <noscript> tag is text that is meant to display in the event that a script is not executed. The <noscript> tag is not meant as a "secret hiding place" for keyword stuffing.

As a rule, anything on a Web page not meant to be seen or detected at any time by your site's visitors is considered spam. Since most browsers support frames and JavaScript, there is little or no need to use <noframes> and <noscript> tags anymore. Furthermore, the search engines have been aware of keyword stuffing in these tags for years, and they place little or no relevance on this text.

Tiny Text

Many spammers understand that hidden text can get their pages penalized, so they will place keywords at the bottom of a Web page. They will format this text with an extremely small typeface and in a color that is not the same color as a background, but light enough so that it is difficult to read.

Even though the tiny text is visible, it is often illegible. In other words, if the text on your Web pages is too tiny for your site visitors to read, then the tiny text is considered search engine spam.

Hidden Links

The legitimate purpose of creating hypertext and graphic-image links is to have people click on them. Unethical search engine marketers who create links that people cannot detect or will have a difficult time detecting, are, in essence, deceiving these people. Therefore, hidden links are generally considered spam.

Ways of hiding links include but are not limited to:

- Using the same font attributes (color, size, etc.) for a hypertext link as your regular text.
- Surrounding a punctuation mark with a hyperlink.
- Surrounding a transparent image with a hyperlink.
- Placing hyperlinks in invisible CSS layers—layers never meant to be seen by site visitors.
- Placing hundreds or thousands of links inside of a small graphic image.

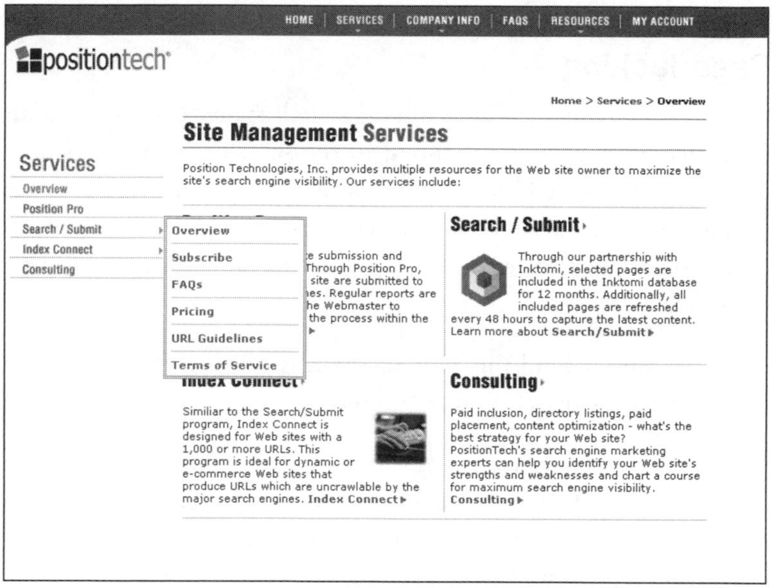

Figure 5-3
A drop-down menu as a navigational element, though initially invisible, is ultimately meant to be seen and to be used by site visitors.

Artificial Link Farms and Web Rings

In an attempt to boost the link component of a search engine algorithm, many spammers create multiple Web sites whose sole purpose is to link with each other. Free-for-all (FFA) Web sites are an example of artificial link farms.

All of the search engines make it very clear that linking to "bad neighborhoods" can get a site into trouble. Though no one can control which Web sites link to your site, you have total control over which sites you link to. Therefore, if your site links to another site that is considered a "bad neighborhood," such as free-for-all (FFA) Web sites, your site can be penalized.

Creating Web rings for the sole purpose of increasing popularity can also be considered spam, especially if the sites linking to each other are not related. For example, a dating service Web site has nothing to do with an auto parts Web site.

As a general rule, if a hyperlink is not created to be followed by humans, or the hyperlink is not designed to be read by humans, then it is probably spam.

Page Swapping, Bait-and-Switch, and Page Jacking

Page swapping, also called bait-and-switch spam, occurs when an optimized Web page is submitted to the search engines, and then the page is "swapped" for a different one after a top search engine position has been attained. Search engines are supposed to view an optimized page; end users are supposed to view a different page altogether.

The reasoning behind this type of spam is to prevent others from stealing a page's search engine "secrets."

Unfortunately, page swapping often happens concurrently with stolen content. Unethical search engine marketers find a high-ranking Web page and copy its content. Sometimes, they will change the company name but nothing else. The page with the stolen content is submitted to the search engines. Once the stolen page gets a top search engine position, a different Web page is placed on the server. The practice of stealing content from other Web sites is called *page jacking*.

Bait-and-switch spam occurs in the commercial Web directories as well. To artificially boost link popularity, unethical Web marketers will submit a "fake" Web site to the directories. Once the site is accepted, another Web site is put up in its place.

Page swapping is a difficult practice to maintain. No one knows when or how often a search engine spider will visit a site. So a swapped page's position is always temporary.

Furthermore, if content is stolen from a Web page, and the original author discovers the online thievery, the spammer could be faced with a copyright and/or trademark lawsuit.

Redirects

Another way that spammers switch Web pages is by using a redirect. A *redirect* is HTML coding, programming, or scripting that is placed on a Web page so that page visitors are sent to a different URL after a specified period of time, often zero seconds. One of the most common ways to redirect is a meta-refresh tag, which looks like the following:

```
<META HTTP-EQUIV="refresh" content="0; URL=http://www.
domainname.com/differentpage.html" />
```

With redirection, spammers create an optimized page for a particular keyword phrase. The optimized page, with the redirect, is submitted to the search engines. If the optimized page gets a top search engine position, anyone clicking on the link to this page is automatically sent to a different page called a *destination page*. The destination page does not contain the same content as the optimized page. In fact, the destination page often does not contain the same keywords as the optimized pages.

To combat this type of spam, many search engines will not accept any type of redirection other than the HTTP 301 (permanent) redirect. Most of the time, the search engines will list the destination page, not the page that contains the redirect. Some search engines allow a 302 (temporary) redirect; however, since search engine spammers discovered ways to exploit the search engines using this type of redirect, I do not recommend using it unless it is absolutely necessary for your type of Web site and individual situation. In other words, using 302 redirects to increase search engine visibility is considered redirect spam.

If you find yourself in a situation where your design calls for a redirect, the redirect timing must last long enough for your site's visitors to read the content. Most of the time, 15 seconds will not cause a spam penalty. With some content management systems, however, a 15-second delay might not be a reasonable solution. To be 100% safe, use a 30-second delay.

Another solution is to place the robots exclusion protocol on any page that contains a redirect.

Mirror or Duplicate Pages

Both search engines and their end users do not want the same Web sites dominating search results. For this reason, most search engines now cluster their search results. *Clustering* generally allows only one or two pages per Web site to be displayed in the top search results.

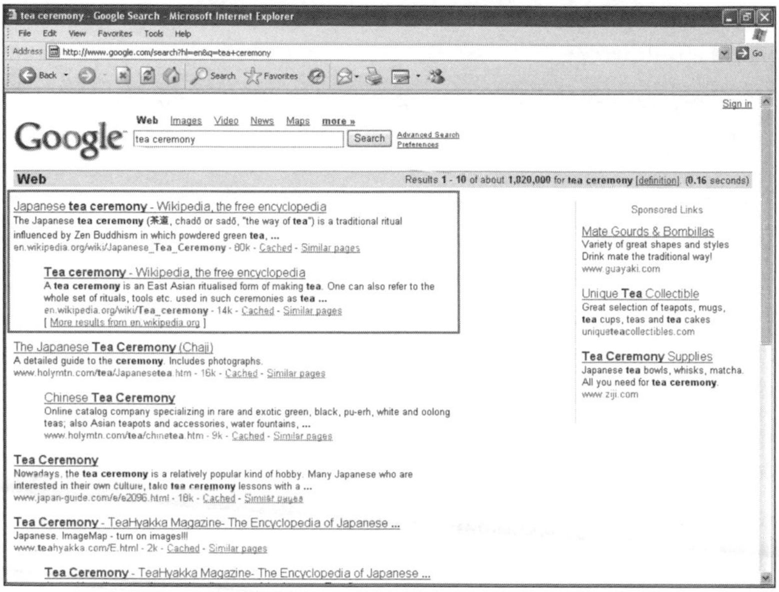

Figure 5-4

Example of clustering Web pages from the same site in Google.

All too often, spammers will duplicate or slightly modify a Web page. Then, the spammers will submit hundreds or thousand of pages with tiny modifications to a search engine. For example, two pages might have identical content and different title tags. And two other pages might have identical content and different meta tags. If any of the submitted pages ranks well for a specific keyword phrase, then all of the pages with slight modifications can dominate a search engine's top search results.

Think about any search you performed that showed the same company over and over again. If you did not like the information the first time you visited the company's site, you will not like it the second, third, fourth, or fifth time you viewed the same information.

Duplicate (or redundant) content is a common occurrence with affiliate and reseller sites. Affiliates and resellers are essentially providing the same information on their Web sites as the original corporate site. Again, if you, the end user, did not like the information presented on the corporate site, in all likelihood you will not like the same information on an affiliate site.

So search engines tend to reject affiliate and reseller sites due to duplicate content. And if they find duplicate Web pages or Web sites, they try to eliminate at least one of them through duplicate content filters.

Doorway, Gateway, and Hallway Pages

Doorway pages, gateway pages, and hallway pages are not created for the benefit of site visitors. They are created specifically for obtaining high search engine positions. That is the main reason the search engines consider doorway pages to be spam.

Doorway page companies generally create thousands of pages for a single keyword or keyword phrase. Generally these pages are fed to the search engines through the free submit pages. Since doorway pages are built specifically to rank, the search engines indices are essentially polluted with Web pages containing unnecessary and redundant information. Doorway pages are generally not very pleasant to look at, and they often contain so much gibberish that they have to be cloaked.

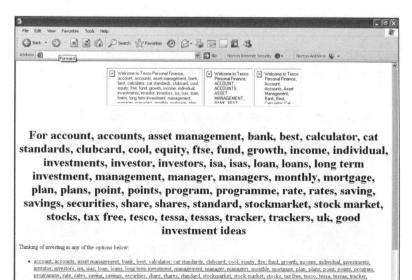

Figure 5-5
An example of an "ugly" doorway page, probably generated by software rather than a professional Web designer/developer.

As companies evolved, doorway pages started to look better. You might be surprised at the well-known, multimillion-dollar search engine marketing firms that utilize doorway pages to generate search engine traffic.

Figure 5-6

An example of a "pretty" doorway page created by an unethical SEO firm. At first glance, most people think it's a normal Web page. Upon further investigation, search engines determined that it was a page created primarily for generating search engine traffic. This page (and others like it) was eventually banned in Google.

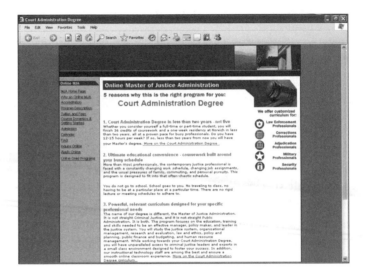

To generate relevant cross-linking to doorway pages, spammers often create a separate site map that links specifically to the doorway pages. A site map to doorway pages is commonly referred to as a hallway page, as shown in Figure 5-7:

Figure 5-7

Hallway page example.

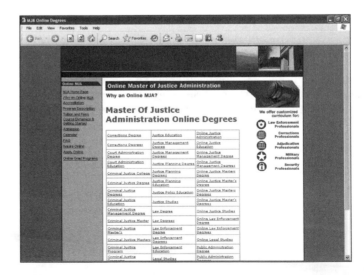

Search engine spammers might not create a stand-alone hallway page to link to doorway pages. They might also put links to hallway pages within an actual site map or site index. Regardless, the majority of doorway pages are considered search engine spam, and this methodology should be avoided.

Cloaking

Cloaking is the technique of feeding search engine spiders one Web page, and feeding all other end users a different Web page. Since the majority (over 95%) of cloaked content is meant to deceive or exploit the search engines, only in rare situations will the search engines allow cloaked content into their indices.

One example of acceptable cloaking is participating in a search engine's trusted feed program. Another might be stripping session IDs from a URL string. However, before implementing parameter stripping via cloaking, make sure you inform the search engines that you are doing so. Search engines have become more effective at stripping session ID parameters off the end of URL strings.

Domain Spam and Mirror Sites

Domain spam is the practice of purchasing multiple domain names and building sites with identical or nearly identical content in them. The purpose of utilizing domain spam is to get multiple listings in Web directories to achieve link popularity and more traffic. The resulting link popularity in the directories helps boost search engine visibility.

A warning sign that you might be dealing with domain spam is if you hear the terms *micro-site* or *mini-site*. This type of spam can also be done with subdomains.

Search engines and directories respond to domain spam by removing all the mirror sites. If the domain spam is particularly egregious, they will permanently remove all the sites from their indices.

Mini-Sites

Mini-sites are small sites created purely to boost search engine visibility. The word *small* is somewhat deceptive because many of these sites might contain 10,000-plus dynamically generated pages.

Other names for mini-sites include:

- Micro sites
- Satellite sites
- Magnet sites
- Shadow domains/sites

Search engine optimization is a service that should always be implemented on pages from your Web site, your domain. Optimization should not be implemented on a new site hosted on the optimization firm's server. Of course, there are legitimate reasons for creating separate sites.

One of the many persuasive sales pitches for creating mini-sites is tracking purposes. How are search engine optimization firms supposed to track their successes if they are unable to determine positioning and the number of clicks that deliver potential buyers to your site? This sales pitch might seem reasonable at first, but when you dig for more information, you might find that the mini-site:

1. Contains thousands or millions of illegible doorway pages.
2. Contains redirects to pages on your Web site.
3. Is cloaked from human viewing.
4. Participates in free-for-all (FFA) link farms to gain link popularity.

Remember, the definition of search engine spam is pages or sites created deliberately to trick the search engine into offering inappropriate, redundant, or poor-quality search results. Since micro-sites are created purely for search engine positioning and not for human viewing, most micro-sites can be considered search engine spam.

Typo Spam/Cybersquatting

Web site owners who purchase domain names for the sole purpose of tricking end users to visit their sites can be considered spammers. For example, a cybersquatter might purchase the domain name Yahhoo.com to try to steal some of Yahoo's traffic.

Google is particularly picky about this form of spam, and will penalize sites that cybersquat. In fact, cybersquatting is illegal in many countries.

Blog/Forum Spam

Since many blog and forum Web sites allow signature files with hyperlinks, including hyperlinked URLs (Web addresses), many search engine spammers post to as many blog and forum sites as possible in order to boost a site's link popularity. In fact, the term *splog* has become a part of the search engine spam vocabulary. A splog is a Web log (blog) site that the author uses primarily to produce false or deceptive link popularity. Splogs often contain gibberish or hijacked content from other Web pages.

Some search engine spammers have even developed software that creates *unlimited variations* of content (so that the variations can slip through a search engine's duplicate content filters), and posts the variations to individual, targeted blog sites.

Fortunately, search engine software engineers caught onto blog/forum spam right away due to rampant abuse. Now, search engines give these types of links less weight than other types of links.

In addition, smart blog and forum moderators realize that these types of links only hurt their sites' search engine visibility in the long run, and they actively remove the links or put a *nofollow* attribute on the link.

Removing a Search Engine Spam Penalty or Ban

In my work, I see search engine penalties and blacklisting all the time. Because most companies are not exposed to this experience on a frequent basis, they might not appreciate how much work Google, Yahoo, and other major search engines put into the quality of their search results. Usually, it takes a spam penalty or blacklist to make them see the light.

Is It Worth the Risk?

Many unethical search engine marketers do not care about getting sites penalized or blacklisted because they merely abandon the domains and set up new ones, essentially playing a cat-and-mouse game. Is being invisible in organic search results pages worth the risk of being penalized or banned? Only a Web site owner can determine whether he or she wants to take the risk or not.

Personally, I have seen how much it costs when a site is blacklisted. Web site owners typically have to spend thousands or millions of dollars in search engine advertising to maintain search engine visibility. Since most searchers click on the organic search results more frequently than they click on search engine ads, one can easily see how quickly advertising costs can accumulate.

Likewise, more costs are accumulated for development time and repairing the damage, especially if a large number of "fake" Web sites and link farms have been created. Legal expenses can be a huge concern. Many search engine optimization firms use other people's or other companies' copyrighted material on the "fake" sites, and no company is prepared for the copyright infringement lawsuit that follows. Both firms can be sued—the search engine optimization firm and the company that hired it.

For these and many other reasons, I do not believe exploiting the search engines is worth the risk.

Nonetheless, I do encounter companies that have hired unethical search engine marketing firms whose actions led to a site penalty or blacklisting. Part of my job is to help these sites get back into the good graces of search engine software engineers. What follows are the steps that I take to assist Web site owners in this process:

Determine Technical Reasons for Blocking Search Engines

Before assuming that a site has been banned or penalized in a search engine, always look for technical reasons that the site might not be included in the index.

Robots exclusion and other technical issues

One of the first steps I take is to review the robots exclusion protocol text file (if used) and the robots exclusion meta tags. Sometimes, when launching a redesigned Web site, developers forget to remove the robots.txt file from the server, or forget to format the robots.txt file to let the search engines know that it is OK to crawl the newly designed site.

Other technical reasons that a site might not be included in a search engine index:

- Site has been recently redesigned or updated with new technology, which prevents search engine spiders from crawling the site (such as requiring cookies).

- URL structure generated from a newly implemented content management system (CMS) is not search engine friendly.

- Using a single navigation scheme that search engine spiders cannot follow, such as a forms-based navigation. Search engines do not fill out forms.

- Log-in requirement—search engines will not log in.

Index count

One way to determine whether a search engine is crawling your site and accessing your site's content is to determine the *index count*, which is the number of URLs in the search engine index. Remember, a Web page cannot rank unless it is in the search engine index.

You can get a general idea of your site's index count by performing the following searches. On Google and Ask, substitute your site's domain name for "yourdomain.com":

site:yourdomain.com

or

site:www.yourdomain.com

Figure 5-8

Example of an index count search in Google. To get a more accurate index count, use Google's Webmaster Central currently available at http://www.google.com/webmasters/.

Microsoft's Live search has a similar query string, and you can also use the Advanced Search page to perform the same query:

site:yourdomain.com

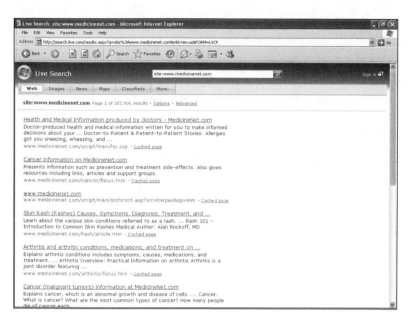

Figure 5-9
Example of an index count
search on Microsoft's Live.

Yahoo recently launched the Site Explorer section of its site to help
Webmasters and online marketers analyze their sites for Yahoo:

Figure 5-10
Example of an index count
search on Yahoo's Site
Explorer feature.

Tip

Reviewing your Web analytics data will also provide clear evidence as to whether the search engines are crawling your site. A drop in crawling is also an indication that a site might have been penalized.

Why is the index count so important for determining search engine spam? A sudden drop in index count without any corresponding technical issues can be an indication that the site has been penalized or banned. However, make sure technical issues are addressed before assuming that a site has been penalized.

Link development

Another indication that a site has been penalized or blacklisted is a sudden drop in link development. In all likelihood, a site will merely disappear from top search results because the search quality team discovered FFA link farms and have banned those sites from the index. Of course, banning links to a site will directly affect a site's search engine visibility.

To determine a site's general link development, perform the following searches. On Google, Live, and Ask, substitute your site's domain name for "yourdomain.com":

link:www.yourdomain.com

Figure 5-11

Example of a link development search on Google. To get a more accurate assessment of your site's link development, use Google's Webmaster Central currently available at http://www.google.com/webmasters/.

Currently, in order to view link development on Yahoo, searchers must use the Site Explorer section of the site.

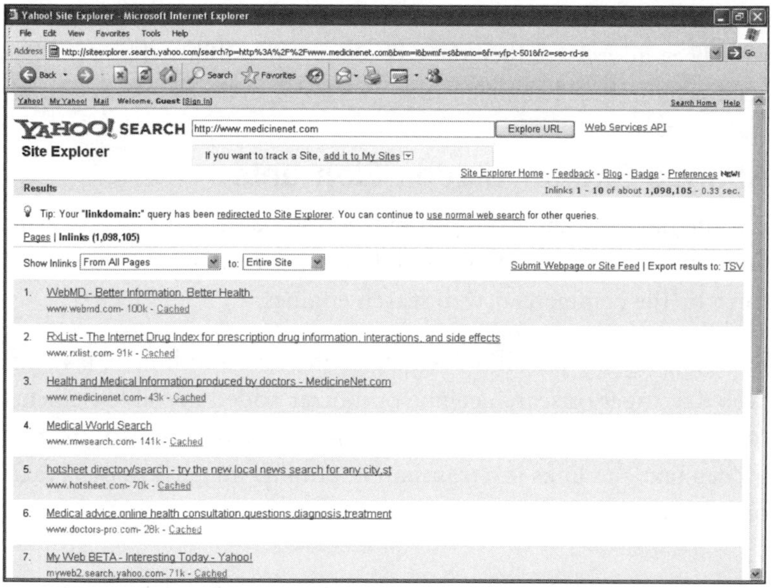

Figure 5-12

Example of a link development search on Yahoo's Site Explorer feature.

A sudden drop in a site's link development usually means that the search quality team has removed poor-quality links pointing to a Web site. If a site's entire link development has suddenly disappeared from Google, for example, the search results will look like the following:

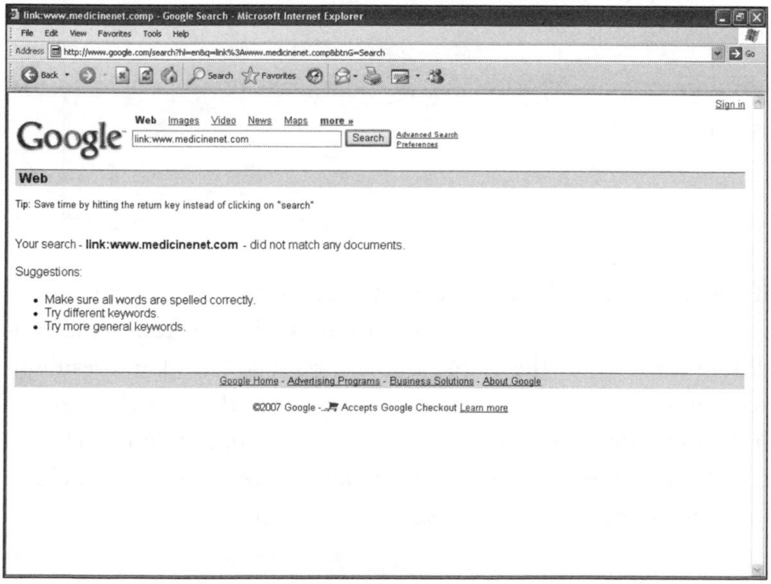

Figure 5-13

If a Google algorithm and/or the search quality team has determined that a Web site has not followed Google's terms and conditions, especially if the spam is due to a form of link spam, the link development to a site will disappear. This is what the link development count on Google would look like if a site were banned in Google.

After all technical reasons for not being spidered and/or indexed have been addressed, then there is genuine possibility that a site has been penalized or banned.

Analyze Site for Hidden Elements

If a site has no technical issues preventing its being crawled, try to find items on a site that might violate the terms and conditions set forth by the commercial Web search engines.

Review your site for all hidden elements: text and links. Has your Web developer or search engine optimizer added invisible elements to your Web site without your permission? One easy way to find hidden text and links in a transparent graphic image is to use a text-only browser, such as Lynx.

Figure 5-14

Screen shot of the Lynx browser. Note how the browser shows invisible text at the bottom of a splash page.

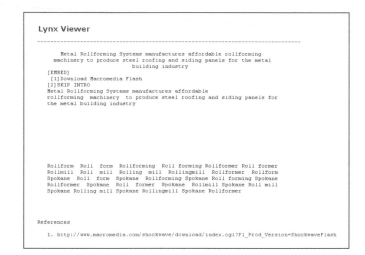

If there are no technical issues that prevent search engines from crawling your site, and if your site follows all of the terms and conditions set forth by the search engines, then go ahead and resubmit your home page and site map (as a backup) in the Add URL forms. In this situation, the search engine had a glitch, not your Web site. It will take time for the search engines to respider your site and include the pages in search results. Be patient.

If your site absolutely requires search engine visibility during this time, then purchase more search engine advertising and participate in any available paid inclusion programs until the site is re-spidered and re-indexed. The beauty of both of these programs is that you can turn the campaigns on and off at a moment's notice.

However, if you find invisible (spam) elements on the page, then it is time to clean up the mess.

Reviewing Search Engine Guidelines

Once you have determined that your site might not be following the terms and conditions set forth by the search engines, then you must modify the site so that it *does* follow the guidelines. Search engine representatives will want proof that you are following their terms, conditions, and guidelines.

Case study: MedicineNet

To be perfectly honest, when a representative from MedicineNet first contacted me, I did not believe that the site had spam issues because the site's content was (and is) extraordinary. My first inclination was to examine problematic technical issues because the site had over 22,000 pages of unique content. MedicineNet is an online healthcare media publishing company established in 1996. The firm also authored Webster's New World™ Medical Dictionary—and the site has a comprehensive online medical dictionary that is searchable. In other words, this is not the type of Web site that typically gets blacklisted.

Figure 5-15a and 5-15b
MedicineNet's home page and online medical dictionary.

After carefully reviewing technical properties of the site, Web analytics data, index count, and link development count, it became clear that the site was blacklisted. The Web analytics data showed a clear drop in Google referrals, indicating that Google was not crawling the site every day, which would be normal on a medical news site. Additionally, the link development count was practically zero, with the only referrals coming from Google's Open Directory listings.

Figure 5-16

At first glance, I did not believe that MedicineNet was spamming Google. This graph showing the sudden drop of Google referrals was a strong indication that the site was blacklisted.

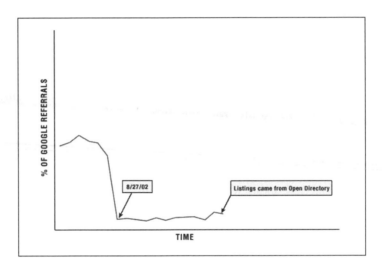

Other clear indications that the site violated the terms and conditions set forth by Google include:

- The search engine optimization firm that MedicineNet hired purchased over 90 domains, which were connected to each other via hidden links (hidden link spam).

- Content in each domain was available on the official, canonical MedicineNet Web site (duplicate/redundant content).

- The search engine optimization firm implemented a link development campaign for all the 90-plus domains, essentially trying to artificially boost link popularity with redundant content. They counted on Web directory editors not checking to see whether the MedicineNet corporate site was already in the directory.

- The search engine optimization firm also participated in free-for-all link farms to boost link popularity.

The result—the MedicineNet Web site was indeed blacklisted in Google.

Repairing the damage

The main issue with Google was twofold. First, the search engine optimization firm was delivering a tremendous amount of redundant content to Google and all the major search engines—over 90 copies of a 22,000-page Web site. Google (and any commercial Web search engine for that matter) only wants one copy of the content. Therefore, the solution was to 301 redirect all 90-plus domains to a single, canonical MedicineNet Web site.

Second, Google clearly had a problem with the substandard link development. Therefore, MedicineNet had to report all known link spam to Google so that the software engineers could track down all remaining low-quality links.

Once MedicineNet had addressed these issues, the next step was to submit a re-inclusion request to Google.

Re-inclusion requests

Even though MedicineNet was completely ignorant of this search engine optimization firm's activities, Google still held the company responsible for hiring such a firm. After addressing all technical issues and eliminating the search engine spam, Web site owners need to contact the search engine directly by emailing a re-inclusion request or filling out a re-inclusion form. The follow-up email or form re-inclusion request should contain the following information:

- **Be polite.** Remember, in a blacklisting situation, you are asking for a person's time. Staff on the search quality teams deserve common courtesy.

- **Acknowledge what you (or your search engine marketing firm) did wrong.** I always feel that it is a good idea to show that you have read the search engine's terms and guidelines, citing URLs and specific quotations. In your email or the comment/details field, clearly communicate to the search quality team that you understand the search engine's terms and conditions.

- **If you hired a search engine marketing firm that spammed the search engines (on your behalf), state the firm's name and contact information.** Helping the search quality team determine how unethical search engine optimizers generate low-quality content resulting in poor search results will generally get their favor. I often provide the search quality team with copies of the spam company's written proposals, contracts, methodologies, and reporting.

- **Explain what you did to remedy the situation—be very specific.** Cite each guideline that was not followed and what you did to fix it. Staff on the search quality team will verify your information. For example, on the MedicineNet site, I gave Google a list of all 90-plus doorway domains and my analysis of the link development to each doorway domain. The search quality team verified that all 90-plus domains had 301 redirects pointing to a single, canonical domain.

- **Apologize.** Admit what you did was wrong, even if the search engine marketing firm you hired did things without your knowledge or endorsement.

- **Provide full contact information in the signature file.** In the event that the search quality team might need to contact you, make it easy. In all likelihood, they will not contact you, but providing full contact information communicates that you are willing to provide full disclosure.

Most of the time, if all goes well, your site will be re-spidered after the search quality team has verified that your site is following all the guidelines. Only in rare situations will a software engineer contact you directly.

Monitor for re-inclusion

To check for re-inclusion, do not bombard the search quality team with emails and form submissions. Rather, review your Web analytics data for spidering activity. You can also perform index count and link development searches provided earlier in this section to determine if pages have been added to the search engine index.

Figure 5-17
Example of a re-inclusion
request page at Google.

In the case of MedicineNet, it took approximately six months for the Google search quality team to allow the site back into the index. Due to the site's considerable size, the entire site was available in Google search results about three months after being re-crawled. Smaller sites might get re-listed, crawled, and added to the index immediately. Larger sites might take longer.

The moral of the story? I do not recommend spamming the search engines. In my opinion, the risk is too great and the advertising expenses are often cost-prohibitive.

Deconstructing Common Misconceptions

Unfortunately, the search engine marketing industry is riddled with myths and misinformation. All too often, search engine marketers mix sales hype with facts just to make a sale. And many amateur search engine marketers rely on their personal experiences rather than tested results over time.

To help you select a reputable, reliable search engine marketing firm, below are some common search engine myths.

Guaranteed Placement or Your Money Back

A credible, experienced, and knowledgeable search engine optimizer can demonstrate results from past performance but cannot guarantee future results. Why? Except for pay-for-placement search engines, no one can guarantee top positions because there are third parties who have all the control: the directory editors and the search engines. In fact, all the major search engines have some sort of disclaimer stating that they ultimately decide which Web sites to include in their indices.

Search engine marketers can guarantee that they will perform proper keyword and category research, optimal HTML coding, submission, etc. in a manner that the search engines find acceptable. But they cannot state, with absolute certainty, that their efforts will result in top search engine positions.

Search engine marketers like to guarantee results so they can tell a target audience what it wants to hear. I often compare search engine marketing to being a stockbroker. No stockbroker can guarantee future earnings. And no search engine marketer can guarantee future search engine positions.

Search Engine Marketing Guarantees Permanent Top Positions

This search engine myth is partly true. Search engine *advertisers* can guarantee top ad positions because the client pays for positioning. In general, the person who pays the highest bid amount will show up highest in the advertising space. Or, as in the case with Google AdWords, the ad that generates the most clicks (in other words, garnering Google a higher profit) gets the highest position.

With search engine optimization, however, no one can truly guarantee top positions. Only one group has final control over what ranks and what does not rank: the search engines themselves. Even though many search engine optimization professionals are very confident in their skills, keep in mind that this guarantee is a sales pitch and not factual at all.

Search engine optimizers have no control over positioning, no matter how enthusiastic and persuasive their sales team is.

Experienced, knowledgeable search engine specialists can demonstrate results from past performance but cannot guarantee future results. In that sense, search engine optimization specialists are like stockbrokers. No stockbroker knows how future markets will perform, and no search engine optimizer knows what future search engine algorithms will be.

In addition, search engines do not want the same sites appearing over and over again in the same positions. They constantly modify their algorithms, sometimes daily, so that the same sites *will not* always appear in the same positions.

New sites and pages are added to the Web all the time, often with better, unique content or a more user-friendly interface than sites already displaying well in search results. How Web pages and sites link to each other also changes. Old and outdated pages are removed from the index. Because of these changes, search engine databases change and constantly evolve. Therefore, positioning always fluctuates. A search engine index is always in a state of flux.

Likewise, many people do not realize that they are querying different data centers at the same time. For example, I might perform a search on Google for "organic green tea," and one of my colleagues might perform the same query, and we will be delivered different search results. I might see a Web page displayed in position #1, and my colleague will see a will see the same Web page displayed in position #6, even though we both queried Google at the same time.

Therefore, to have a goal of "permanent" top positions is an unrealistic expectation. Positioning and traffic fluctuations are perfectly normal. A more realistic expectation is to have consistent, qualified traffic from the commercial Web search engines over time.

Unfortunately, a large number of the search engine optimization firms that offer guaranteed search engine positions are spammers. To achieve top positions, thousands, even millions, of doorway pages are submitted to search engines. If one such doorway page gets a top position, even if only for a few days, the search engine optimization firm fulfilled its end of the contract.

Understandably, many Web site owners like the comfort of a guarantee. They believe that a guarantee demonstrates the search engine optimization company's confidence in its skills and expertise.

A guarantee is merely an attractive element of a sales pitch. The same guarantee that convinces you to sign a contract may very well result in spam practices that will get your site penalized or banned by the search engines.

The Goal of Search Engine Optimization Is To Achieve Top Positions

This myth is widespread and inaccurate. The partial goal of search engine optimization is to make a Web site more "findable" in the commercial Web search engines. If a Web site receives consistent, qualified traffic from the search engines over time, then the search engine marketing campaign is successful.

Generally speaking, most Web sites receive 6% to 7% of overall traffic from the commercial Web search engines. A successful search engine marketing campaign should deliver qualified traffic at least in the double digits. I typically aim for 10% to 30% of Web traffic to come from the search engines, though every site is unique. A publisher Web site will typically receive far more search engine traffic than an ecommerce site.

I tend to focus on site statistics, Web analytics, and usability testing data rather than positioning reports. I then update a site based on what visitors are communicating. If I know that a considerable number of site visitors land on a specific products page and leave, then maybe the information on the product page is not communicating the right message. Maybe the page is too hard to read. Maybe the product photo was blurry. Maybe the price was too high. Maybe site visitors needed more information about the product. Maybe the shopping cart was hard to use. Maybe the page does not appear focused enough (i.e., does not provide clear "you are here" cues) and more user-centered keyword phrases are needed.

There are so many variables to a successful Web site. Making a site easy to find is only part of the equation. As a Web designer/developer, I am fortunate enough to have marketing and usability skills in addition to my design and technical skills. I only change a Web page if I believe it will benefit my target audience. If that change generates a higher search engine position, which it often does, then great! If the change does not generate a higher search engine position but the sales conversions are higher, then who cares if the Web page isn't in a Number 1 position?

Having the right perspective is key to achieving search engine visibility and generating a positive user experience. Having a narrow focus on positioning generally leads to a negative user experience.

Top Search Engine Positions Equal Top Sales

The sales process has never been a one-step process. Not only should a Web site receive qualified traffic from a variety of resources (search engines, public relations, advertising, etc.), it should also:

1. Deliver useful information and value to site visitors.

2. Compel site visitors to take a desired action.

For example, on an ecommerce site, the desired call to action might be Add to Cart. If a Web site is offers online courses, the desired call to action might be Register for Class.

"Top search engine positions equals top sales," is a gross overgeneralization. Many sites achieve top search engine positions and no sales. Many Web sites do not have any top-10 search engine positions and generate millions of dollars in sales.

Furthermore, many online marketing professionals honestly believe that top search engine positions generate a positive branding experience. This belief is a partial truth. I would modify this statement to say, "Top search engine positions equal a *temporary and initial* positive branding experience."

What if clicking on a top search result link delivers searchers to a page that takes a long time to download? What if the landing page does not contain a clear call to action or scent of information? What if the searcher is delivered information he or she is not expecting to see based on his or her keyword query?

Once searchers click on a link from the search engine and land on a Web page, they want to see their query words appear on that landing page. Seeing those query words makes them feel more confident that they arrived at the most appropriate page on a site, and prominent, focused keyword phrases help encourage searchers to take a desired action or to continue navigating the site. However, if a searcher is dissatisfied with what he or she sees, the searcher hits the Back button in the browser and goes to different sites displayed in search results.

Moreover, if the searcher refines the keyword phrases to get better, more accurate search results (which is often the case) and sees the same unsatisfactory Web site appear in search results, is the searcher likely to click on the link to that Web site? Of course not— the searcher remembers the initial negative user experience.

Top search engine positions might generate an initial positive branding experience, but Web site usability, pricing, and customer service will ultimately determine the final outcome. No top search engine position can take the place of a positive customer experience.

Therefore, instead of being overzealous about maintaining positions, online marketers should spend more time on analyzing visitor behavior and sales conversions. Web site usability has a direct, positive impact on search engine visibility.

If Web designers/developers, usability professionals, and search marketers would focus more on delivering keyword-rich content, they might find their sites can easily generate targeted search engine traffic and convert visitors into buyers within a single site.

Submit Your Site to Thousands of Search Engines

The majority of Web sites receive qualified traffic from only a few commercial Web search engines, Web directories, and industry-specific sites. Submission software claiming to submit your site to 10,000 search engines will get you listed in many FFA (free-for-all) link farms.

An FFA link farm is a collection of Web pages that contains indiscriminate, often unrelated, links to other Web pages. For example, a site that sells golf balls has nothing in common with a mortgage or gambling site. FFA link farms are used to artificially boost link popularity and are considered spam by all the major search engines.

In addition, many search engine marketers will not tell you that a single search engine supplies results to other Web sites. For example, Google currently supplies search results to America Online (AOL), yet many search engine optimization experts consider a ranking in Google to be completely different from a ranking in AOL Search.

Instant Link Popularity

Any search engine optimizer that promises instantaneous link popularity is probably spamming the search engines. In all likelihood, search engine optimization firms that promise instantaneous results build link farms to artificially inflate link popularity.

Quite often, these firms rely on expired domains on Yahoo and Open Directory. Many of the link farm sites are not even in the same industry. Why would a real estate site link to a site that sells baseball bats?

Some search engine optimization firms purchase links to generate instant link popularity. Some link purchases are legitimate, such as a link from the Yahoo directory. And some link purchases are clearly meant to exploit the search engines.

For example, news publications often sell text-link ads, ads that are formatted in such a way that Google, Yahoo, and the other major search engines cannot tell if the ads are truly ads or are part of the site's main content. The salesperson for the news publication is only trying to do a job—sell advertising space to generate income. The search engine optimization firm is trying to get the client instant link popularity by getting links from a "legitimate" source—the news publication. The problem with this scenario is that the link is not from an objective third party. The intent is to exploit the search engines, not to benefit the user experience, especially since the ad is often not placed next to a relevant, topic-related article.

The search engines have known about news-site link purchases for years, and they are actively working to eliminate these types of paid links when they compute link development properties as part of the search algorithm.

Results people see from link farms are generally short-lived. Search engine software engineers discover the link farms and promptly remove all of the sites from the search engine database.

Though no one can control which Web sites link to your site, site owners have complete control over which sites they link to. If a site links to another site that is considered a "bad neighborhood," such as free-for-all (FFA) link farms, the site can be penalized.

Quality link development takes time.

Search Engine Visibility Reports

If you receive an unsolicited "visibility" report in your email, you are probably not dealing with a reputable search engine marketing firm. Here is why:

- The report you received was unsolicited. If you really wanted a search engine visibility report, you would have requested one.

- The company that sent you the report probably selected a very general keyword phrase or a set of keywords that is not important to a your business. No one knows what keywords are your most profitable selections just by viewing your Web site.

- If you actually perform keyword searches on the search engines, you will find that your site is appearing more frequently than indicated in the visibility reports. Many of these visibility reports are inaccurate. The search engine marketing company is just trying to scare you into using its services.

- If you have a new Web site, in all likelihood, your site will not appear in the search engines for at least one to three months. All search engines have lead times, which is the time between Web page submission and when the page appears in the search engine index. Again, this is a tactic used to scare you into using their services. Your site will probably appear in the search engines after the lead time has passed.

So don't fall for the sales hype from any company sending you visibility reports. Your site-statistics software will tell you whether your site is receiving search engine traffic.

Search Engine Optimization Does Not Deliver Good Return on Investment

Currently, there is a widespread belief that if a company can pay for a position, why should the company bother embarking on an SEO campaign?

Search engine optimization and search engine advertising are two different online marketing strategies.

Search engine advertising relies far more on payment than relevancy. Granted, search engine representatives will not allow advertisers to buy any keyword they wish. The landing or destination pages for the advertising must contain some relevant content. However, nothing on the landing page determines positions. Ultimately, what determines positioning is how much the advertiser is willing to pay or generate for the search engine.

Search engine optimization designing, writing, and coding (in HTML) your entire Web site so that there is a good chance that your Web pages will appear at the top of search engine queries for your selected keywords and keyword phrases. When a site is properly optimized, search engine spiders do not have a difficult time finding and spidering a site. Quite often, with a search engine friendly site, paid submission and paid advertising are not necessary.

Many businesses never use pay-per-click advertising and get excellent ROI. I have witnessed many sites receiving millions of dollars in increased sales within months of launching a search engine friendly Web site. Some of the Web pages used as examples in this book have generated this type of ROI.

Search Engine Traffic Is Not as Good as Leads from Traditional Marketing Methods

Search engine traffic is often better than leads from traditional marketing and advertising (direct mail, radio, television, etc.) because people who come to your site via the search engines are actively seeking information about your products and services.

When analyzing the data comparing the cost per lead, costs can be much lower for search engine marketing than more traditional marketing methods.

Search Engine Marketing Equals Search Engine Advertising

One of the most widespread beliefs about search engine marketing is that search engine advertising equals search marketing. For example, if an online marketing firm runs advertising campaigns on Google and Yahoo, the firm often promotes itself as specializing in search engine marketing.

Search engine marketing encompasses a variety of skills. The main forms of search engine marketing include:

- Search engine optimization
- Search engine advertising
- Web directory paid inclusion
- Search engine paid inclusion

- Vertical/specialized search services (news/blogs, shopping, travel, etc.)

- Link development

- Local search optimization (geo-targeted)

- Image search optimization

- Multimedia (audio, video) optimization

The reason this myth is so widespread? Search engine marketing has become a hot new agency service. Unfortunately, many ad agencies have few or no search engine optimization skills. Writing keyword-rich text is a foreign concept to them. Juicy sales hype and buzzwords are the norm. Agency site designers are often more concerned with Flash sites or sites with "pizzazz" than with search friendliness.

Additionally, many new search engine advertising firms consist of former search engine employees. This group specializes in search advertising—not optimization, paid inclusion, or vertical search.

If you hire a full-service search engine marketing firm, make sure you hire one that has experience in all forms of search engine marketing. Do not hire a firm that specializes in advertising when the service you need is search engine optimization.

Search Engine Marketing Should Always Be Done In-House by the Webmaster

Most companies delegate search engine marketing responsibilities to a single Webmaster or Web site developer. In my experience, the IT department is a poor selection for this task. The IT department might be responsible for creating a search engine friendly Web site that downloads quickly, but the IT department is not usually responsible for a Web site's content. Usually an Editorial or Marketing department is responsible for a site's content. And the content of the page is as important as the design.

Furthermore, an effective search engine marketing campaign also involves link development, a responsibility that usually falls under the Marketing department.

The fact is that search engine marketing involves talent in Web copywriting, site design and layout, technical skills, site submission and monitoring, analyzing site reports, and so forth. In all likelihood, one person with multiple responsibilities will not be able to effectively handle all of these responsibilities and keep up with the ever-changing search engines. Many search engine marketing firms specialize in all aspects of optimization and submission.

You Don't Have To Change Your Site To Achieve Top Positions

This statement is rarely true. If you hear this type of statement from a search engine marketer, often you are dealing with a cloaking company. Since all the major search engines consider cloaking to be spam, work with cloaking companies knowing that your site can be penalized for spamming.

If you are purchasing positions via search engine advertising, you might not have to change your site. However, if you are purchasing a search engine optimization campaign, you will have to modify your site.

A search engine optimization campaign involves rewriting some of your content so that keywords are more prominent and frequently used. A site's navigation scheme might not deliver the keyword-rich content to the search engines. Either the navigation scheme should be modified, or you can participate in a pay-for-inclusion (PFI) program.

A Web site is always a work in progress because the Web is constantly evolving. Browsers are constantly being updated to support improved HTML, Cascading Style Sheets, scripting, and multimedia files.

Therefore, always be prepared to modify your content in places that will have the highest impact, which will be in your HTML title tags and visible <body> text (headings, paragraph tags, hyperlinks, table cells, ordered and unordered lists, etc.). Modifying content in your meta tags alone will not make a Web page appear more focused, which brings me to the myth that will not go away.

Meta Tags Are the "Secret Ingredient" To Getting Top Search Engine Positions

A few years ago, a spam technique called keyword stacking or keyword stuffing became popular because people did not want to change their visible Web page content in order to rank well in the search engines. Keyword stacking in meta tags became so common that the search engines gradually downgraded their importance over the years.

The title tag is much more important than meta tags because all the major search engines use title-tag content to determine relevancy. Very few search engines use meta-tag content to determine relevancy. Even if a search engine (such as Yahoo) uses meta-tag content, the content is nowhere near as important as the HTML title tag and main content.

Change All Text to CSS-Formatted Text and Use Web X.X Standards and Your Site Will Get Top Search Engine Positions

Part of this misconception originates with Web standards evangelists with a personal agenda. They seem so concerned with promoting their personal beliefs that they do not view searcher behavior as part of the big picture.

Web sites do not exist in a vacuum. If visitors cannot find a site through searching, browsing, and link development, Web standards are not going to matter.

Additionally, through usability testing, clickstream analysis, and Web analytics data, Web site owners often find that site visitors genuinely prefer graphic images over CSS-formatted text in many instances. Making a blanket statement such as "format all text via Cascading Style Sheets" is a poor marketing and usability decision.

Granted, converting a graphics-only Web site into a site with CSS-formatted text and graphic images will certainly help a site's search engine visibility. Remember, primary text is text that all the search engines use to determine relevancy. Alternative text (the text in graphic images) is secondary text, and search engines do not use alternative text to determine relevancy in text-based documents. Nevertheless, search engines want what users want. So if you determine that your target audience genuinely prefers a graphics-only Web site? Then give them a graphics-only Web site. If they want a combination of graphic images and CSS-formatted text? Then give it to them. But do not accept overgeneralizations and blanket statements. Always test and measure results.

Though search friendly site designers are learning about Web standards and applying those principles to sites, Web standards advocates do not seem to understand the search industry. Search is such a huge component of usability, sales, and design. To ignore search (or diminish its importance) is somewhat troubling.

You Only Need To Optimize Your Home Page

Many Web hosting companies offer this sales pitch: If you cannot afford full site optimization, the next best thing is to optimize your home page only.

Unfortunately, many Web hosting and other Web design firms have limited knowledge of search engine optimization. The function of a home page is to act as a site's Table of Contents, and a limited Table of Contents at best. All too often, a home page's content is not focused on targeted keyword phrases.

Additionally, a home page does not close a sale. Very few site visitors will Add to Cart, Sign Up for Newsletter, or Enroll in Class from a site's home page.

Which pages are the best pages to optimize on a Web site? Pages that are focused on targeted keyword phrases that are likely to convert visitors into buyers—these pages deliver qualified traffic, leads, and final sales conversions to your site. The types of pages that tend to rank well and deliver sales are:

- Product pages (for a B2C site)

- Service pages (for a B2B site)

- Category pages

- Help pages (FAQs or frequently asked questions, customer service)

- Media pages (press releases, testimonials, case studies)

- Informational pages (articles, tips, and tools)

Product, Service, and Category pages often contain focused content and are most likely to close a sale. Help, Media, and Informational pages can also deliver focused content. However, these pages guide visitors to more focused pages.

Of course, a home page should be optimized to the best of your ability, but do not expect that a one-page optimization strategy will deliver the same results as a site with fully optimized Product, Service, Category, Help, and Media pages.

Always optimize your most important Product and Service pages first. Home page optimization is a poor substitute for optimized Products and Services pages.

Buying Search Engine Advertising Will Improve Your Site's Rankings in the Main Search Results

This myth is based on an erroneous cause-and-effect occurrence. When a company launches a new Web site, the company often purchases search engine advertising for increased visibility. After checking to see how the ad appears in search results, people at the firm notice that their site URLs appear in the main search results area. "Wow," they think. "All we have to do is purchase search engine ads and our Web site appears in the main search results." Correct assumption?

No. Purchasing Google AdWords will not make a site rank higher in the main search results. Purchasing Yahoo ads will not make a site rank higher in the Yahoo results. The algorithms for displaying search engine advertisements and for displaying URLs in the main search results are completely different.

The main reason that ads display is payment. The main reasons a page ranks well in the main search results are the three building blocks that I discuss throughout this book:

1. **Keyword-focused content:** The Web page contains words and phrases that people type into search queries.

2. **Information architecture and user interface:** The site designer has given search engine spiders easy access to the words on the page via a spider-friendly navigation scheme, URL structure, relevant cross-linking, a well-organized site architecture, a strong sense of place, and clear scents of information.

3. **Link development:** The number and quality of relevant links pointing to a Web site (or page) are in place and show positive growth over time.

Even Google states, "Advertising with Google neither helps (nor hurts!) a site's rankings on Google" (www.google.com/webmasters/facts.html).

We Know the Algorithm from (Google, Yahoo, MSN/Live Search, Ask, etc.)

Whenever any search engine marketing professional makes this statement, do not believe him or her. No one knows exactly how search engines rank pages.

Search engine algorithms change constantly. Some of the changes are subtle, and some of them are more apparent. Search engine algorithms are applied differently to different elements in search results pages. For example, the algorithm for news search results is different from the algorithm for advertising results. The algorithm for the main search results is different from the algorithm for image search results.

At many search engine strategies conferences, search engine representatives have publicly stated that algorithms contain over 100 components. Any search engine marketing professional who claims to have reverse-engineered a search engine algorithm is essentially claiming that the firm knows all 100 components of the mathematical equation that constitutes a search engine algorithm. Do they know all of the mathematical equations for the duplicate/redundant content filters? Do they know how search engines determine boilerplate elements? How are outliers determined? And, when a search engine marketing professional claims to know the answers to these questions, they often make a bold statement that they have the algorithm in a "black box."

Even if a search engine marketing firm hired a former search engine employee, do not be impressed. In all likelihood, the search engine marketing firm hired a representative from the advertising department. An ad representative does not have the same knowledge as a software engineer.

No search engine is going to publish all components of its algorithm in patent files, scholarly publications, or anywhere for that matter. Therefore, no search engine optimization professional knows all of the mathematical equations that constitute a specific search engine algorithm. And if a search engine marketing company makes claims that it knows a search engine's algorithm? The search engine marketing company has a well rehearsed, but false, sales pitch.

A Client List and Testimonials on a Web Site Indicate a Reputable SEO Firm

Just because a search engine marketing firm displays an impressive client list does not necessarily mean that the firm practices "ethical" search engine marketing. Big-brand companies desire search engine visibility as much as small- to medium-sized companies. Many big-brand sites often get banned or penalized by the search engines due to search engine spam.

To be sure, ask a search engine marketing firm if any of their strategies have resulted in any spam penalties. If a search engine marketing firm is constantly building micro-sites or purchasing domain names specifically for search engine positioning, you might not be dealing with an ethical search engine marketer.

Also, many reputable search engine marketing firms sign nondisclosure agreements (NDAs) with their clients. So they are not permitted to display all or part of their client lists on their Web sites.

However, since most firms that wish to hire a search engine expert will ask for references, firms that have NDAs should have at least three references they can give you.

Conclusion

Using spam techniques does not guarantee that your Web pages will get top search engine positions. Even if spam techniques work, the search engine positions are short-lived. Once the search engines or your competitors discover the spam, the site(s) using spam are either penalized or permanently banned from the search engines. Then you, the Web site owner, and the spammers will have to build another Web site, another set of Web pages, and begin the whole search engine marketing process all over again. This "cat-and-mouse" game can become time consuming and expensive.

Are these myths and misconceptions applicable 100% of the time? Of course not—I do not believe that something is true or false 100% of the time. There are always exceptions. For example, some search engine optimization firms might offer a money-back guarantee because the firm is confident of its ability to get results, not because the firm practices unethical techniques.

However, many optimization firms know how desperate people are to obtain top search engine visibility, and they prey on that desperation. If you hear any of these myths, misconceptions, or spam methodologies as part of a sales pitch, proceed with caution. Read the fine print in the contract. Getting sites unbanned and unpenalized has never been a quick and easy process.

Web pages with unique, high-quality content and an acceptable search engine friendly design consistently perform better on the search engines than spam pages. Because the pages contain quality content and the search engines have access to that quality content, the cat-and-mouse game is unnecessary. Sites that are optimized from the beginning of the design and redesign process need little tweaking once the foundation is in place. Building a site for your target audience and following search engine best practices is one of the most cost-effective components of a search engine marketing campaign.

Index

L